PRAISE FOR WHISPERING BACK

'Adam and Nicole remind us of the fundamental reason for being involved with horses – because we are in awe of their magnificent nature and are drawn to form a partnership with such a [...] willingness to learn and experiment whilst they are on [...] journey is an inspiration, and their humanity and courage [...] through. You may learn a lot about horses reading this book, but you will also learn about persistence and a clear intention, valuable lessons, whatever your life's journey may be.'

Tina Sederholm, author of *Words of a Horseman:*
The Life and Teaching of Lars Sederholm

'This book is the chronicle of a journey into knowledge. Their teachers are Monty Roberts, Kelly Marks, and Mary Wanless. They are pledged to improve the lives of traumatised equines. In the course of their journey they find self-awareness, recognizing weaknesses and strengths in them, which belong to us all. We have all pretended to understand something and that pretence has covered up potentially dangerous ignorance. With humility they note: "some horses never have a fair chance to do anything right enough to avoid being punished." This is no wishy-washy, idealistic sugar-food, but the strong story of two intelligent and committed young people. It kept me awake all night.'

Bula Brazil, *British Dressage magazine*

'I think I may be suffering from an overload of Christmas sentimentality, because the first two chapters of your book made me cry twice – firstly for old Rupert overcoming his life-long fear, and then for Nicole fulfilling her life-long desire. Both of you write so beautifully, and with such honesty and feeling, that I'm sure it'll be a book to tie knots in many horse owners' heartstrings, as well as educating us with much-needed insight.'

Fiona Walker, author of *Kiss Chase* and *French Connection*

'This book tells their [...] of larger than life character [...] *der magazine*

READER REVIEWS

Whispering
BACK

NICOLE GOLDING
ADAM GOODFELLOW

EBURY
PRESS

First published in the UK in 2003
This edition published in 2004

1 3 5 7 9 10 8 6 4 2

Ebury Press
Random House, 20 Vauxhall Bridge Road, London SW1V 2SA

Random House Australia Pty Limited
20 Alfred Street, Milsons Point, Sydney, New South Wales 2061,
Australia

Random House New Zealand Limited
18 Poland Road, Glenfield, Auckland 10, New Zealand

Random House (Pty) Limited
Endulini, 5A Jubilee Road, Parktown 2193, South Africa

The Random House Group Limited Reg. No. 954009

A CIP catalogue record for this book
is available from the British Library

ISBN 0 09 189544 8

Jacket design by Two Associates
Interior by seagulls

Printed and bound in Great Britain by
Bookmarque Ltd., Croydon, Surrey

Papers used by Ebury Press are natural, recyclable products
made from wood grown in sustainable forests.

This book is dedicated to the memory of our fathers:

Robert John Golding (1936–1999)
Mark Aubrey Goodfellow (1931–1999)

Contents

Acknowledgements

This book might never have been written without the help, advice, and encouragement of our friend Matthew Parker. In addition, we would like to thank Thomas Wilson at Ebury Press and Rachel Leyshon for their editing expertise.

Many friends helped us to edit and compose the book, especially Annabelle Harling, Maggie McDonnell, and Jeannine Golding. Our thanks also to Julia Scholes, Andrew Golding, Laura and Veronica Deacon, Elizabeth Reynolds and Mark Rashid for their suggestions, and to Guy and Adele Nevill for giving us the use of their bolt-hole. Diana Maclean deserves much credit for her patient photography, and also Paul Thompson for so much help and so many pictures.

There are many people who have helped us along the way, including Linda Ruffle, Lorraine Fidler, Richard Searight, Meg Jackson, Dido Fisher and Henry Robinson. We are indebted especially to Jo Lindsey and many of our helpers and working pupils, particularly Helen Whittaker, Kate Reece, Brian Mortenses, Lisa Mygind, Carrie Milton and Ella Wall, who enabled us to concentrate on writing while they looked after the yard. Thanks also to SCSI – Andy Hughes, Simon Messenger, Huw Parry and Tim Hills, who work tirelessly to desensitise the horses.

For their never-ending support and encouragement, we owe our mothers, Lynn and Jeannine, undying gratitude. Without the generosity of Derek Partridge, we might never have been anything more than a one-horse family.

Finally, we would like to thank all of our teachers, especially Mary Wanless, Kelly Marks and Monty Roberts, without whom we wouldn't have a story to tell. In particular, Kelly's support, inspiration, encouragement and belief have helped us achieve things we would have never thought possible.

Nicole Golding & Adam Goodfellow
December 2002

Note

Monty Roberts®, Join-Up® and Dually™ are service marks, trademarks, and/or trade dress of Monty and Pat Roberts, Inc.

All events described in this book are true, to the best of our recollection. Some names have been changed.

Introduction
BY MONTY ROBERTS

I first met Nicole Golding and Adam Goodfellow in 1996, at a time when my life was changing rapidly. Having worked with horses since I was a child, I was now embarking on a new career, with the launch of my first book, *The Man Who Listens to Horses*. For me, years of frustration and rejection were about to be turned around to an extent that I could not have even dreamed of. When I had first discovered join-up, as a young boy up in the big country in Nevada, I knew I had found a way to train and communicate with horses that could revolutionise the way horses are treated. But the reaction of my father and others made me hide this discovery for decades, and I did not even show my methods outside my own operation for many years. I would never have guessed that it was to be in England that my methods would be accepted and adopted first, not so much by established trainers, but by ordinary people such as Nicole, a talented amateur with an unbridled passion for horses and an instinctive mistrust of the violence which she had been told to use by her instructors.

It was in 1989 that I first came to England at the invitation of the Queen to demonstrate my work to her. At that time I was completely unknown in this country, and although I had spent years in competitive horsemanship in the States, my methods were no better known there. At the Queen's behest I toured several venues in the UK, appearing before audiences often numbering no more than a few dozen. But the seeds had been sown, and it was not long before I met Kelly Marks. Through her ceaseless hard work and dedication, my dream of passing on what I had discovered and proved in training many thousands of horses began to become a reality. Kelly taught the first new generation of eager students, among whom was Nicole.

Like myself, they saw no place for violence in horsemanship, nor in their lives.

When my first book was launched, it became clear that we were not alone. At the time, autobiographies of horse trainers/books about horses were considered a great success in publishing terms if they sold more than 10,000 copies. The first print run of *The Man Who Listens to Horses* was therefore only a few thousand copies. Such was the outpouring of enthusiasm by a world sick of violence, that to date my first book has sold more than 4.5 million copies worldwide. No one could be more astonished by this turn of events than myself. But what particularly surprised me was how many of those readers were people like Adam, animal lovers who rode horses as a hobby, if only to spend some time with their girlfriends! It's remarkable to me to hear that it was discovering my work that caused Adam to want to change a hobby into a whole way of life.

It takes more than good intentions to make a good horse trainer. I often tell people who want to learn my methods that before they try to run, they must learn to walk, and before that, learn to crawl. This book tells the story of two young people doing just that, finding their way through the challenges of working with problem horses. Being among the first graduates of Kelly's courses, they have been thrown in at the deep end, being asked to train horses that would test any horseman. Of course, there are mistakes and misjudgements along the way, but at the heart of their journey, as in mine, lies a burning desire to do what's right for the horse.

It was my goal from the beginning to make the world a better place for horses and humans, and to apologise to Equus for the thousands of years of mistreatment and misunderstanding, which he has suffered at the hands of man. I hope that I have helped to do so. But I also know that for my contribution to make a lasting impact, I must rely on others taking my work on and bringing it to those who share the same convictions as myself.

Therefore I wish all the best to Nicole and Adam, for them to achieve continued success in their ventures with horses, and with this, their first book.

Monty Roberts
December 2002

ONE

Rupert meets the luckiest man in the world (Adam)

It was one of those perfect summer days that English people never seem to mention as they set about the national tradition of complaining about the weather. I slung my kit bag into the car and looked out across the fields at our horses. Quietly grazing or dozing in the sunshine, they made a picture of absolute tranquillity. Consistency might not be the strongest point of our climate, but no country in the world could produce a finer day than this without clouds of insects to go with it. In any case, it would have taken more than a cloud in the sky to dent my good mood, for I was on my way to work with two of my favourite clients, Linda and Colin, a retired couple who like myself had recently moved to the West Country. I had worked for them before, with great results. This time, they wanted me to have a look at a retired schoolmaster called Rupert, who had a problem with tarpaulins and plastic.

Any horse owner knows that many horses have what seems to be an unnatural fear of plastic, and won't go near it unless they learn that food is sometimes to be found in plastic bags. Monty Roberts's autobiography, *The Man Who Listens to Horses*, includes the story of his first horse, Brownie, who had been phobic all his life about paper after Monty's father had forced him to endure a practice known as 'sacking out'. Having secured him to a strong post, Monty's father had, over a period of several days, repeatedly thrown a paper sack over his back, in an effort to break his spirit of resistance to humans and to teach him 'respect' for the pressure of the rope restraining his head. It had left a scar so indelible that even though he owned him for many years thereafter, Monty was unable to persuade Brownie that it would never happen again, and the horse would worry at the slightest rustle of paper. This didn't bode well. If the famous Monty Roberts couldn't eradicate Brownie's phobia, was there any way I would be able to cure Rupert of a similar fear?

When I arrived, Colin came to meet me and shook me warmly by the hand, but my heart sank when I saw Linda. Her face was creased with worry and her voice strained as she explained the origins of Rupert's problem.

When he was four years old and only recently broken in, Rupert was being ridden back into the yard by his young owner. A tarpaulin was lying on the ground, and he had accidentally stepped on it. When his foot came down, making a sharp rustle, he suddenly spooked and shot forward, unseating his rider, who fell off. This was probably a good thing, because he galloped right across a cabbage field, and jumped a wall on the other side, landing in a heap on the road, where he slipped and fell over. He scrambled to his feet and stood panting, probably wondering where on earth that noise had come from, and why his rider had dismounted so gracelessly.

That might well have been the end of it, since many horses spook at such objects without developing a major problem about them. But this young girl's father had been standing nearby and thought he'd teach Rupert a lesson, which indeed he never did forget. He strode across the field to where Rupert was still standing and, grabbing him by the bridle, dragged him back to the spot where the incident happened. Facing Rupert at the tarpaulin, he tried to pull him across it. When Rupert refused, the man twitched him, tightening a cord around the end of his nose so tightly that it bled. He forced him to stand on the plastic sheet, beating him so badly that for the next twenty-three years of his life, Rupert had refused to go near a tarpaulin, and was terrified of the sound of plastic. Although he was perfect in every other way, he resisted any effort to come to terms with the phobia that had been so mindlessly beaten into him. On one occasion, Linda had been persuaded by her instructor, an experienced horse-woman, that she could sort out his problem, and she proceeded to try to ride him forcefully over a tarpaulin using a whip, making him re-live the trauma all over again. After this he was worse than ever.

'I'm not sure if I'm doing the right thing by asking you to work on this,' she explained. 'He's retired so it's not as if I have to worry about him spooking at a plastic bag in a hedge and running into the road with me. I just make sure that he never has to go near a tarpau-lin. We keep all the plastic bags in the feed room so he doesn't have to deal with his problem. It's just he has such a terrible fear lurking at the back of his mind. He won't be with us much longer, and I wish he could go to horse heaven without the unresolved memory of that terrible beating. But I'm worried that you'll make it worse for him, like the last person who tried.'

I'd never before dealt with a horse who had a specific, deeply ingrained phobia about tarpaulin. I wasn't exactly sure what my plan should be, but I knew that in the end, it would have to be Rupert's choice. If he just couldn't deal with it, and was getting more trauma-tised, I would have to stop, and leave him to live out his days without ever coming to terms with his fear, and the great injustice that had been done to him so long ago. I assured Linda that I felt exactly the same way as she did and would stop immediately if she wanted me to.

Colin and Linda had just constructed a huge outdoor arena, which was magnificent. Built of sand and rubber, it was perfectly flat and was surrounded by a high post and rail fence. They stood near the gate and Colin hid the tarpaulin I had brought with me while I led Rupert in. He was a handsome bay, about 15.2 hands high, with a kind eye. He seemed very relaxed and happy to be handled by a stranger, as if he hadn't a care in the world. He had never been in the arena before, and although it had materialised right next to his paddock only a week or so before, he didn't bat an eyelid as he walked in confidently, hardly bothering to sniff the ground. Obviously he had been in a few schools in his time, and knew the firm, crunchy sand was not, unfortunately, raw cane sugar. Even so, I walked him around it for a few minutes.

I was planning to do join-up, the method discovered by Monty Roberts, which uses body movements to communicate with a horse in his own language. The starting point is to give the horse the choice to stay with you or to move away. I let Rupert loose and walked away, inviting him to follow me. He broke away immediately and cantered off to the far side, hoping to find a way to get back to his friends in the adjoining field.

I was instantly reminded of why it is easier to do join-up in a 50-foot round pen than an Olympic-sized school, for within seconds Rupert seemed like a dot on the horizon, but as I had been trained to do, I sprinted after him, using assertive body language to tell him to keep moving away, since that was where he had decided to go. Leaving a trail of deep holes in the surface as he went, he reached the far corner of the school well before me and stopped briefly to tear a few chunks out of the pristine fence. I glanced across at Colin and Linda, whose faces bore a look of resigned stoicism. They'd known their new school wouldn't stay perfect for ever, but perhaps they'd hoped it would last longer than two minutes!

Rupert was clearly determined to make me work hard for my money. Although, at the age of twenty-seven, he was old for a horse, he seemed to want to prove that he was still a few years younger than me. Not being outstandingly fit, I was soon out of breath, but Rupert was also beginning to have second thoughts about the wisdom of his policy of flight, as he was doing a lot more running than me, and it was only bringing more pursuit. Despite his attempts to evade me, he could not pretend I wasn't there, for as far as I could in such a large space, I was asserting my authority over him by making him move in the direction I chose. As he ran up and down the fence I would sometimes block his movement and keep him away from the field, which seemed to make him focus on me a little. Then I began to see signs that he was starting to change his mind. First his inside ear began to flick towards me, as if to say, 'I don't know who you are but you're clearly after me for something.'

He began to slow down, and seemed more regular in his movements, breaking into a canter less frequently and then settling down into a trot, which became increasingly steady. His flight instinct was beginning to subside and his head began to come down, as his adrenaline lowered. Finally he was walking, licking and chewing as his anxiety receded, so I changed my body language to mirror his. It was as if he was saying, 'OK, I give up. Let's just stop and eat, shall we?' Or in Monty Roberts's words, 'If we could have a meeting to renegotiate this deal, I'd let you be the chairman.' With his attention fully on me, I moved away from him, dropping my eyes and changing my stance completely, showing him my shoulder, to invite him to come over and join-up with me. He stopped, and it seemed as though the world stopped with him.

But off he went again, obviously thinking that was enough of a meeting. He'd still rather consult with his mates, although they hadn't done much to help him, having continued to munch the grass on the other side of the fence, with only the occasional bored glance in our direction. OK, I thought, setting off after him again, with Monty's words again ringing in my ears: 'If you want to go away, then go away, that's fine. But don't go away a little. Go away a lot.' I sent him off round the school for another minute or two. He was soon showing signs of regretting his decision and the moment he made the slightest effort to change his mind, I went back to my passive stance, looking down at the ground near him so I could still see what he was doing.

This time he did not run off, but stood and looked at me for a second before turning back towards his friends. When he did I immediately turned to him again, looking him in the eye and making a 'tscch' noise, which startled him and brought his attention back to me. Before he had even finished turning his head to look at me, I had already dropped my stance back to passive, in a much-practised move. He stared at me, responding as if caught by the hypnotic rhythm of an inaudible tune. I began to move in an arc around him, and he followed me with his head, looking at me with both eyes, until his feet finally had to move towards me. A tentative step or two in my direction, but then he moved off, and once again I explained my position: 'Everything's nice when you're with me, everything's tough when you go away.' Finally he seemed to conclude that although I looked like a human, I was acting like a horse, communicating in the same way a horse would, and using exactly the same method another horse would to get him to accept me as his leader. He took another, hesitant step towards me and I rewarded him by remaining absolutely still for a moment, and then moving around him in a series of curves, gradually decreasing the distance between us until I was close enough to touch him. I gave him a gentle rub on the forehead and he relaxed further, licking and chewing, showing that he was happy to be with me of his own choice.

We had formed the basis of a new relationship, the bond that was essential if he was to trust me sufficiently when it came to the tarpaulin. While I had not run him around to anything like the point of exhaustion, the fact that he had already been through his adrenaline reaction and flight instinct meant he would be calmer and better able to deal with his fear.

When I moved away from him, he followed me as if on an invisible lead rope, turning sharply when I did, stopping with me, showing no further inclination to leave. We walked together all around the arena, his head by my shoulder, and came to a rest in the middle of the school. Still with nothing attached to his headcollar, I spent a few minutes just touching him all over to reassure him that I had no intention of hurting him. I also picked up each of his feet, for although this had been done to him thousands of times before, it would remind him that it was safe to trust me to hold the tools that were the key to his only real means of defence – flight. As we stood together, the contrast between fleeing away from me (and having to work hard), and standing quietly if he chose to stay with me, made it clear that I could be a safety zone for him. He relaxed further and I spent a few more minutes enhancing his appreciation of this with more 'follow-up'.

As we marched along the other side of the school, I asked Colin to set out the tarpaulin on the ground close to where they were standing. At the sound of it, Rupert's head shot up and he broke away, rushing to the far corner of the school, where he stuck his head out over the fence in a last, feeble effort to get away. I followed him over and looked directly at him, before lifting my hand and rustling my fingers, until he looked at me again. This time when I turned passive, he couldn't manage a step towards me, but I sidled up to him, and gave him a stroke on the forehead, murmuring to him, 'It's all right, it won't be so bad. You don't have to do it. Let's just see if you can.' I knew he didn't understand my words, and that really I was saying them to myself. Rupert was staring past me at the plastic sheet. Although Colin had put sand along the edges to hold it down, and folded it to make it narrower, there was no way Rupert would fail to recognise what it was. The sun reflected brightly off the blue material, making strange ripples of light.

On the other side of the fence, Linda was holding her hand to her mouth. Colin put his arm around her, but his expression was full of doubt. I couldn't help thinking that Rupert immediately knew what this was all about. His head was raised and I could hear his breathing was shallower and more rapid. Although I had a headcollar on him, I decided not to use it, as I wanted him to be free to express his fear if he needed to run away, without feeling under any pressure. I reminded myself that I had to work with his consent, that there was no way I could force him towards the tarpaulin without triggering all the bad memories he had of being bullied in the past. Keeping Rupert's attention on me as best I could, I approached the area in a roundabout way, while he continued to follow me without a lead rope. He had so much confidence in me already after our join-up that he went quite close to the tarp, and I rewarded him by asking him to follow me away from it every time he made any effort. It was as if you could see that in his heart, he really wanted to face this fear. All I needed to do was to help him.

He got close enough to sniff it, tentatively lowered his head towards it, then couldn't cope any more and broke away from me. I turned and looked towards him. He stood anxiously in the furthest corner, shifting his weight from foot to foot, taking another chunk out of the new fence. I approached him, took him by the headcollar and turned him towards me, then immediately walked away, listening to him follow. A moment later, we were back at the tarpaulin, and this time he stopped. It seemed as though he was willing, but couldn't summon up the courage. I asked for a rope.

Attaching it to his headcollar, I led him around on a loose rope for a moment before approaching the tarpaulin. But every time I went directly towards it I could feel the fear rising in him, so I would change course, leading him around or away, gradually asking for a little more effort until after a few minutes he could walk past it quite calmly. Finally, giving him a rub on the neck, I turned directly to it, stepping on to the crisp sheet. At the noise he jerked his head away, but did not make a serious attempt to escape. He stopped dead in front of it, while I walked to the other side. Gently tugging on the lead rope, I tried to invite him forwards but he pulled away. I held on when he pulled against me, but when he made the slightest movement towards me, I released all the pressure, gave him another rub on his forehead and led him away. The next time we came to the tarpaulin, he hesitated for a moment, and then, without any contact from the lead rope at all, he stepped forward, onto the bright blue sheet. His eyes showing white and bulging with fear, in a sudden rush, he was across.

Linda gasped with amazement and broke into tears. Colin beamed. Even I couldn't believe what I had just seen. Rupert seemed so pleased with himself, arching his old neck proudly as he came back down to a walk. I gave him another lovely rub and rewarded him in the best way I possibly could, by taking him right away from the tarpaulin and allowing him to rest for a moment while I somehow kept myself from following Linda's example. I took him over to the fence and we all made a big fuss of him. As we approached the tarpaulin again, I wondered how Rupert would react. Would he feel he'd done enough by going over it once? Sometimes the second time is harder than the first. But this time he crossed it almost without hesitation, and much more slowly. We practised it again a few more times, and then I unclipped the headcollar. If he really didn't want to go over it, there would be nothing to make him. We walked forward and I crossed it confidently.

For a moment he stopped. He knew he was loose, and looked away at the other horses as if to check whether they were looking at him, thinking he must be mad to go anywhere near one of those blue things where humans beat you up. I went back and stroked his head, then, gently pulling his headcollar to get his attention, walked away. We went in a small circle and came back to the tarpaulin. This time, he hesitated, but then put one hoof deliberately on it, and came over to me, with only a shadow of the fear he had shown before. Within minutes I had unfurled the tarpaulin to its full size, and he was standing calmly in the middle all by himself.

I invited Linda to come over and see if he would follow her. At first she was reluctant, fearing that she would make a mistake and undo my work. I reassured her that if she just walked at full speed, turning in arcs as I had done, he would confidently follow her in the same way. So she set off around the arena while Rupert happily walked after her, without a lead rope, as if he had been doing this all his life. When they came to the tarpaulin he walked straight over it, completely trusting her leadership just as he had trusted mine, in spite of the fact that she could hardly see for the tears in her eyes.

'Why don't you see if you can ride him over it?' I suggested after they had gone over together a couple more times.

'You must be joking!' Linda began, before reminding me of Rupert's last negative experience, when her previous riding instructor had tried to ride him over a tarpaulin. She was worried that if she didn't ride well enough, his fear might return. She also hadn't ridden him for a while and, she protested, he was supposed to be retired.

'If he doesn't want to do it, we won't make him,' I reassured her. 'But wouldn't it be a wonderful thing to do the last time you ever ride him?'

She nodded and started to lead him off to the stable to put on his saddle and bridle. 'Why don't we just go bareback?' I suggested. 'You must have ridden him without a saddle before.'

She agreed. 'I think he'll be fine.'

I gave her a hug and she put on her hat. We tied two lead ropes on to the headcollar to use as reins, and I gave her a leg-up. She settled herself onto his back, and held on to his mane as we set off around the school again, with him following me loose.

As we approached the tarpaulin, I could hear her holding her breath, and for a moment, a doubt crossed my mind. But Rupert was following me bravely and continued to walk straight over it. Linda couldn't believe it, and burst into tears again as she leant down and hugged him around the neck. We walked around and crossed another time.

'Would you like to try by yourself?' I asked her. 'Just trust him, he won't let you down now. Don't bother using your leg much, just point him at the tarpaulin, look up ahead and see what he wants to do.' She took a deep breath as they approached it. He looked down for a second, then walked over it as though he had never been the slightest bit worried. He tried to look as if he couldn't understand what all the fuss was about as we all gathered round, patting and congratulating him. It was an unforgettable moment. The whole session had taken less than an hour.

As Linda dismounted from him for the last time, she gave me a long hug. Her voice was breaking. 'You know, I can't believe it, I never thought he would get over it. I am just so happy that I've made it up to him, paid him back for all the pleasure he's given me over so many years. He will not go to his grave carrying that fear, which he has held inside for so long. Thank you so much for helping him to come to terms with it. That was amazing.'

Rupert was amazing. But I was just putting into practice principles I learned from a man who has turned the violence meted out to him in childhood by his father into something really special, a mission to show the world that violence and fear are tools we must leave behind if we are to forge the only bond that is worth having – one of trust and love.

What was perhaps most amazing was that I had ever met this man at all. For Monty Roberts comes from a world so different from my own, a world of cowboys and cattle, ranches and rodeos. After almost a lifetime of rejection and ridicule, he has travelled halfway around the world to show people how to listen to horses. As a result, I now had the chance to help horses like Rupert to overcome terrible problems. As we shared the moment and a cup of tea afterwards, I could not help but send a silent message of thanks to Monty for giving me this wonderful opportunity.

One of Monty's sayings is there's no such thing as luck, but I can't think of any other word to describe how I came to be doing this work. As a child, I lived in cities all over the world, being the son of a diplomat, and I only rode a horse once. I was about five years old but I still remember what a sense of achievement it gave, for I managed to get this old black riding school horse to take a few strides of canter, in spite of his being absolutely enormous, at least to my young eyes. My little legs flapping furiously against the saddle as he lumbered down a country bridleway, his bouncing, banging trot gave way to a few wonderful, smooth strides of canter. This was my only equestrian accomplishment by the time I met Nicole in 1988 at university. The fact that, against all logic and her better judgement, she then fell in love with me, made me the luckiest man in the world.

Nicole had spent her childhood cleaning out stables in her home town of Milton Keynes, looking forward to her weekly riding lessons and endlessly re-reading *Black Beauty* and other horse books to fuel her limitless enthusiasm. But her childhood was unfulfilled in this sense, for although they loved and supported her in every way, her parents never bought her the one thing she wanted: a pony. Her dream was to own a grey Welsh Mountain pony, whom she would call Misty, but a blind, three-legged pony named Buck would have done.

When we first met, I had no idea that Nicole's childhood passion, which seemed to have waned at that point in her life, would turn into a full-blown adult obsession that would later overcome even me, for she only spoke of horses once in the first year of our relationship.

'It's Badminton this weekend,' she said on this occasion.

'We're playing badminton?' I muttered incredulously, wondering what this could possibly have to do with my preoccupations at the time, which could neatly be described in the words of a famous Ian

Dury song. Perhaps she had arranged a new drinking game in keeping with the general debauchery of the times?

'No, Badminton Horse Trials. I usually go. Didn't I tell you I'm crazy about horses?'

I didn't recall her mentioning it, but then I hadn't brought up my own embarrassing childhood dream of becoming a General. That was the end of the matter, and for the next year she didn't refer to it again, just as I resisted the temptation to educate her in the statistics of the First World War, battle by battle.

Sensi changed all that; but then I only have myself to blame.

TWO

Nicole falls in love
(Nicole)

I watched as the battle developed between the horse and the human. The horse stood at nearly 17 hands high, bold and strong, bright bay in colour. The rider was a young man, tall, but slight. Recent heavy rain had caused the bridleway in front of them to flood, and the horse was refusing to go through the muddy water. He couldn't see the bottom, and although another horse had stepped through just ahead of him, he seemed determined to find another way around. There wasn't another route, however, and the man seemed equally determined to persuade the horse through.

He started by kicking his legs against the horse's sides. The horse ignored him, and tried to move away from the puddle. Each time he turned away, the rider pulled his head roughly back towards the water, and kicked him again. The more he was pushed, the less confident the horse seemed to be. Eventually he took a tentative step forward, and the man dug his heels into the horse's side, urging, 'Go on!' The horse backed away suddenly, getting further away from the obstacle. The man lifted his whip.

A light smack across the horse's side, and the horse jumped

forward, stopping suddenly just at the edge of the water. The rider hit him again, harder this time, and the horse bucked in protest, tipping his rider forwards. He whipped the horse for bucking, but he bucked again. Another smack, and the horse reared this time. Again, he was punished for this disobedience. The rider seemed more determined than angry. The horse looked resentful. It had become a battle of wills: if the rider stayed on and forced the horse across, he would win. If the horse could get rid of the man on his back, he would be the victor. As the man continued to hit him, by now with all his strength, and the horse plunged and squirmed in an effort to get rid of this aggressor, I couldn't keep quiet any longer.

'Come on, Adam!' I cried. 'Show him who's boss! Don't let him get away with it! He's got to do what you ask. Put a bit of effort into it. *Get angry*!'

'Get angry, Nicole!' was what my riding instructor would repeatedly shout at me throughout my childhood. I was often timid and ineffectual, and spent many a lesson spectacularly failing to get the pony to do what I wanted him to. My instructor would exhort me to greater effort, and when all else failed would threaten to hit the pony herself if I didn't start 'giving him a good wallop'. I wanted the pony to do what I asked, but not because I forced him. If I couldn't demonstrate that I could achieve my goals by fair means, then I would be told to 'get tough'. Sometimes, hitting the ponies did work, and they reluctantly submitted to my clumsy requests. Often it didn't, and I would end up on the ground, unceremoniously dumped by a pony well practised in the art of child disposal.

It was years ago that I told Adam to get tough with Wilberforce to get him through the puddle, and I really believed it was the right thing to do. We'd followed the advice from the hundreds of horse books I'd read: we'd asked him nicely, we'd tried to get him to follow another horse, we'd 'encouraged' him with a bit of stick, and we'd stayed true to the maxim 'never let the horse win – make sure he knows who's boss'. As a result, we'd naturally progressed, in this instance and in others, from gentle requests to brute force. We were following Monty's father's way: 'Do what I say, or I'll hurt you.' And we were doing it with the approval of just about every horse institution in the country, if not the world. I didn't feel angry that Wilberforce was disobeying Adam, I just believed that if we let Wilberforce 'get away with it', he would have no respect for us at all, and would never obey us again. I didn't like seeing him hit, but I believed it was an inevitable part of every horse's life. Without the insights and strategies we later gleaned from Monty Roberts, it was almost the only way we had of communicating. Far from 'whispering' to our horse, we were screaming. We had no idea that Wilberforce was trying to communicate with us. We were only interested in telling him how it was.

Wilberforce went through the puddle in the end, and we had the good grace to reward him with much patting and praising. We took him backwards and forwards across the water a few more times, to make sure he no longer had a problem with it, and he soon walked through as if it had never been an issue. He was a tremendously forgiving, almost thick-skinned horse, and seemed to bear Adam no grudge as we completed our ride, despite still bearing the marks of the whip on his flanks. I'd like to think that even then we had some ability to 'read' a horse. It wasn't right to hit Wilberforce, but we knew it wouldn't deeply traumatise him, as it might so many other horses. (We had generally managed to avoid such bullying tactics with Sensi, our first horse. Once, in a similar situation, we went for pure stubbornness: asking her to cross a ditch, and waiting patiently for two hours before she made the decision to comply. But with Wilberforce we were out of our depth, the strategies we had used to good effect with Sensi failed, and we tried to intimidate him into submission, largely because we felt so intimidated by him.)

It's very easy to judge others, and to despise them for resorting to violence. Like many horse owners, we used excessive force in this instance because we rapidly ran out of options, had ineffective methods at our disposal, and felt that any evasion had to be confronted and defeated at any cost. Conventional tools such as the whip were so easy to abuse. We often remember the ordeal to which we subjected Wilberforce. We loved him, and we treated him badly. There'll never be a chance to make it up to him.

As Adam mentioned, my parents didn't buy me a pony when I was a child, not because they were being mean, I now realise. At the time they had no idea how long-lasting my interest would be. As the obsession grew, they worked out the ramifications: if I had a pony, would they ever be able to get me to go to school again? What about family trips away? I already resented being dragged away from my local stables for the occasional weekend visit to relatives. And what would happen as I grew older? Would I be able to bear selling an outgrown pony? Obviously, I would rather sell my brother. There was also the issue of cost. 'Not just the initial outlay,' my dad patiently explained, as I challenged him on the vast sum he had just spent on a state-of-the-art Bang and Olufson music centre, 'but the upkeep. The stereo really won't cost much to maintain, you know, and it's something we can all enjoy.' It was no good arguing that I could get a job (not much work going for eight-year-olds, and besides this idea didn't make my promises about keeping up the school work sound any more plausible), nor insisting that everyone could enjoy the pony. Both my parents had watched me being bitten, kicked, trampled on, and thrown off far too often to believe that there was any enjoyment to be gained from being anywhere near horses, let alone being 'saddled' (this sort of cruel pun went straight over my head) with the responsibility of actually owning one.

No, they had worked out all the downsides, and decided it simply wasn't practical. No amount of pleading, manipulating, or laying on of guilt on my part had any effect. As I got older, they gradually convinced me that I didn't want to spend the rest of my life shovelling horse muck (although strangely, they were proved wrong in this ...) and that I should concentrate instead on getting a good education. 'As a doctor, or a lawyer, you'll have lots of money and you'll be able to keep your horse in absolute luxury in a livery yard somewhere.' It seemed to make sense, though I knew even then that I wouldn't want to be a 'weekend owner', and have someone else looking after my horse. As the years passed, my obsession grew, fuelled by the mountains of horse-related information I avidly consumed, ingrained more deeply with every precious hour I snatched at my local riding school. At eleven years old, I thought I knew everything there was to know about anything.

'You know,' I announced loftily, 'I think the importance of a good education is vastly overrated.'

'You could be right,' my dad said, 'but you'll only be in a position to judge that once you've actually got one.'

Then we moved to Canada. 'You see,' they pointed out, 'what would we do now if you had a pony?'

I couldn't understand their point. Obviously, I would stay behind with it. Or, if they really insisted we come with them, they could pay the very reasonable few thousand pounds it would cost to transport it across the Atlantic. What problem?

I was devastated at leaving my weekend 'job' and all my favourite ponies, not to mention my best friend, Ciara, who shared my obsession. From 7 a.m. until 6 p.m. every Saturday and Sunday, and each day of every school holiday, we would work at the riding school, and then hand over our pocket money for one lesson a week. And when I say worked, I mean worked. We would muck out stables, empty wheelbarrows, sweep yards, rake the school, fetch, groom and tack up the horses and ponies, fetch bales of hay and straw, fill haynets, scrub feed buckets and water drinkers, wash doors, clean tack and do any other job we were asked – and we loved it. We felt it was a privilege to be allowed to spend time on the yard, and we were extremely grateful.

Our weekend experiences would sustain us through an entire week of school, and when we weren't talking about horses we were pretending to *be* horses. Neighing to each other when we met, cantering over the log seats at school, and prancing around an imaginary dressage ring in the playground earned us a reputation for being 'different', and of course we came in for a fair bit of stick. We filed our fingernails into sharp points, and literally fought tooth and claw until we were left alone. In the evenings after school, we forced our dogs endlessly around courses of fences and through dressage tests. (Actually, I didn't have a dog and had to borrow a neighbour's, who could never work out why he was so tired after his 'walks'.) When it was dark, we knitted rugs for our plastic toy horses, and even knitted miniature horses. Ciara constructed the stables, and I knitted the saddles for my show-jumping hamsters (her gerbils were considerably less compliant). I couldn't imagine finding another friend like her.

All the same, we moved to Quebec, where I immediately encountered a difficulty. I couldn't speak French. Worse, I had to learn it. With liberal amounts of help from my parents, a dictionary, a table of verbs, and a lot of hard work, I scraped through my first year.

I didn't think much of Canada. The winters were too cold (minus 20°C), the summers were too hot (plus 30°C), and the riding was different. For a start they called it 'horseback riding' – as if there was any other part of the horse you would ride on! The chocolate tasted weird, and they didn't have smoky bacon crisps. A washout, as far as I was concerned. The only good thing was that Dad worked for Air Canada, which meant regular free flights back to England.

I was on a riding holiday at my old stables, during one summer visit to England, when my parents came to see me, saying they had something very important to discuss. My heart skipped a beat. Perhaps my riding instructor had told them how well I had been getting on with the horse I had for the week – a 16.2 hands high gelding by the name of Bank Robber. I could just see it: 'Yes, Mr and Mrs Golding, they really have built up a very strong bond, and in such a short time, too. Quite unusual. I think it would really be very much the best thing for both of them if you were simply to buy her the horse.' Surely they couldn't turn her down?

In fact, it was the next best thing – they were thinking of moving back to England. At least, Mum and I would return; Dad and my brother might have to stay in Canada. We'd still be able to see each other all the time, because of the free flights, and this way I'd be able to go to an English university. I wasn't listening to the details: I was just glad I'd be able to go back to my old stables.

The effort involved in learning French to the standard required in Quebec had given me a real taste for learning. I found time for one riding lesson a week, but otherwise I transferred my equine obsession to an academic one. My state school, which was considered almost dangerously radical, was extraordinarily accommodating, and arranged the timetable to allow me to do all sorts of extra exams, and to earn the sort of grades that impressed the entrance committee enough to earn me an unconditional offer from Cambridge to read Engineering.

I was nineteen, free and single, studying at one of the best universities in the world, but I had lost track of my purpose in life. I was further than ever from getting a horse, and I hardly even rode any more. Strangely enough, it was a skinny, musical intellectual, who didn't know one end of a horse from another, who changed all that. When I went to Cambridge, I didn't mean to find a 'husband' and settle down. It had been more my intention to take full advantage of the very favourable male to female ratio, and enjoy being single. I thought I'd give it another ten years or so, and then start looking for a serious partner. But as 'Golding' and 'Goodfellow', Adam and I were standing next to each other for the Matriculation photo, and so I suppose we were bound to meet, although, on that particular morning, we were both too hung-over to take much notice of each other.

Adam was charming and intense, prone to quoting long passages from *King Lear*, and with a disarming interest in what people really thought about the 'Meaning of Life'. To my mind the 'what's it all for, anyway?' questions are answered very conclusively with reference to the existence of chocolate, tea, and horses. He wasn't quite sure what to make of me, either.

We had our first all-night conversation mid-way through the second term. I was due to go rowing the following morning. Adam clearly thought I was mad when I began to get ready to go, particularly as it had just started snowing, but when you row as a team you have no choice but to turn up. The Cam is never too warm at six o'clock in the morning, but on a sleeting February morning the chill goes right into your bones. The strenuous effort of rowing warmed me up in a superficial way, but the very core of me stayed frozen.

I went straight to an Engineering practical afterwards, and cycling back to college on roads that had become treacherously icy, I had my mind full just trying to stay upright. When I started climbing the stairs to my room, however, I surprised myself by hoping that Adam was still there. He was, and after that we more or less moved into the same room together, which considering that the rooms were just big enough to fit a single bed, a desk, a chair and people only if they were on top of those pieces of furniture, was quite remarkable.

It was a chance encounter that re-ignited my passion for horses. Adam and I were in our second year, and living together in a village outside Cambridge. One fine day in early spring, I decided to go out for a bike ride and since Adam stared at me wordlessly from the sofa in utter disbelief when I suggested we go together, I set out alone. A couple of miles from home, I noticed a horse in a field. In fact, there were two, but I only had eyes for one, a bay mare. She was beautiful, young, and inquisitive. She had that bold-shyness typical of a young horse – she wanted to see what this new person was all about, but was not quite confident enough to come right over. She peered at me from under her forelock, her black-edged ears flicking backwards and forwards, and I fell in love. Eventually, I was able to stroke her neck from over the gate, and feed her handfuls of grass. I cycled home, wistfully, filled with that old familiar longing.

'I've just met a couple of really nice horses,' I said when I got back. 'Uh.'

Adam and I were both struggling with what can most politely be described as 'lethargy' at the time – bone idleness might be more accurate. I guess he was probably meant to be writing an essay, so any diversion was welcome. There being no chance of getting him to use a bicycle voluntarily, we got into the car his parents had lent us and drove back to the field. The horses had moved away, but came over when they saw us, keen on the idea of more hands picking them grass. There was a public footpath running through the field, so we went in. The two horses followed us. Reaching a high bank on the far side of the field, we clambered up it. They came too. As we ran down again, they broke into a canter and the gorgeous bay leapt off the bank and cavorted around us, bucking and leaping with excitement before running off with her friend. I explained to Adam, 'They're only young – I don't suppose they've been broken in yet.' (I'd had a quick peek at their teeth.) 'They're nice types, too, although this one is much better put together, and a lot more friendly.' Having long given up on the idea of having a horse, I was simply making idle conversation of the type horse people simply cannot resist. We started walking to the car.

'Well, how much do horses cost?' asked Adam. 'Perhaps we should buy her.'

I was dumbstruck by this idea. Then it became clear: I was living with a genius!

'Although, I suppose they must be quite expensive to keep?' he retreated, gripped by an unusual sense of practicality.

I thought back to all the long conversations I'd had on this topic with my parents: the vet's bills, the feed, the bedding, the shoes, the insurance, the saddle, the tack, the transport, and all the things I didn't know much about: chiropractors, massage therapists, dentists, not to mention riding lessons.

'Oh, no.' I flicked it all away with a contemptuous wave of my hand. 'Not really. They just live off grass. A bit of hay in the winter, a set of shoes now and again, nothing much. Besides, I could use the horse to teach on, and she'd earn her keep – might even bring some money in.'

I wasn't being deceitful. I really believed it.

The next day I set off resolutely to track down the owner. There was a large mansion overlooking the field, and I cycled tentatively down the long, winding drive. There were peacocks and statues everywhere, but no sign of any human activity. I was secretly relieved, left a note, and carried on.

The next property was located on the river that ran along the edge of the horses' field. The owner was a bright, cheerful man, and he directed me a couple of miles along the road to a house on a corner. 'There's a couple of horses in the field next to the house – you can't miss it.'

As I drew nearer the house, I grew increasingly nervous. It was all very well, as an abstract idea, to fulfil a lifetime's longing, but as the prospect of actually discovering the identity of the filly's owner grew nearer, I began to panic that my dream would never turn into reality. Until I found out one way or another, there was always the possibility that my dream might come true. Finding out for certain could mean the end of my hopes. It was probably best not knowing, I decided.

I was wrong about that, though. It turned out that the field owners were not in. I bumped into the postman who informed me they were away. I left a detailed note, describing precisely the location of the field, more than a mile from their house, and asking if they could give me the name of the horse owners who rented the field from them. I then waited for them to come home. It turned out to be ten long, agonising days.

Of course, we should have done the sensible thing and not visited the horses until we knew one way or another. Instead, we went every day and fell deeper in love. We visited late one night, 'on our way' back home from college. It was a wild, windy night, with a full moon. We stepped to the gate, and called out, and almost immediately there was a thundering of hooves and two horses materialised out of the darkness. They were restless and stopped only a moment to say hello before hurtling off around the field again. I couldn't bear the idea that all this might have to stop, that someone might take this perfect horse away, and I might never see her again.

The call came the next day. 'Yes, I know the mares you mean. Two in a field together, one with a star and a sock, the other without any markings. Two bays. That's right. No, I'm afraid they're not for sale. Old favourites of mine. Sorry.'

I couldn't trust myself to speak. The man by the river must have been wrong. She did own the horses. There couldn't be another pair to match the description. I mumbled my goodbye, and burst into tears. There was nothing to be done.

'I'll go to see her,' Adam volunteered, desperately trying to find a way to stop me crying. 'Try to change her mind.'

'She sounds pretty sure about it.' It felt like my life was falling apart.

With the gallantry for which I have always loved him, he insisted. 'I'll do my best, but don't expect too much,' he warned. 'It's not like we have unlimited funds to offer.' He added, under his breath, 'God, this is going to be embarrassing.'

He came back half an hour later, a half hour that seemed the longest of my life. I knew as soon as I saw his face that it was no good. He put his arms around me, but I was inconsolable.

Some hours later, my mood had still not improved. In an attempt to find a way of breaking the gloomy silence, Adam spoke, hoping to make me laugh but worried that I might hate him for ever if he didn't.

'But I thought you said you knew a bit about horses,' he offered tentatively. 'You said that they were thoroughbreds, and young, about two years old. It turns out that they're New Forest ponies, that the oldest one is eighteen, and she's eleven months pregnant – just about to give birth, in fact!'

I looked at him through my tear-bleary eyes as he waited nervously for my reaction.

'Oh, my God – she's got it wrong!' I shouted.

'I don't think so, Nick, I think she'd know her own horses ...'

It took me some time to make myself understood. 'No, she's talking about the wrong horses – she means the ponies next to her field, not the ones at the end of Long Drove. She didn't read my note properly! Call her up, and tell her not those bloody horses!'

On reflection, it was hardly surprising she'd thought I'd meant the two mares next to her house, as they matched my description almost exactly. I watched intently as Adam spoke politely to this woman, who seemed quite unperturbed about the fact that she had nearly killed me with grief.

'Sorry to bother you again, I think there's been a funny misunderstanding.' I harrumphed loudly in the background. 'Did you think we meant the ponies next to your house? In fact there are some others, in a field a couple of miles away. Yes, that's right. They're not yours? I wonder if you could possibly give us the number for the person who owns them. That's terribly kind of you. Thank you.'

I snatched the number from his fingers, and had started dialling almost before he had hung up. I got through to the owner straight away.

'You're interested in the older of the two? Well, no, she's not really for sale. I was going to break her in myself and sell her afterwards. But I suppose I could let her go, if you're really interested. When would you like to meet?' I looked at my watch, I could be there in five minutes. 'Would Wednesday suit you?'

Wednesday! That was two days away! But I didn't want to seem too desperate, and agreed.

I must have been hell to live with for those forty-eight hours. I was worried about the cost. Adam had kindly offered to liquidate his Post Office account, paying me back as he'd demolished my savings from my 'year out' working, but he only had £500. Would it be enough? If not, how could I get more? Prostitution, robbery, drug trafficking? There had to be a way.

I tried to appear non-committal when I met the owner, Wendy, but it was a difficult position to maintain. I had clearly gone to a lot of effort to track her down, and it didn't help that the horse – we'd already named her Sensi, the Japanese word for 'teacher' – was clearly fond of me, and wouldn't leave us alone. I couldn't pretend that I'd only noticed her in passing. The owner wanted £800 for her, and I managed to negotiate down to £750. That still left me £250 short. I would have to call my parents.

They were both living in Canada again, so I had to wait until it was evening over there, Montreal being five hours behind England. They were taken aback, not having heard this familiar request for nearly three years, but they tried all the usual objections.

'Well, I'm going to get one as soon as I graduate anyway, this is just a little sooner,' I protested. No, of course I didn't think getting a horse in my second year would distract me from my work. 'If anything, it will keep me fresh – stop me getting too intense.'

They didn't sound convinced, but promised to call me back the next day. I could, however, detect a hint of resignation in Mum's voice. I was no longer asking for permission to buy the horse, just the loan of some money. She was worried about how else I would raise it, I guess. I knew she could talk my dad around, and I was delighted, but not surprised, when they phoned back the next day to say they were sending a cheque over. And, as is so typical of their generosity, they never asked for it to be paid back.

It took a month to release Adam's funds from the Post Office, but I put down a deposit, and took over paying for the field. I got a job cleaning a house nearby, just a few hours a week, which covered the field rent of £6 per week.

On my twenty-first birthday, 12 May 1990, Sensi became my first horse, and I became the happiest person alive.

THREE

Starting Sensi
(Adam)

Looking back on it, it was madness. Or at least, naive optimism, for me to have any involvement in 'breaking in' a young horse. By now I just about knew one end of a horse from the other. But I had never taken the time to consider quite how powerful, heavy and easily frightened any horse – especially a young one – can be. This might seem an obvious fact, but my education had not always been of the most practical nature. Had I been fully aware of what we were taking on, I would not have made such a careless remark in that field in Cambridgeshire.

Although Nicole had a great deal of knowledge and experience of riding ponies and horses, she had never been involved in starting a youngster. However, there were three factors in her favour: Sensi was as willing and intelligent as any horse could be; Nicole had plenty of time to spend (if one ignored the work she was supposed to be doing for her degree) and she already had an almost encyclopaedic knowledge of every conceivable fact known to man on the subject of horses, except, as we were to discover so much later, the ones you really need to know. On the other hand, she had no facilities to work with, and was to be assisted by me, an incompetent, extremely amateur, fair-weather enthusiast of someone else's hobby.

The most useful of Nicole's books was Lucy Rees's *The Horse's Mind*. I remember being shown pictures of horses demonstrating various facial contortions with descriptions of what emotions they denoted. Even back then, when horses weren't yet my hobby, just my girlfriend's obsession, this really did appeal to me, much more than the difference between various types of nosebands, bridles or bits. I was intrigued by the idea of what was going on in a horse's mind.

Thanks to Nicole's patience, and the guidance of Lucy Rees's book, Sensi's early education was successful. During the summer break, we moved her to a field near Milton Keynes. Nicole took Sensi out for a lot of walks in hand, to see the countryside, and gradually expose her to traffic, dogs and all sorts of other sights and sounds. By taking her time, Nicole reduced the stress of each new procedure so much that nothing seemed remarkable to Sensi. I can hardly remember the first occasion when she put on a saddle it was so uneventful. Some time later, Nicole backed her for the first time, one baking hot summer's day in a friend's little paddock.

'What do you reckon?' Nicole asked me. 'Does she seem calm?'

Sensi was so hot and full of grass that she was having trouble not falling asleep.

So I gave Nicole my expert opinion. 'I'd say she's on the verge of losing consciousness.'

Nicole got me to lead Sensi up to the fence on which she was perching precariously. She patted Sensi's back a couple of times, sort of hugged her around the neck, leant across her back, and finally scrambled on. Still lying low on her neck, she stroked her gently. Sensi turned her head lazily, and sniffed Nicole's ankles. Nicole's face was just one ecstatic grin. Bareback and with just a headcollar, it was hardly a conventional backing, but it worked and we were happy. At least Nicole remembered to wear a hard hat, although I probably didn't.

In our final year we moved Sensi to a yard near Cambridge, where there was a tiny riding manège, fenced off in the middle of the field. She was not very well co-ordinated and found it difficult going around it, even in trot, as it was so small. One afternoon, Nicole arrived to find that Sensi had let herself in by limbo-dancing under the cross-rail, and was practising the work they'd been doing the day before! By making everything they did together so positive, and always ending on a good note before Sensi got bored or tired, Nicole had brought out the best in her, preserving her enthusiasm and the essence of her character.

We left Cambridge in 1991, with honours degrees in Social and Political Science, and were therefore unemployable. Nicole had switched from Engineering after one year, and I had left English after the second year, but I suspect it wouldn't have made much difference what our degree subjects had been. It was the height of the biggest recession since the 1930s, with unemployment amongst university graduates standing at 90 per cent. This was just as well, since neither of us really wanted a job. Nicole had already achieved her life's ambition, and mine – that of being the next Jimi Hendrix – was unlikely to be served by getting a conventional job. We signed on and moved to Milton Keynes, staying with Nicole's parents, who had by then moved back to England from Canada. It was now clear that living with Nicole was going to involve horses. 'If you can't beat them, join them' was the only option, I felt. I tried to sell myself for a price, though, and eventually we came to a reasonable compromise. I would learn to ride; she would learn the guitar. She mastered a few chords, even a song or two (probably 'Mustang Sally' and 'Wild Horses'), but her enthusiasm petered out after about a month. Perhaps things would have been different if there were more popular songs about horses.

Even at this early stage, however, it was already clear that I had a close affinity to horses – at least, they seemed to like me. A year after we had graduated, I went to a house party in Norwich, leaving Nicole to look after Sensi. The day after the party, my friends and I went to a pub for lunch and were walking back through a field, home to three huge Shire horses. One came over and wanted some attention, probably used to being offered treats by people using the public footpath through his paddock. He was so big that I practically had to stand on my toes to scratch his wither. He loved it, sticking his nose into the air and wibbling the end of it around, showing clear evidence of the evolution of the elephant as he stretched his lip out in ecstasy, mutually grooming the space in front of him and turning to nuzzle me, asking me to scratch harder. My friends had moved off, but as they turned to tell me to come on, they all burst out laughing at the sight of this huge animal as he contorted his face comically. Or so I thought. His belly was so big, it filled my line of sight and it was not until I had walked a few metres away that I could see just why they were all laughing. My new friend liked me so much he had let down his undercarriage and was standing on what appeared to be five legs, wistfully looking at me as I left.

But it was on a trip to Wales the autumn after we had graduated that I came to realise the full extent of Nicole's single-minded focus. Taking only mild interest in the castles and hill forts I had thought we were planning to visit, she came up with 'a much better idea'. Looking up from a sea of books and maps spread out on the table, she said, 'Did you know, Lucy Rees lives somewhere in North Wales. Perhaps we could go and find her on the way to one of your castles?'

From photos, diagrams and descriptions in two of Lucy's books, Nicole had narrowed down the location of her house to somewhere in the vicinity of a mountain called Cnicht, in the heart of Snowdonia.

In those days, our options for holiday destinations were severely limited. However, living as we were with Nicole's parents, the idea of some time to ourselves held a lot of appeal, especially as most of our friends had gone off to Thailand, Australia or Japan. We hardly had enough money to fill a car with petrol, let alone buy one, and an overseas adventure was completely out of the question. We decided to visit a friend who lived at the foot of Cader Idris. His cottage, built with stones from a nearby castle, the last stronghold of Welsh nationalists, which had been comprehensively demolished by the English in 1283, made up exactly half of the houses in Llanfihangel-y-Pennant (excluding the church). The hamlet nestles into a perfect valley near the coast, and is overhung with crags echoing to the calls of buzzards and red kites. Its claim to fame is as the only village in the country with twice as many letters in its name than it has inhabitants. Clearly it was not going to be accessible by public transport.

A friend from Cambridge, my old schoolmate Dom, had got himself into the unenviable position of owning a clapped-out Ford Escort estate, which needed constant repairs to keep it on the road, and for which he did not possess a licence to drive. It was almost old enough to be a collector's item, except that nobody in their right mind would collect such a desperately unstylish car. Nearly a year before, it had somehow passed an MOT test, but this did not necessarily mean it was roadworthy. In any case, it had been sitting outside Dom's flat for months, quietly detracting from Cambridge's tourist attractions, and utterly redundant. Therefore it was not terribly difficult to persuade him to let me borrow it, and I took the bus over to Cambridge and drove it back to MK to pick up Nicole for our ten-day trip. It was a rusting death trap, and suddenly I wasn't so sure that Dom was doing me a favour when it failed at first to start. He sounded unusually sober as he wished me good luck and added, 'Take care.'

Unable to reach 60 mph, the car only just made it to Milton Keynes and the brakes were decidedly dodgy, so we held off a couple of days until they had been fixed. Although our extremely limited holiday budget had not included the costs of repairing Dom's car, this was, in retrospect, probably the best money I have ever spent. We set off across the English Midlands, following the Roman road, Watling Street, which runs from almost outside where we were living, right to the middle of Wales. From here, we found ourselves struggling to get up the steep inclines of the Welsh mountains, even though we remained on A roads. The traffic built up behind us as the Escort toiled up to the crest of each ridge, at one point needing to be put into first gear as we urged it on like cheerleaders, looking desperately for a roadside parking space to let the long line of cars past.

We managed to reach our destination, and from there, a few days later, decided to make an excursion to see one of Wales's magnificent strongholds. Or, as it turned out, Lucy Rees's house, 'on the way'. After an hour's drive, we left the main road and headed for a village that appeared to be in the right area. Of course we got lost, although to say we got lost implies that we actually knew where we were trying to go, which we did not. After many embarrassing conversations with local shepherds and shopkeepers, we came across a couple of farmers who were standing by the side of the road. They seemed to know who we were talking about, although we found their accents almost impossible to interpret. 'Up that road,' one of them pointed. 'Go past the village Lleffiddillich bllah bllah and then when you come past a house, go left, Ddyllian lleyn bllah bllah and she's the second house llan Gw llar the valley.' Having asked him to repeat himself once, we pretended to understand, thanked him and set off.

For those who may not have visited the charming vicinity of Cnicht, there are not many roads, houses, or villages, but still we managed to take a wrong turning. We came to a house, expecting there to be a drive. There was a muddy footpath leading through some trees. I suggested we park and have a look down it.

'Nonsense,' Nicole stated, so firmly that anyone might have thought she knew what she was talking about. 'Where's the driveway? It must be up there,' she said, indicating a stony track which continued beyond the house. 'She does say in the book that she lives halfway up a mountain.'

Ignoring the voice in my head, which was getting a touch uneasy about this little jaunt, I turned the car up the track, which was not immediately too steep for a mountain goat. As we came out of the trees, however, all I could see ahead was a barren mountainside, strewn with rocks, the odd scrap of vegetation clinging to its near-vertical face. 'Are you sure?' I asked, knowing full well that she wasn't. 'I don't see how she could possibly live up here.' I glanced across the car towards the valley in which two other houses could now be seen. 'Perhaps it's one of those.'

'Look, let's just see if it's round the next corner.'

But the next corner led only to more bleak cliffside, and the gradient of the track was now so steep that the car was having trouble climbing any further. So was I, as my ears popped with the altitude and my vertigo began to make me feel that I was about to veer off the road and down the precipice that loomed just inches from the passenger side wheels. Oblivious to the danger, Nicole was humming cheerfully. By now, I was starting to pray that our destination would be just around the corner, because hopefully there would be somewhere to turn around, and I would not have to go down this slippery track backwards.

'Look,' I said as calmly as I could, 'this is ridiculous. How could anyone live up here and not die from exposure?'

'Well, why do you think there is a track, if nobody lives up here?'

Nicole had a point, although I found it hard to believe anyone would build, let alone buy, a house stuck on the side of a precipice when there was a perfectly cosy valley a few hundred feet below. I agreed to keep going and look around the next corner, and then the one after that. Reversing was the only option, anyway, as the track was only just wide enough for the car. With a cliff going down on one side, and up on the other, I was seriously toying with the idea of abandoning the vehicle, escaping on foot and making up a story as to what had happened to it. I was just thinking up my excuses when, around the next corner, we came to a passing place, cut out of the rock on the side of the track. It looked just big enough to turn the car around, and I pulled in.

'What are you doing, it can't be here,' Nicole protested, but I categorically refused to drive any further, and as she didn't have a driving licence, there was no arguing with me. 'It's probably just around the next bend,' she protested. 'Well, then, we'll know when we get there,' I said, turning off the ignition and getting out. The air was cold and clear, and although I wouldn't let myself go closer than 5 feet from the edge, I could see we had gone a lot higher than I had thought.

'Aren't you going to lock it?' Nicole said as I put the keys into my pocket. 'It isn't our car, after all.'

'If anyone is stupid enough to steal it, they can have it,' I replied, remembering that Dom had said exactly the same thing to me when I left Cambridge. 'Come on, let's go.'

So we continued round that bend, only to see another one a few hundred metres ahead, beyond which we couldn't see. We continued walking until we reached that, to find yet another stretch of road that led around a corner. Nicole was beginning to accept that this wasn't likely to be where anyone but a mad hermit would live, or possibly a buzzard or two, but having come this far, we were curious to find out where the road led. It seemed impossible that it didn't go somewhere, as it had clearly taken a huge effort to build it out of the solid granite mountainside. Eventually, after we had climbed about twenty minutes, we came around the final bend. There in front of us, behind large gates imposingly blocking the path, was a disused slate mine, perched on top of the cliff with a long chute leading into the valley, down which the quarried stone must have been thrown. There was no sign of any Welsh mountain ponies, nor anyone to ask where a woman called Lucy lived.

It turned out, when we actually did find her house, that she was in Portugal, buying Lusitano horses.

'Never mind,' Nicole said cheerily, 'at least it was fun trying to track her down. Wasn't it great going up that hill?' I looked at her sharply, trying to detect sarcasm in her voice, but there was none. 'Maybe next time we could bring Sensi to Wales, and ride her up to the very top.'

Returning to Cnicht didn't appeal to me, but the thought of going there with Sensi made the prospect much more inviting. It was absolutely wonderful to have the companionship and love of this beautiful creature in my life, and Sensi had already done us a great service by preventing us from drifting into London along with most of our other friends. Instead, we had settled for living in Milton Keynes, where we rented a little flat, close to some paddocks where Sensi could live. Through her, I had begun to appreciate for the first time the beauty of the English countryside, for seeing nature from the back of a horse is a very different experience than travelling on foot or by bike. Above the level of the hedges, I could see so much more. And I soon discovered that wildlife viewed me in a different way when I was on top of a horse – not so much as a fearsome predator, but more as a fellow creature, and I spotted foxes, deer, hares and birds at much closer quarters than ever before.

But it was not a good combination, a complete novice learning to ride on a recently started young thoroughbred. With characteristic grace Sensi put up with me banging about on her back, farcically bouncing as I tried to sit to her trot. Sensibly, I got some riding lessons at the local school where Nicole had learned as a child.

Like most English riders, I religiously carried a whip at all times, although I did not find with Sensi that I needed it for its original purpose, getting her to move forward, which she was always keen to do. In fact it would have been of more use to me if it had been capable of getting her to stop. In my first emergency situation it did not help me in the slightest when, on a blustery day, she cantered off with me down a bridleway. I had asked for a trot but was soon out of control, as, with the wind under her tail, she headed for a narrow gap in a line of trees, through which the bridleway ran. Nicole, on foot behind me, could do nothing but watch helplessly and wince as I was unceremoniously dumped when Sensi shied just in front of the gap. I too had known intuitively that she was not going through, and despite having already learned that much of good horsemanship is 'anticipation and feel', this was of little help to me. Although I could 'anticipate' that she was going to stop suddenly, this did not prevent me from having the unmistakable 'feeling' of having a bridleway in my face. Sensi seemed very surprised that I had decided to get off and worship her so suddenly. She stood a few yards away, sniffing the earth in case I had found something worth eating. Shocked but not injured, the first thing I saw when I looked up was my whip. When she saw me reach for it, Sensi decided it might not be in her best interest to stick around, and ran off half a mile across the field, eventually to be retrieved with the help of a friendly gardener and his carrots.

This was my first fall, and I learned a lot from it, but was only slightly comforted by Nicole's words.

'Well,' she said knowledgeably, 'at least you're not a complete beginner any more. They say you aren't a good rider until you've fallen off seven times.'

I replied that if this was what was required, I would just as soon never be a good rider. And anyway, surely a really good rider wouldn't fall off even once!

Of course, Sensi was just young and inexperienced, and could not be blamed for what had happened. But as time went on, and she continued to spook at lots of things, such as plastic, paper, leaves, flowers – in fact, everything except the one really dangerous thing she came across, cars – I began to get frustrated. I also had another, very nasty fall in which, cantering down a bank, I lost my balance and flew straight over her head when she put in her characteristic duck out to the side. As with my first fall, I knew I was going to come off a long time before I did, but lacked the ability to do anything about it. It was probably a good thing that I was resigned to my fate and did not try to stay on, for doing so might well have been fatal. I flew through the air for what seemed like ages, and landed on the top of my head like a human cannonball, feeling a sickening jolt go up my spine. My first thought was, This is what it's like to be dead. Then, lying still, I realised that it was remarkably similar to being alive and I was able to feel my fingers and toes. I stood up, leaving a helmet-shaped imprint deep in the earth, and got back on my bemused mount. Unbelievably, I was not seriously injured, as the ground was very soft following several months of constant rain, and the force had gone directly along my backbones in a perfect line. Otherwise I would have been, at best, in a wheelchair for the rest of my life. I was incredibly lucky. Of course, this accident was also my fault entirely. But after that, I was anxious about having another fall and was less patient with Sensi. I started to tap her neck with the whip when she spooked. At times, this was relatively successful, as it could bring her attention back to me, but if I was in the wrong mood, I would sometimes use it inappropriately, antagonising her and making her more nervous, simply because it was there in my hand and I didn't realise how many other tools were at my disposal. I never considered how Sensi must have viewed the whip.

Of course, my early years of riding were peppered with incidents in which I nearly came to grief. One of the more memorable happened when one of my old friends, Ben, visited with his future wife, Louise. We had taken Sensi with us to the pub, half a mile from her field, one balmy summer's evening when Nicole was away. She was all tacked up, and seemed to be enjoying visiting the pub, where we sat on the benches in the garden. Ben had bought her a pint of beer, thoughtfully presented in an old ice cream tub, which she sniffed, slobbered in and then ignored while she began to tuck in to the lawn. The scene was one of absolute peace. The type of situation that any horse can turn into an emergency in the blink of an eye.

Standing nearby was a bin, which consisted of a steel cylinder held within a frame, made up of vertical strips of metal that ended in decorative curls. Smelling the salt from packets of crisps, Sensi began to investigate by sticking her head in. Before it even happened I knew she was going to get her bridle caught and I leaped up to disentangle her, too late. Feeling a jab on her mouth, she lifted her head sharply, only to find the bin came up with it and bashed her in the face. Panic set in immediately as she tried to get rid of these rather cumbersome blinkers. She reared up, with the bin still hanging off her mouth, banging up and down within its holder, showering her face with rubbish that only added to her shock. She wheeled round as fast as she could in an attempt to escape, while I held on to the reins, and was lifted bodily into the air, until I found myself flying round her in a circle, parallel to the ground.

Thankfully the bin somehow fell off her face and we stood there, shaking, while Ben and Louise, their faces ashen, emerged from under the table to check that we were OK. The rest of the pub's clientele, being English, pretended that nothing untoward had happened, and they had not, just seconds before, been in danger of having a man, a horse and a large bin fly into their laps, or through the huge plate-glass window they were sitting next to.

But, otherwise, things went very well with Sensi until she reached the age of about five. It was then that Nicole, encouraged by textbooks and peers, decided it was time she moved on. This meant getting her to 'work in an outline, on the bit'. In theory this would mean her using her hindquarters more, and keeping her nose vertical. Common advice was to 'push the horse forward from the leg into a restraining hand' – seven pounds of pressure in each hand, according to the only book that quantified what a 'restraining hand' should be. In practice, this meant desperately trying to kick her every step of the way, and pulling her mouth all the time. She disliked this, as well as the side reins we bought her, and would constantly move her head around, trying to get rid of the pressure. It also made her mouth less sensitive, which in turn led to her being harder to slow down, although she remained amazingly forgiving and never really threatened to bolt. The crazy thing was that Sensi had previously been working really well – using her back and actively engaging her hindquarters. She was responsive, reasonably balanced, and obedient in every way. She just didn't have her nose on vertical. Sensi quite literally got all in a lather over this dubious ideal, which she resolutely refused to submit to.

At around this time, we gradually began what would probably have been the smallest business in the country, except that so many businesses were already evaporating in a sea of bad debt, for it was the early 1990s. Trading under the name 'Sensi's School', at first it was only Nicole, having taken her BHS Stage 1 and 2 exams, who gave lessons to a few children. Then my godfather kindly offered to buy us another horse, and this was when we bought Wilberforce, the bay hunter with a dislike for puddles, who was far too large for most of our clientele, which strangely did not include a large percentage of heavy adult males. Much more suitable was my godfather's next gift, Cobweb, an old palomino schoolmaster, 14.2 hands high, very pretty and popular with young girls. He never put a foot wrong in the whole time he worked, and is the only one of our horses who could possibly be said, on balance, to have actually made any money for us. By this time I reckoned I could say, 'Sit up straight, heels down, now ask for a working trot along the far side' as well as the best of them, so I started giving the odd riding lesson myself, to beginners. At times my Cambridge degree definitely came in handy as I not only had a nearly inexhaustible ability to pontificate on any subject (regardless of lack of knowledge), left over from the days of discussing and writing at length about books I had usually not read, but also the arrogance to pretend I actually knew what I was talking about, which was not often the case.

I had already discovered, of course, the extent of Nicole's shocking cover-up on the costs of keeping horses. Making any money from the business was implausible to say the least, but the income from lessons helped to offset the ridiculous overheads. But I was not sure my godfather was doing us a favour by buying the new horses, for it meant there were yet more expenses involved. Nicole got a part-time job as a cashier at a building society, which paid some of our basic expenses. At a time when we did not have the money to go to the pub or cinema, the six-weekly shoeing costs alone were appalling, particularly given how infrequently either of us would get new shoes for ourselves.

The only sense in which we found the horses to be naturally productive was in creating massive quantities of manure. This endless disposal problem, however, led me to a lifelong interest. Until that time I had never had any appreciation of plants and would just as soon have watched paint dry as visit a garden. It all began because one of the old boys from the local allotments came and asked if we would mind him taking some manure away. As we gathered it frequently to combat parasitic worms, but had nowhere to put it, we were more than happy to let him take all he wanted. This led to Nicole making a throwaway comment of similar magnitude to the one I'd made in Sensi's first field a few years before.

'I wonder where the allotments are? Perhaps we could get one, and grow some potatoes or something with all this muck?'

Within a year we had four, very well-fertilised allotments, producing dozens of varieties of vegetables, fruit, herbs and flowers, as well as billions of well-fed, happy slugs. At first, I literally didn't know a radish from rhubarb. We set to work digging up the thick clay in a vain attempt to destroy the invading hordes of couch-grass and nettles, plastering chemicals on the insects and slugs that devoured most of what we planted. It was hard work, but when we had our first harvest of ten, fresh sweetcorn, it was all worth it.

We began to discover new ways of gardening, and eventually abandoned the traditional methods of soil preparation for a no-dig, organic approach. This did not come easy to Nicole, who had by now got into the almost endless task of turning the soil to knock back the weeds, which somehow always seemed to thrive more than any expensive, vacuum-packed seeds bought in the shops. We could almost hear the old boys tut-tutting as they continued their time-honoured practice of digging the heavy clay, while we would simply empty a barrow of nearly-rotted manure onto the surface of a bed, and sling a carpet over the top to stifle the weeds until spring, when we would lift off the cover to find abundantly healthy soil, ready for sowing, with the manure mixed in by worms who had been working hard all winter. The warm, dry micro-climate produced by our carpet mulch also encouraged beetles, who gradually reduced the number of slugs to a manageable level. Our favoured method in the end was to raise plants in biodegradable pots on the tiny windowsill of our one-bedroom flat, before planting them, pots and all, through holes in the carpets, using a bulb-planter. This gave us amazing results for much less effort. It was not the last time we would find that 'alternative' ways of doing things actually made the most sense. However, the old boys got the last laugh. They generally had wives back at home who would prepare a meal from the hard-earned fruits of all their labour. Nicole and I were usually so exhausted by a day riding, shifting muck, planting and harvesting, that if we had the energy to bring some produce back up the hill from the allotments, it would usually begin the long, slow process of rotting in our fridge, before eventually being taken back down to be composted. Meanwhile we would scramble to shove some bread into the toaster and a tin of baked beans into the microwave, to stop ourselves fainting from hunger. This was our contribution to nature's never ending cycle of growth, decay and renewal, which, although immeasurably satisfying, rarely put a decent meal on our table.

And so it was that one afternoon, I came in from the allotment with a bunch of ill-fated, optimistic vegetables, to be told by a breathless Nicole, as she fumbled a tape into the VCR, that there was this amazing guy on TV. He could get a horse to follow him around without a lead rope, and put on the first saddle, bridle, and rider in about thirty minutes. They called him 'the man who listens to horses'.

I sat and watched the first QED programme about Monty Roberts in stunned silence. It was as if a whole new dimension opened up in my appreciation of horses, indeed of life. Suddenly I realised that there was so much more to understanding a horse than I had thought. And such benefit to be gained from that understanding. So much of what Monty was saying seemed equally applicable to people. Using nothing but a rope, body language, and an acute understanding of the horse's psychology, he created within minutes a bond with a horse he had never met before, bringing out the best in the horse and also in himself through his fundamental commitment to non-violence. The results were almost unbelievable, but it all made perfect sense. It was as if he and the horse were holding a rational conversation, all of their own. Spellbound by how he was generating such a calm presence around himself, and producing such an amazing response, I found myself being drawn into a new world, a world of relative speeds and movement, eye contact and angles, of pressure and release, advance and retreat. The world of a language he called Equus.

FOUR

When the student is ready, the teacher will appear (Nicole)

For me, the ten-week Monty Roberts Preliminary Certificate of Horsemanship course was like dying and going to heaven. From 8.45 in the morning until 5 at night my day was filled with nothing but horses, and I was surrounded by people who shared my obsession. It was just as I'd imagined going to Cambridge would be: bright articulate people tossing ideas around, sharing thoughts, discussing finer points, having brilliant insights. University had been a big disappointment in that regard, not just because I'd chosen Engineering and discovered that the loading weight of a plank of wood didn't fascinate me that much after all, but also because it didn't appear to fascinate many other people either. Even in the more intellectual subjects, like political science, philosophy, or English, where people would get really fired up and fiercely debate the issues of the ages, for many students there was still an underlying lethargy, a commitment to doing the least work (and the most drinking) possible, fuelled perhaps by a post-adolescent existential crisis. My biggest regret some years on was wasting the opportunity to pick some of the finest brains in the world. I wasn't going to make the same mistake again.

One of the aspects of the Cambridge environment I particularly disliked, but quickly found myself colluding with, was the level of intellectual aggression. Undergraduates wanted to be seen to be clever, and this sometimes made them extraordinarily closed-minded and judgemental. Rather than listening to other points of view, they generally wanted to trash them, using the most obscure, esoteric language possible. I suppose it was partly because there were a lot of shocked, unnerved people; they were used to being the cleverest people in their school, and now all of a sudden 5 As at A level was nothing special.

But this intellectual ferocity was nothing compared to the deeply-held, never-to-be-challenged views of many in the world of horses. Over the course of the next few years, both Adam and I would come face to face with this resistance time and time again.

Not that the learning environment at West Oxfordshire College was perfect, either. There was scepticism from tutors on other courses, and right from the very start students were desperate to impress Monty with their skills and knowledge. This competitiveness was hardly conducive to learning.

I very nearly didn't go on the course. Like so many others, I'd seen Monty on the first QED programme, and been amazed. But it didn't seem like a possibility to meet him. In my mind, he became the equine world's equivalent of David Bowie – an utter genius, well out of reach. Then I saw a small advert in one of the glossy horse magazines I bought from time to time: 'Ten-week course on the techniques of Monty Roberts to be held at West Oxfordshire College, Witney'. I looked it up on the map – definitely within travelling distance, if I had a car.

'I don't know,' I said to Adam, 'I'd have to give up my job.'

He looked at me in astonishment. 'Are you mad? You work as a cashier at a building society. Part time. This course is about horses! You'll get another job.'

Then I spoke to my mum. 'I know it's great value for money' (the course was just £750 for the entire ten weeks), 'but it's still quite a lot to find all at once.'

She looked at me oddly. 'Oh, don't worry about that, we can always lend you the money if you don't have it to hand.'

'But ...'

'No problem.'

I tried again.

'Dad, I want to go on a ten-week course about the methods of that American chap we saw on TV, remember, the one who listens to horses. I'd have to give up my job, I don't have the money to pay for it, and I'd have to somehow get hold of a car. What do you think?'

I knew he would say no. He hated anything that looked like a 'scheme'. After all, there's no money to be made from horses, and it's not a good idea to change jobs too often. Looks bad on the CV. Besides, he would think it crazy to invest even such a reasonable amount of money in what essentially amounted to a hobby. The part of me that didn't think I deserved to go on the course knew I could rely on my dad to back me up. Even more conveniently, I could blame him for holding me back.

'Yeah, sounds great! Don't worry about the money, I'm sure we could help out. I've been thinking about getting a second car anyway. You could take the black one. Witney, eh? Not far out of Oxford, I think, let me get the map ...'

I was astonished. Resigned, I pointed out Witney to him.

I don't know why I experienced this reluctance to go on the course. I do know that we often resist the things in life that would benefit us the most. Also, that the fear of success can be greater than the fear of failure. Whatever the reason, in the face of such over-whelming support from Adam and my parents, I could think of no convincing excuse. I had missed the deadline for the first course, but was in ample time for the second. I took greater care over the application form than I ever had for any job or university entrance, and waited anxiously. By now, all my hesitation had dissolved, and I was desperate to go. When the acceptance came through, I could barely contain my excitement. I couldn't wait to get started. Since then I've met many people with similar stories. Sometimes it's taken them several years to come on the courses. I fancy I can see the same look of slightly stunned disbelief and relief on their faces that I must have had when I found myself sitting in the classroom that first morning: they can't understand why they nearly let such a fantastic opportunity slip through their fingers.

The course started in October 1996. As I drove the circuitous route to Witney, I could barely contain my excitement and curiosity. It was one of those stunning, bright autumn mornings, and I was on my way to meet one of the greatest horsemen of all time. I had just finished my first reading of his book, and I was enthralled. Not only was he a genius horse trainer, but he had clearly led a fascinating life as well. I was determined not to be overwhelmed, but I still felt pretty daunted.

I arrived at the college and was shown into a large room. A few students were already there, and more kept arriving as we started to go through the inevitable administrative tasks. Kelly Marks, the course organiser, was there, being bright and friendly and efficient. I had thought that she simply did the administration for the courses, and that someone else did the actual teaching. She looked to me far too pretty and feminine to be any good with a horse. Little did I know just how much I would learn from her over the years, nor what a profound role model and friend she would turn out to be.

We had about half an hour to have a coffee and meet each other before Monty arrived. There were eighteen of us. The atmosphere was electric. I think we were probably all worried that we would say the wrong thing, create a bad first impression, and were anxious to establish allies straight away. Questions sparked around the room: 'How many times have you read the book?' 'What do you think he'll be like?' 'Have you seen a demonstration?' 'What sort of horses will there be on the course?' 'Will we have to show him what we can do today?'

Then all of a sudden he was there. We all sat down, Kelly introduced him, and he started talking.

'I feel very humbled,' he began, 'to see you all here today. To have such young, bright, enthusiastic students on a course to learn my methods is a great honour.'

I looked around the room. Not everyone was under sixty, but Kelly later informed me that anyone under fifty-five is a kid to Monty.

As he continued, I felt a surge of happiness. I was in the right place, I was doing the right thing, I was going in the right direction. Ten weeks of self-indulgent learning stretched out ahead of me. For once, I was studying something that I really wanted to know about. But would I be any good at it?

Kelly then asked us to introduce ourselves, and say a little about our experience with horses and what we hoped to get out of the course. I was very impressed by the other students – it seemed they had all done much more exciting things than I had. I mentioned starting Sensi, and having my own small business. I'm sure Monty and Kelly gave me the same reassuring smiles they gave everyone, but I wouldn't have known, staring as I was at my hands the whole time. Monty often laments the fact that the English don't seem capable of looking people in the eye and giving a firm handshake. I've often felt like contesting this notion, but I can't honestly say that anyone in the room that day actually met his gaze and spoke confidently to the room. It didn't seem to occur to Monty that his presence might have been the cause of such shyness.

After lunch we went to the stables, and Monty worked with three horses, introducing the first two youngsters to their first saddle, bridle, and rider, and putting the first saddle and long-lines on a third. It was fascinating, and I got my first glimpse of his incredible energy.

When the day was over, I reluctantly drove home, head buzzing, trying to imprint every last detail in my mind.

As I told Adam all about my day that evening, I was already feeling the first pangs of nostalgia. One day was over, the course wouldn't last for ever, what was there afterwards? Would I ever have this sort of opportunity again?

After the morning lectures the next day, we headed out to the stud stables again. I had noticed that on the first afternoon Kelly had done something that struck me as curious: she had asked for volunteers to take her car to drive Monty to the stable yard. What she wanted was for people to get the chance to have an informal chat with Monty on the way over, to get to know him as an individual, and not be too much in awe of him. I was very dubious about this idea. Although I'd passed my driving test in a manual car by this time, I was used to driving an automatic. I could envisage the embarrassment of repeatedly stalling Kelly's rather sporty car, grinding the gears, or perhaps even crashing it. I hid at the back when Kelly asked for volunteers, careful not to meet her eye. It didn't strike me as a good omen, though – if I couldn't bear to expose even my driving skills to scrutiny, what would I be like in the pen?

That afternoon, we worked on the horses again; the two that had been sat on briefly the day before, by an assistant tutor, were this time taken through the process by students. Monty called instruction from the outside of the pen, and the students concerned did an admirable job. I was one of several people who had leapt at the chance to 'have a go', but as I watched a fellow student become only the second ever person to sit on the first youngster, a three-year-old thoroughbred called Candide, I felt no sense of being left out. It was as fascinating to watch as it was to do, and I was sure we'd all have a chance. Walking back to the car park, however, I realised with some surprise that not everyone felt the same way. I could hear mutterings of 'It's not fair' and 'Why were those students chosen?' I closed my ears to the negative words, but they were like pinpricks threatening to burst the balloon of my happiness.

On the third afternoon, I caught a glimpse of the frustration that can result from wanting to impress. One of the students, Janet, was working with Magic, one of the other youngsters, and she was doing a good job, following Monty's instructions carefully, but not always moving at the right pace or in exactly the right direction. As it was Magic's third time in the round pen, he was getting more familiar with the process, and was finding the student's occasional small mistake somewhat confusing. Tension was creeping into Monty's voice, and he was clearly worried about undoing the progress made in the first two sessions. To prevent any further confusion, he stepped into the pen, and took over that part of the join-up process. For those of us watching, it was immensely valuable – we could really see the difference in what Monty was doing. For Janet, though, it was a disappointing moment. She watched carefully as Monty demonstrated what he had been trying to explain, and then she took over for the rest of the session. I thought she'd coped with the situation brilliantly, and was very impressed with her resilience.

As it happened, she and I ended up driving back to the college in the same car with the student, Anna, who had worked on the horse the day before. Janet was giving herself a hard time over the mistakes she'd made. I tried to reassure her without offending Anna.

'Well, from where I was sitting, it didn't look as if you made any more mistakes than Anna did – sorry, Anna. It's just that because it was the horse's third time, it was even more critical not to confuse him. If you'd done the horse yesterday, and Anna had done him today, I'm sure the outcome would've been the same.'

Although Anna agreed wholeheartedly, we couldn't shake Janet's persistent feeling that she'd somehow failed. I could really identify with this feeling, particularly given my reticence to get behind the wheel of Kelly's car, but it occurred to me in a sudden flash of insight, that the whole point of receiving help and guidance was to have your mistakes exposed. If you managed to conceal them, you would never get the information you needed to correct them. I was reminded of one of my most absurd Cambridge experiences: I was struggling with an exercise paper on Thermodynamics, and although the answers were printed on the back, it was taking me about four hours per question to arrive at the correct answer. And even when I'd finally contorted my calculations so that I came to the right conclusions, I was never able to remember the process of how I'd got there. Yet, rather than explaining my difficulty to the tutor, I spent an hour trying to convince him that I understood it, when in reality, it had made no sense to me at all. Janet wasn't much cheered when I recounted this experience, especially when I told her how dismally I'd done in the exams at the end of my first year, before giving up Engineering. But from that moment on, I resolved that I would never try to cover up my inadequacies when I was receiving instruction with a horse, and I would never again pretend to understand something I didn't.

At the end of the first week of the course, Monty did the last few dates of his 'book launch' tour, a series of demonstrations to promote his work and his book. When Kelly told us that we were welcome to come along to any or all of the demonstrations for free, it almost seemed like too much indulgence. As a child, I once had the experience of going to Horse of the Year Show the night before a riding holiday. Having two such momentous events happening so close together was almost unthinkable, like having two Christmases at once. To see Monty start a horse in front of 1,800 enthralled spectators made me realise just how privileged I was to be on the course. And even though the graduates from the first course who were now helping on the tour clearly felt that as new students our group were all impostors, I felt a tremendous sense of belonging.

A common student fear was that once Monty left, at the end of the first week, the rest of the course might seem a little flat. We needn't have worried. Kelly stepped into the fray, and we got straight back into the swing of things. It soon became clear why Monty considers her the best teacher of his methods anywhere in the world, and whilst I may have initially felt a little regret that I wasn't chosen to work in the pen while Monty was on the course, I quickly realised that having Kelly teach me didn't constitute 'second best'. My concerns about her unhorsey feminine appearance quickly dissolved. There was serious horse work to be done on the course, and Kelly was more than up to the job.

The weeks settled down into a steady rhythm: Tuesdays to Fridays at the college, then the weekend teaching riding, with Monday to myself to catch up on the muck clearing and to try out new techniques. Sensi was astonished when I started visiting her every morning at 6 a.m., practising halt transitions by the circular light of the street lamps that overhung the edges of her field. Monty had told us that he had taught his horse Dually how to do those amazing sliding stops by riding straight at the walls at the end of the school. As the horse gathered himself to stop, Monty would sit back and say 'whoa!' Once Dually understood the association, Monty would sit back and say 'whoa' before Dually reached the end of the school. The idea was that the walls were quite a long way apart, and after a while the horse would eagerly start anticipating the command. If, however, he failed to stop, Monty could push him on until he reached the wall. The field where Sensi lived had tall hedges all around the edge, and I would ride her at these as fast as I dared on the frosty grass. She very quickly got the idea, and would do some pretty convincing transitions from canter to halt.

It was fascinating to see how the horses on the course developed over the ten weeks. The two 'starters', Candide and Magic, which Monty had worked with on the first day, progressed steadily, calmly, with no problems. The third horse, Rosie, turned out to be quite a challenge. Athletic and sharp, she was wary and distrustful of everything. It soon emerged that she wasn't a 'normal starter', but was in fact 'remedial'. The owners had already had a go at breaking her in, but by the time she had reared over backwards twice on long-lines, they had decided to send her away to the course. They hadn't explicitly lied about her background, but they had omitted to tell us some very important facts. Then, in my naivety, I was shocked. Now I know this is commonplace, and we always ask very specific questions before horses arrive with us for training, and take the horse's word for it rather than a human's. Even the most honest owner may not have been told the truth by those who have trained or owned the horse in the past.

Other horses arrived on the course – four more starters, a terrified pony, a huge two-year-old with attitude, and a napping horse that wouldn't nap. I soon got my time in the pen. I was lucky enough to be closely involved with two of the starters, and spent a lot of time working with the nervous pony, particularly in the evenings after the course. It was fascinating to see how Kelly approached the training of each horse, treating each as an individual and adjusting the technique accordingly. Even though I felt that I had finally found a teacher who felt the same way about horses as I did, I was occasionally surprised by the choices she made. It worked out every time and I found myself having to reconsider the 'truths' in which I believed.

The drive to and from Witney became an important part of the course in its own right. Dad had the car serviced, new tyres and brakes put on, and the eccentric electrics sorted out. He hadn't been able to get the fan fixed, however, and this meant that to avoid the car overheating, I had to drive with the heater on full. This made it noisy and hot, so I'd drive along with the windows and sunroof open, music blaring away. It was pretty cold out on those frosty November mornings, and I got some very strange looks. I loved driving through the gently rolling countryside of Oxfordshire and Buckinghamshire, and there was still enough of the child in me not to get miserable about winter until after Christmas. My brain whirred constantly, mulling over the details of what I'd seen and heard, while the intense music seemed to echo what was happening in my life. Had my drive been shorter, I think I would have learned far less from the course.

Another memorable part of these journeys was an audio tape of Jonathan Swift's *Gulliver's Travels,* which I had borrowed from the library, on Adam's insistence that I fill in some of the literary gaps left by my 'radical' education. In the last section of the book, after his escape from the little men in Lilliput, and many other adventures, Gulliver arrives at an island ruled by horses, called Houhynhyms. So pure of thought and spirit, despite their advanced scholarship, they have no concept of, nor word for lying, simply calling it 'to say the thing which was not'. The non-violent civilisation they have created would be perfect but for the presence of the human 'yahoos', who live and breed like vermin, exhibiting all the vices of mankind.

Increasingly, as I drove, I felt ashamed at what we have done to the world, not least to horses, and to each other. From the time of Swift, when horses were so universally enslaved for the use of man, to the present era, horses, still deeply misunderstood by so many people, seem to represent one of the last windows left open onto our rustic past. Our partnership with the horse has been at the centre of that nostalgic dream-idyll, blown aside by the relentless pace and mechanisation of our culture, but for which so many of us yearn. The simple lifestyle of a horse, the peace we find in their company (when we have time to feel it), their profoundly generous nature, point us to a more honest existence than our own.

FIVE

Adam joins up
(Adam)

During that first week of Nicole's course we both attended Monty's demonstration at Addington Equestrian Centre. Naturally I had been keen to see him in action, having been told so much about him. But, like the hundreds of people in the audience that night, I was astonished by what I saw. 'It's like magic,' I said to Monty when we met him afterwards.

The first horse accepted his first saddle, bridle, long-lines and rider in half an hour. The last had previously taken hours to load, but was soon following Monty into a trailer without a lead rope. With Dually, his quarter horse, he also gave a demonstration of 'cutting cattle' (separating one out from the herd) without a bridle. Particularly impressive was the obvious enthusiasm of the horse as he went about this incredibly difficult task. I had no idea a calf could move so quickly, and change direction so sharply. Monty got his horse to cut the calf all by himself and was 'just' sitting there as he did so, without interfering. And all the while he kept up a monologue that had the audience spellbound.

Although I had never seen anything like this before, I could see immediately why he was able to make such an impact, and make better progress than any conventional horseman. As I've said, Monty doesn't attempt to teach horses our language, he simply tries to use their own and he gives the horse confidence in his ability to take them through whatever problems they have. With a keen sense of discipline and great self-confidence, as well as an aura of unflappability and calm, he also has a ready response for whatever happens in the pen, which takes away any incentive for the horse to continue his unwanted behaviour. That night we saw how he created an environment in which the horse could easily learn. 'There's no such thing as teaching,' he suggested, 'only learning.'

> *The choice is his. If he does what I want, I'll make him comfortable. If he does what I don't want, he'll be made uncomfortable – he'll have to work harder, for example. I'm not going to take away the choice from him. He can do anything he wants. But he has to be responsible for his actions and I'll be responsible for mine. If I take away his chance to do something wrong, then I also take away his chance to do something right. It has to be his decision.*

Like so many of Monty's sayings, it is no less relevant to life in general than to training horses.

All the time that I'd spent fighting the system at boarding school, I'd been vaguely aware that the rules and the way they were enforced pushed me into a corner. You either conformed or rebelled. There seemed to be no middle ground in which to establish your own personality. As a pupil, you were constantly lectured about being 'responsible', but were not given any real responsibility for your actions or choices. Instead, by means of near-constant supervision, the authorities tried to stop you from doing 'wrong' things, which made me, at least, want to do them so much more.

A perfect example of the reverse psychology Monty uses when starting a young horse is teaching it to go backwards. Conventional horsemanship would have you avoid ever asking a young horse to go back, thinking it might cause napping (refusing to go forward, or backing up without the rider's control). This is a common problem in the UK, perhaps in part for this very reason. Monty's explanation was typically deft:

> *It's like this. 'Johnny, I've got to go into town. You stay here in the house. You can do anything while I'm away, but don't go in that room.' Now you haven't even got to the end of the drive before Johnny's looking through that key-hole.*

A ripple of laughter went through the audience. But I was shocked by the gulf between my approach and Monty's. I would never have allowed a horse the choice to go back if that's what he decided to do. I would have tried to make him go forward. But the logic of Monty's approach was so convincing. He would allow the horse to go back, but take all the benefit out of that behaviour by making him back up far more than he wanted to. When training a confirmed napper this might have meant backing up more than a quarter of a mile on the first day. But eventually the result would be that backing up came under the control of the rider, instead of being something the horse could do to evade the rider.

We had no idea how this man's philosophy was going to change our lives, but it was an irresistible pull. It was fascinating, powerful, and above all, accessible. I didn't see any reason why I couldn't learn to do the same things he was doing. And it didn't just seem like a way to becoming a better horseman, but also a way towards becoming a better person. I thought of how I'd whipped Wilberforce to make him go through puddles, and was deeply ashamed at the thought of how cruel and pointless it had been. What kind of a leader had I appeared to him? Insensitive. Domineering. Stupid, violent and obstinate. All the things that I had so long ago resolved not to be, right back at school, and that I so loathed in other people. Mixed with revulsion at my own behaviour was anger that I had allowed conventional 'wisdom' to influence me, which would have me pick a fight, when it came down to it, 'to show the horse who's boss'. What right had I to hit a horse? What right had I to be the boss, if that was how I was prepared to enforce my authority? Perhaps my aggressive, catch-him-doing-something-wrong-and-punish-him-for-it attitude had taught Wilberforce who was boss, but it had probably also made him less likely to genuinely respect me or co-operate voluntarily with trust. And, if I could not motivate my horse to do things for me willingly, I would never get the most out of him. He would never want to go through water if I was beating, forcing or even just threatening him. In fact, next time he saw a puddle, he'd have a real reason to be scared of it. I couldn't have known then how often I would find myself repairing the damage inflicted by others, phobias beaten into horses by people keen to teach them 'who's boss'.

I vowed at that demonstration never to use a whip again, not only so that I would never again be able to misuse one, but also because Monty had made me realise something fundamental both to horsemanship and every relationship in the world. If I needed to use force to get my horse to do something, then I should never have been asking him to do it. Common sense, perhaps, but as someone once said, common sense isn't always common practice. Somehow I had not noticed that, when dealing with an animal weighing about eight times more than oneself, the *only* way you can work is with his consent. But I had often been demanding, petty, rude and harsh in how I got that agreement. It was given grudgingly, after sometimes spectacular scenes of dissent, which could have seen either one or both of us badly injured. It was like the political prisoner who signs his untrue confession in a gesture of consent – he picks up the pen, but only as a result of the tortures he has been subjected to, and which he knows will continue if he does not sign. Some horses, dogs, and humans never have a fair chance to do anything 'right' enough to avoid being punished. But surely the key is to avoid disagreement in the first place. The crucial ingredient was trust. And every time I hit a horse, or even threatened or thought of hitting him, I was doing so simply because I had no better method to get what I wanted, and had listened to some bad advice.

The results Monty achieved were magical, but the methods were logical, relying on a sound understanding and application of body language and psychology rather than force. Instead of getting a horse to do things, Monty was getting the horse to *want* to do them. I came away resolved to change the way I treated horses, having learned more valuable information about how to train horses in that one night than I had in all the years before.

SIX

More teachers appear
(Nicole)

As if the course wasn't already the best thing I'd ever done in my life, it was also to give me the chance to meet two of my most inspirational horsewomen. Every Tuesday morning, we had a guest lecturer, an expert in their field, a top farrier, for example, or physiotherapist. The lectures were always interesting, adding another dimension to our understanding. I couldn't believe my luck, however, when I discovered I was going to meet my childhood heroine, Lucy Rees, whose book had been so important in starting Sensi. Adam and I had once spent a most agreeable afternoon trying to visit her in Wales.

As if that wasn't enough, Mary Wanless, ground-breaking riding coach and author, would also be lecturing. Reading Mary's *Ride With Your Mind* books had already made a tremendous difference to my riding and I was able to disentangle myself from the disheartening struggle riding had become. Hearing her speak on the course was incredible. Here was someone who knew the biomechanics of what good riders actually do *and* how to teach it. To a non-rider this might not sound so remarkable, but it is incredibly rare to find these two things in the same person. Perhaps more astonishing is the fact that almost no one else in the horse world seemed even to recognise that this information was lacking. For years, it was acceptable to repeat the same worn-out, largely meaningless phrases, and when they didn't work, say them louder before blaming either the pupil or the horse. So much of what I heard that morning related as much to life as to riding. Mary's own story was an inspiring tale. She had come to horses comparatively late, not starting riding until the age of fourteen. She claims she was just an average rider, with no discernible talent, working her way through the system until she finally became a BHSI. At this stage, however, she hit a plateau, which two years of training with a top classical rider wasn't able to get her through. She had got the job on the strength of a half-halt she'd ridden during the interview, which she was never able to reproduce in the two years she was with this trainer. This struck a deep chord with me, and I believe it's typical of so many riders' experiences – a brilliant moment, a sudden coming together of all that you've been striving for, a sudden 'A-ha! I've got it!' that turns out to be elusive. You haven't got it after all, and the more you try to find it again, the further it slips away, disappearing perhaps for years. After two years of having the same commands barked at her, of trying her hardest, of being lunged late into the night, continually failing (she felt) her horse, her instructor, and herself, she gave up in despair and moved to London, supporting herself (more or less) by selling fire extinguishers.

Friends began to pester her for help with their horses, and financial desperation led her gradually back into the world of horses. But this time it was different. Distrustful of all the old 'truths', she approached her new learning in a thoroughly experimental manner. What if, she thought, I tried doing the opposite of what I've been told all these years? If what I've been doing for all this time hasn't been working, I've got to try something else. She discovered to her astonishment that when, instead of relaxing and 'going with' the horse, she engaged all her muscles and tried to keep still and strong on the horse, she immediately became significantly more stable. Having achieved this, she was much more in control of her body and more able to influence the horse. If there was such a huge gap between what she was being told to do, and what actually worked, what did this say about the teaching that was going on? Was she actually being told to do the wrong thing, or was there a massive failure of communication? When her instructor said 'sit up straight and stretch your legs down' did he mean what she interpreted him to mean? Was it what he was really doing? It often seemed to work for him – that is, it had the desired effect on the horse – so there must be some 'slippage' of meaning in the communication. Of course, if ever he were struggling with something, then perhaps his understanding of the biomechanics was at fault.

Solving this riddle took her down some seemingly tangential routes. She studied the Alexander technique, Feldenkreis bodywork, Neuro-Linguistic Programming, martial arts such as Tai Chi, dance, massage, anatomy, sports psychology and Educational Kinesiology. She discovered how the body worked, how people learn, how to communicate. And she also decoded the horse-rider interaction: how what the horse does affects the rider, and how what the rider does affects the horse.

In essence, she discovered the language of riding, Equus on horseback, and, in my opinion, her revelation was as significant to the world of riding as join-up is to the world of 'breaking'. And just like Monty, she has struggled for years to have her methods recognised and accepted.

In real life, she was just as she appeared in the book: small, intellectually formidable, focused, articulate.

'If you have a goal you wish to achieve,' she said, 'you need to know where you're starting from, where you want to get to, and the steps involved to take you there.'

Blindingly obvious, perhaps, but it was the first time I'd heard this

information presented in this way, and to me at the time it was reve-
latory. The idea that there are different 'maps' of riding, and that
some of them are more useful and accurate than others, had never
seriously occurred to me. Applying this model to life, and recognising
that adapting your approach to its different challenges could funda-
mentally change your experience of the world, was very exciting.

'If you want to navigate around New York, it will help to have a
street map. But if your map is of Chicago, it won't help you at all. If
you never notice that you're equipped with the wrong map, you'll be
doomed to confusion and frustration, and if you ever get to where
you want to go, it will be purely by chance.' She went on to remind
us of the joke about the traveller who asks an Irishman, 'How can I
get to Dublin?' The Irishman replies, 'If I were going to Dublin, I
wouldn't be starting from here.'

About halfway through the course, in November, another student,
Sarah, and I were working with Candide, one of the horses that had
been started during the first week. Sarah hadn't had much to do with
this particular horse, and as she rode her around the pen, she exclaimed
with pleasure, 'Oh, she's really sensitive. I think it would be really quite
easy to teach her bridle-less riding. Why don't I teach you how to do
it, then we can show Monty when he comes back next week?'

This seemed reasonable. We knew Monty was coming back for a
couple of days, and would be seeing some more students work in the
pen. We only had a week to work with the horse, but we weren't
expecting to achieve that much – we could just show him what we'd
been doing so far.

I got on the horse, and Sarah told me what to do. I tried to keep
in mind my Mary Wanless knowledge, too, making sure I stayed
aligned over the horse's centre of gravity, not pushing her off balance
by leaning over too far on the turns, and trying hard to keep my body
as stable as possible. By the end of that first session, we had taken off

her bridle, and were able to get her to halt just from the pressure of a rope tied around her neck. We could also turn her quite reliably, changing direction across the middle of the pen. She was a bright horse, and seemed to find this new game fun.

'Let's ask Kelly if we can be the only ones to work with her for this week,' suggested Sarah, 'but let's make it a surprise to show everyone at the end of it.'

I didn't think there would be a problem with this. In fact, Candide had started off as quite a 'sour' horse – she had quickly grown tired of the pen, and although she picked up a great deal when we started to hack her out, she still tended to drop off the bottom of the list of horses to be worked if we ran out of time. On the Tuesday after a three-day weekend, we asked Kelly if we could work on Candide in secret, in the afternoons after the course. Kelly agreed, intrigued. Then one of the other students who hadn't been very active on the course suddenly decided she'd like to ride her in the afternoon. Candide came back quite hot (she was unclipped and it was a lovely, surprisingly warm, November afternoon), and we decided she would probably not be in the right sort of mood to do more work. Never mind, there was still Wednesday and Thursday. We were confident.

The Wednesday session went well, but we made a real error of judgement. In her enthusiasm, Sarah tried to teach me how to move Candide sideways along a pole, a standard move in Western training. I was too uncoordinated to explain to the horse what we wanted, and the three of us got quite frustrated. We were sensible enough to recognise our mistake, and went back to working on the simpler things – transitions from trot to walk, and trot to halt, changing direction, and cantering. I'd ridden without a bridle before, in the way that many people do – riding a pony down to the field in just a headcollar as a child, and on one memorable occasion during a riding holiday when we jumped on some ponies in the field. (Mine had taken great exception to this arrogant intrusion, and promptly bucked me off.)

I'd also hitched a lift with Sensi across the field a few times, but I had rarely cantered on her without her bridle, at least not intentionally. It was exhilarating to be deliberately cantering in the pen with nothing but a rope around the horse's neck. I enjoyed the feeling that although she couldn't go very far, equally I couldn't really control her if she decided she didn't want me to. It felt strangely liberating after all the hand-dominant instruction I'd been given as a child. We finished the session in high spirits.

Even more exciting was the prospect of meeting Lucy Rees. Kelly had asked for a volunteer to collect her from Oxford train station, and I had jumped at the chance. I don't consider myself much of a celebrity buff. I don't read about the lifestyles of the rich and famous, for example, and am not particularly impressed by ostentatious displays of wealth, power or influence. I am, however, impressed by achievement, and love watching people who are masters in their field, whether that's comedy, acting, singing, or horse training. I'd always felt surprisingly little desire to meet any of my heroes, partly through a fear that they might not live up to my expectations, and partly through a sense of unworthiness. What could I possibly have to say to these people that they would find interesting? What did we have in common? Now, five years later, I feel completely different. If John Cleese wanted to come on a course, I'm sure he'd find us all perfectly charming, amusing, interesting. Should David Bowie suddenly develop an interest in horses, I'm sure we'd be able to help.

Now, Lucy Rees is not exactly as famous as David Bowie. Not even everyone in the horse world has heard of her. But she had been the single most important influence in my life with horses before I met Monty Roberts. As a teenager I had stumbled across a documentary on TV, in which she and another person were breaking in two mustangs. He was using traditional methods of force and violence, and she was using her own unique blend of patience and ingenuity. Initially, he seemed to be making much more progress than her – he already had the saddle on his horse before she had even managed to touch hers. But ultimately, his horse never really accepted being ridden, while Lucy just hopped on hers in a stream and went straight out across the Arizona desert. That she was a woman operating in the macho world of cowboys made this achievement all the more remarkable. I couldn't wait to see what she was like in the flesh.

'I'm sorry I'm so horribly late. Are you the poor student they've sent to fetch me?'

She was tall, slim and strikingly good-looking, with wild, long blond hair. The sort of person you might call eccentric.

'That's right. I mean, no. I volunteered. I'm a big fan.'

We headed out to my (dad's) car, and I tried to think of something to say. I didn't want awkward silences, but on the other hand I didn't want to appear inane. At times like these, Adam is brilliant. He always can think of something to say, and has a whole range of manners, from condescending (he's not very good with children) to courteous, and every shade in between. The more I tried to think of something intelligent to say, the more paralysed I became by my own thoughts.

'So what exactly are you expecting me to say?' she asked.

I was startled. This thought so mirrored my own I thought perhaps she was reading my mind.

'I mean, what do you want me to talk about? Is there anything specific? I don't want to go over anything you've already heard about.'

'Oh, I see. Well, Monty's here this afternoon, and also tomorrow. It's Thanksgiving, and there's a cake and everything. I think the idea is that we have a fairly free-roaming discussion. Questions and answers, lively debate. Differences as well as agreements, that sort of thing.'

'OK. So tell me a little about this Monty, then.'

A hint of scepticism? Professional jealousy? I pushed the thought from my mind and enthused about Monty, Kelly, the course, the horses, what I'd been learning.

She interjected the odd question, then said, 'Of course, none of it's new, you know. This sort of thing has been going on in the States for decades, centuries maybe. I've seen Monty work, and he's an extraordinary horseman, but it's not as revolutionary as you think.'

'Well, it's new to me,' I said, perhaps a little petulantly. 'I understand that people have known about advance and retreat since the days of the Native Americans, and the concept of the release of pressure is well understood in the States, but to almost everyone in this country, this stuff is new. People may have noticed certain things happening in the round pen or on the lunge – ears locked on and head lowering, for example – but it's Monty who's taken it to the next stage, who's worked out what to do with the information, as a structured way of communicating with the horse, and he's brought it to the attention of large numbers of people.'

'Yes, that's true,' she conceded. 'But I was doing this sort of thing years ago. We didn't need some flashy American to come here and show it off.'

I couldn't think what to say. 'Well,' I started, as gently as I could, 'the reason this has suddenly become so popular is because it's exactly what so many people have been waiting for. For years and years people have been looking for a kinder way to deal with horses.'

Maybe Monty finally found himself in the right place at the right time. But it hadn't always been that way. Even just a few years previously, when the Queen, astonished by his skill, had arranged for him to tour the country to demonstrate his techniques, audience numbers were small. It was clear, too, that Kelly had been enormously instrumental in Monty's UK success. But I could sympathise with Lucy. She was an exceptional horsewoman, who had been working with problem horses for almost as long as Monty. She had written books, appeared on TV, and lectured at colleges, but she was experiencing nothing like the recognition that Monty was receiving. I could understand her frustration, but I also wanted her to appreciate the frustration that many horse riders had been experiencing, too. If there had been a ten-week course on Lucy Rees's horsemanship, I would have been the first to sign up. To hear that she had been doing lectures that I hadn't even heard about was no comfort at all.

I was dispirited by this conversation. Kelly had said that Monty was particularly keen to meet Lucy Rees, and it was a pity if she didn't feel the same.

In the end I needn't have worried. Once Monty and Lucy were in the same room, conversation flowed. Lucy had some controversial revelations about stallions and their behaviour in the wild. It turned out that 'rival' stallions would often come to quite amicable agreements about wife swapping, and that quite often two stallions appeared to share groups of mares. This fact was often missed by observers, she said, because they would see one very well-muscled stallion, and assume he was the only one. People usually saw what they were looking for, I couldn't help thinking. If scientists, who receive a certain amount of training in objectivity, couldn't even be open-minded enough to spot a second adult stallion in a herd, then how likely were we to 'read' each horse we were training? How could we ever know if any of our assumptions were correct? It's a question that's bothered me ever since, and it always worries me when people state, 'Oh, I know he's not really frightened because ...' I've become almost politician-like in my reluctance to state categorically the reason why I think a horse doesn't want to do something. I guess Stantonbury, my old school, is partly responsible for this. If someone hadn't done their homework, lack of motivation was considered as good a reason as 'my cat died'. The teachers would look for a way to inspire motivation, rather than blame the student for being awkward.

Another shocking revelation of Lucy's was that much of the 'documentary' footage of stallions fighting comes about as a result of the documentary makers driving one group of horses into the territory of another. So many of those vicious encounters are simply avoided in real life, but can easily be set up for the cameras. Horse life is actually pretty dull: eighteen hours a day of steady munching, sex once or twice a year, and only the occasional bout of spectacular aggression.

I had previously discovered that one of my horsey friends from the 'pony paddocks' in Milton Keynes knew Lucy Rees. In fact she had spent large chunks of her childhood in Wales with Lucy, learning to ride on nearly wild Welsh mountain ponies. Lucy didn't have any concrete plans for that evening, so I suggested she might like to come to Milton Keynes to meet her old friend, since I was driving that way anyway. I was immensely thankful for my pretty reliable ability to remember a phone number having only rung it a few times, and I called Jane. She was (unusually) at home, and delighted at the prospect of seeing her old teacher again. We just had to nip out to the stables first, and do a little training with Candide …

We'd arranged with the college staff for the key to the tack room to be left somewhere accessible. When we got there, it was nowhere to be found, and we couldn't get the lights to work. Bridle-less, bare-back, and in the dark? Maybe not. We spent some time with the nervous pony, then Lucy and I headed for Milton Keynes.

All the awkwardness of the first drive had disappeared. As we drove through the cold, dark, windy night, rain splattering against the windshield, it was obvious that she'd really warmed to Monty, and had even asked to come back on the next day of the course.

Before we went around to Jane's, we stopped by to check on the horses. It was dark and windy in their field, and when they saw us they came charging over, snorting playfully, manes blowing wildly, curious about this new person.

We collected Adam and went off to the pub for a few beers before ordering a take-away curry. One glass of wine followed another, each anecdote rolled into the next, and before we knew it, we'd reached that time of the night where six hours' sleep suddenly becomes an unattainable luxury. I hadn't been drinking, but I'd hit the level of tiredness that's almost intoxicating.

'I'll pick you up at seven-thirty then?' I asked doubtfully. 'In the morning?'

'No problem,' Lucy assured me.

Adam and I reflected on the strange turn our lives were taking. Who would have thought we'd spend the evening drinking with the author of my all-time favourite childhood book? Still, in the back of my mind, I was hoping she wouldn't be ready to go to the college in the morning as Sarah, Candide and I were to give our presentation in the afternoon. The idea of exposing my riding skills – let alone my bridle-less ones – to her was not appealing to me. I'm the sort of person who, if I were an actress, would never allow friends and family to come to the opening night, or possibly not any other night either. When things go well, I always regret that friends weren't there to witness it, but I'd rather that than be horribly embarrassed by screwing up in front of them.

To my surprise, and slight dismay, she was ready promptly, just those few short hours later. Perhaps she hadn't gone to bed at all. Conversation was a little more subdued on the way into college.

In the morning, we had another meeting with Monty, as he explained more of his concepts and training techniques. There was a BBC film crew there, and I began to get a little nervous. Surely they would get their filming done in the morning and not bother to stay for the afternoon? I hoped so, but it seemed improbable.

Sometimes I'm astonished by my profound lack of understanding of a situation. Once, at university, I suddenly realised that the Engineering student against whose stomach I was lying might be expecting something more from the situation than I was intending. (This was before Adam and I got together.) The fact that we had gone out for several meals, including a 'study picnic' at Grantchester meadows, and that we were lying on the same bed studying didn't strike me as particularly significant. Cambridge has a ratio of about four men for every woman, and I was quite used to being the only woman in a roomful of eight men (more than which constituted a party as far as college authorities were concerned, therefore requiring written permission from the Porter's Lodge). I was the only woman on my course of twelve students. It seemed inevitable, then, that a large proportion of my friends would be male. I was very fond of this person, and going through a particularly tactile phase, but that was it, as far as I was concerned. Looking back I'm astonished at my stupidity. The strange thing is, I don't consider myself to be particularly naive in such matters. It's as though my brain had all the relevant information, and just didn't bother to process it.

So it was with Candide. With a little mental clarity I might have been able to see the situation for the daunting task it was. There I was, on the strength of two actual sessions, about to show Monty Roberts, Kelly Marks, a BBC film crew, my childhood heroine Lucy Rees, and all the other students on my course, the principles of bridle-less riding. At least Mary Wanless wasn't there.

By the time we went out to the stables in the afternoon, I was feeling a little other-worldly. Not just that I was tired, but I felt distanced from my body, as if it was happening to someone else. As I warmed Candide up, I was aware things weren't going too well. She was distracted, and even a little bored, and my signals to control her speed and direction weren't getting through. I could see from Sarah's face that she was worried.

'If things look like they're not going too well,' she advised, 'make sure it's not too obvious from the outside that you're trying to control her. If she canters off, just go with it, like it's what you intended to do, and if you want her to stop, say "whoa" quietly enough that no one on the outside can hear, otherwise they'll know it's all going horribly wrong.'

I smiled weakly. A vision of me galloping around for what would probably seem like eternity, trying to pretend all was going according to plan, floated in front of my eyes. It wasn't a positive image. 'Promise me that if that happens, you'll come in,' I pleaded. 'You can slow her down with body language, and we can start again.'

I couldn't understand what was keeping them so long. Monty was meant to just be taking a quick look at the horse in the stables next door. It seemed they had been ages. Candide was really going off the boil, and as a three-year-old, her concentration span was short enough as it was. I didn't want her to 'peak' before they came through to watch her. I also didn't want to get off, in case she assumed the session was finished, and then felt cheated about being asked to work again. I could feel a tight knot of tension and impatience clenching in my stomach.

Finally, the crew came through, set up the camera, and we could start. The students filed in and sat on bales of straw round the edge of the pen. By this time, Kelly was in on the secret, too, although she hadn't actually seen us working. As she and Monty came in, I hoped fervently we wouldn't let her down.

Then I started riding, and talking, and it began to feel all right. I explained what we'd been doing, how we'd been pairing the 'new' signal on the rope around her neck with the 'old' rein aid. As I demonstrated, Candide began to pick up interest, getting more responsive as we went on.

'Once you're confident the horse can respond to the neck rope alone,' I said, and by this time the reins were just resting knotted on her neck, 'you can take off the bridle.'

Monty came into the pen to remove the bridle, and as he approached us, I tried to read his expression. It was impenetrable. His face was blank, and I had to quell the foreboding feeling that he was annoyed. After all, who was I to be explaining bridle-less riding to him? Of course, I was really explaining it to the others on the course, but would he see it like that? Would he think I was just an upstart, arrogant student trying to impress him? The nervousness came flooding back.

But Candide behaved impeccably. It was an amazing feeling to be riding along with no contact at all on the horse's head, but being able to control her so closely with my seat bones, using the information I had only recently learned from Mary Wanless. Aside from an uncomfortable moment when we struck off on the wrong canter lead twice, it all went better than I could possibly have hoped for. There was a polite smattering of applause, Candide did a sort of bow after the last halt, and Kelly said something to Monty that I didn't quite catch. Then I found myself leading her out of the pen, taking her back to the quiet of her stable and untacking her, feeling pleased and relieved, but not at all sure what Monty's reaction would be. Sarah came up to me, delighted with how it had gone, and one or two other students congratulated me. It seemed childish to ask, 'And what did Monty think?' so I didn't say anything and went back to the school to watch the other students being filmed doing join-ups and interviews. I was thankful it was over, and pleased that it hadn't been a complete disaster, but I couldn't quite shake the memory of Monty's face, completely expressionless, as if set in stone.

When all the horses were finished, Monty called everyone into the pen.

'What we've seen here this afternoon, this … bridle-less riding, this, this display of horsemanship is really one of the most …'

I shut my eyes. I felt seriously dizzy. Surely he wouldn't tell me off in front of the entire group?

'… amazing feats I've seen in a long time.'

I breathed again.

'That someone could take my concepts and apply them so quickly, to such good effect, and explain them so clearly. Well, I'm overwhelmed.'

He said much more, too much for me to remember, and aside

from stating rather too emphatically that I wasn't a professional rider ('far from it, in no way could she be described as such'), it was complimentary, embarrassing, but lovely, too. I couldn't remember ever feeling more pleased with an achievement.

Candide might have been the high point of the course for me, but the last few weeks were precious, too. I spent a lot of time with the nervous pony, going out for walks, and sitting in his stable. I offered to continue working with him, for free, over Christmas, but the owner was unconvinced. He had made great progress on the course, but she wasn't satisfied. I was devastated when I learned she was seriously considering having him put down due to his unpredictability. It was so frustrating to feel I could help him, but wouldn't have the opportunity. I never did find out what happened to him.

I couldn't bear the thought of the course ending. The last day was 20 December 1996, and I think if it hadn't been so close to Christmas, I would immediately have succumbed to a serious depression. We went to Windsor Castle to receive our certificates from Terry Pendry, the Queen's Equerry. It was like a sort of pilgrimage, returning to the place where it had all started in this country. The last thing I said to Kelly before I got in my car to drive back to my old life was, 'If you ever need any help, any sort of help at all, please ring.'

However, we had another problem to occupy us – a 16.3 hand high problem.

Wilberforce was never really the horse for us. He was aggressive (we clearly weren't the first people to have hit him), and unpredictable. We didn't have perfect control when riding him, but even less from the ground, especially when we first got him. Sometimes he charged at us in the field, and he once cornered Adam in the stable, threatening to kick him. He would strike out with his front legs, and sometimes when we were leading him, we had to let him go. At times, we resorted to carrying a whip in one hand, smacking him smartly across the legs if he struck out. In the year or so that we had him, we did manage to improve our relationship, and even took him on a long holiday, riding the length of the Ridgeway. He loved the views, and would stare into the distance for ages, while Sensi stuffed her face and admired the only view she cares about – a close-up of the grass! This experience definitely brought us closer to him, but we decided he might be better off with someone else. Just before I went on the Monty course, we put him on loan, but he came back with lameness problems. When the course ended, I decided to try out my newly acquired skills.

Wilberforce responded to join-up in almost textbook fashion. Despite my fears about being charged at, he didn't challenge being sent away, and very rapidly gave all the signals. When I invited him in, he walked straight up to me, stopping a respectful distance away. He followed me meekly as I walked in circles, and lowered his head for me to rub it. It was almost as if he was saying, 'This is how I should be treated.' When I attached a long rope, I was able to lead him wherever I wanted, with no sign of that nasty tendency to strike out. Finally, we were communicating.

Shortly after that we discovered that Wilberforce had Wobbler's disease, a progressive degeneration of the spine, which eventually leads to the horse being unable to control its movements. We watched as he became gradually less co-ordinated, and when I saw him fall over in the field, I knew it was time to act. The illness is incurable. He was fully insured, but we couldn't claim unless we let him get so bad that he had to be destroyed on humane grounds. We couldn't let that happen to him. Phoning around the local slaughterers is one call you wish you never have to make. I felt literally sick with fear as I walked down to his field to wait for the knacker man. I gave him one last feed as I said goodbye, filling the bucket with all his favourite foods. Adam stayed at his head, whilst I held Cobweb, Wilberforce's field mate, a safe distance away. The anticipation of waiting for the shot to be fired was nearly unbearable. Adam had made me promise not to watch, but it was almost impossible not to look over. Wilberforce wouldn't keep his head still, and it hadn't occurred to me to save any of his feed from earlier. Finally, he stood still, looking off into the distance, and the man fired the bullet through his brain. Cobweb and I jumped as Wilberforce crashed to the ground. Adam knelt by his head, stroking his neck, until his heart stopped beating. We walked over to say good-bye. Cobweb sniffed him all over, and I patted his neck one last time. Then he was winched into the lorry and was gone.

SEVEN

Student at work
(Adam)

Every night, when Nicole returned from Witney, she would tell me in detail about her day. I heard all about the starters, the problem horses, the nervous pony, and her achievement with Candide. I saw her wake at some ungodly hour of the morning, and leap out of bed with enthusiasm for the day ahead. I shared her pleasure in meeting Lucy Rees, and was thrilled that Mary Wanless had some positive things to say about her riding. It was clear that the course was a high point in Nicole's life. I was worried how she would cope after it ended.

And, of course, Nicole did come back from the course in a despondent mood. Then, one day after Christmas, the phone rang. She launched herself into the room, suddenly cheerful.

'That was Kelly Marks! She's asked me to go and help on the first day of the next course – assist with the admin, and maybe say a little about my experiences on the course. Good, eh?'

This continuing connection with the course, Kelly and Monty was a huge boost, and having something positive to focus on helped her to deal with the pain and distress of having to have Wilberforce put down in January.

She came back from the first day in an ebullient mood, but there was just the hint of resignation in her manner, and the following evening I found out why.

'It was lovely to see Monty again, and fascinating to see him work – there are some unhandled yearlings at the new place – you know – Willow Farm, where the courses are being held now, and Monty says it's the nearest thing to a mustang that you'll get in this country. He says it's like a university, there's so much learning to be had. Anyway, he remembered who I was, which was great, but he didn't mention anything about the Candide thing. I half-expected him to, because he was so complimentary about it at the time. So I got to thinking it was deliberate. He was trying to tell me that what I did was good, but I can't expect to continue receiving praise and approval on the strength of one achievement. I got the impression he knew what I was think-ing, and that I expected him to say something, and so he wasn't going to. And that was all right.'

She paused, and took a swig from her pint of tea.

'I mean, I think it's really important that we don't do these things just for the recognition, you know? It's that old school thing of only being motivated to write an essay because someone is going to mark it. If the subject really interested you, you'd write it for its own sake.'

'I guess so.' I wasn't entirely convinced that anyone would be that intrinsically motivated, or that they'd be quite right in the head if they were. The thought of all the Cambridge essays that I never wrote even though I had someone waiting to mark them loomed guiltily from my conscience.

'So, I'd just got around to accepting the fact that my moment of glory was past, when Monty said to the group of students, "Do you all know Nicole and what she did on the last course?" I looked at my feet, and he launched off into an explanation of the whole thing. It was really nice, in an embarrassing sort of way.'

She looked at me and grinned.

'The thing is, it did go really well with Candide – I mean, I was really pleased, and we did trot to halt transitions, turns and canter and stuff. But to hear Monty tell it, we were doing canter pirouettes, sliding stops, flying changes, turns on a dime ...'

I raised an eyebrow. 'Did you correct him, then?'

'Oh no! Heavens, who am I to contradict him? It wouldn't have been appropriate ...'

Not long after this first conversation, Kelly rang again. When Nicole hung up she was almost dancing. I was beginning to think that whenever she talked to Kelly it was good news.

'Kelly's asked me to start a pony for her! The idea is to bombproof her, make her safe for a young kid, Kelly's niece. You'll have to help.'

And so, on 2 February 1997, Nessie arrived at our paddock at Milton Keynes. Only 12.2 hands high, she was tiny, and like a miniature version of a racehorse, with a fine head and beautiful dark, intelligent eyes. Not what either of us had been expecting. Nicole took one look at her legs and said, 'Oh, my God, they'll break if I sit on her!'

It was fascinating to see Nessie progress. Nicole and I both worked with her, together and separately, as often as we could. Somewhere along the way, Kelly added in the goal that we should try to get her so good she could be used in the next set of demonstrations, which started a month later in March.

Nicole had started a new job, working as a Communications Operator in the Control Room for Thames Valley Police, and although the job was part-time, she had to go on some lengthy full-time training courses. She ended up doing a lot of work with Nessie after dark, training under the glow of the street lamps that lit the footpaths around the outside of the paddock. Nessie was quite ear-shy, and we worked on getting her good at having her ears handled, and taught her to lower her head for the bridle. We introduced her to as many scary things as we could, including plastic bags, tarpaulins, fluorescent sheets, stones in tin cans (which make a great noise), bicycles, cars, motorbikes. We took her out for long walks and let her meet sheep, wooden footbridges, and sailboats. We didn't have a school or a round pen, just our stable and small paddock with trees and water troughs and other immovable objects in it. We had to get her as calm and accepting as possible before we could even think of getting on her. Luckily, Monty had been at Henley where Nessie had been kept, and had already done a join-up and introduced her to her first saddle. We did also long-line her, but as she was so small, it was just as easy and perhaps even more useful to simply stand by her shoulder and use the reins as one would when riding her, and in this way we taught her to turn, halt, and rein back.

As it happened, Nessie had been with us for more than a fortnight before it felt appropriate to back her. Nicole was working on her own, and I kept watch nearby. She placed a bucket beside Nessie, and stepped up and down on it, getting Nessie used to the idea of someone suddenly rising up above her. Nicole lowered herself across Nessie's back, gradually letting more of her weight rest on the saddle. When she finally took her feet off the bucket, Nessie staggered a little under her, and struggled to gain her balance, but she soon relaxed.

At the time, I was working very long hours, often fourteen a day, at a nearby Japanese international school, so Nicole worked with two very capable young riders for the next few days, progressing to leading Nessie out with one of the youngsters on board.

About three weeks after she had first arrived, Nicole took Nessie to Campbell Park, one of Milton Keynes's lovely, landscaped, public parks, through which a bridleway runs, in fact the very same bridleway where Wilberforce and I had our big fight about the puddle. As part of her bombproofing process, she led her up some steps, through a bus-shelter, and straight up the side of a steep hill to the viewing point. Nessie was behaving so impeccably that Nicole decided it would be an appropriate time to ride her for the first time with no one at her head, and also to trot her for the first time. She reasoned that the park was enclosed, and well frequented, so even if she fell off, Nessie would be safe and Nicole would be found quite quickly. What she didn't tell me until several years later was that she hadn't brought her hat with her, but had decided to ride the pony anyway. This was out of character for Nicole, who is a very safety-conscious person, and luckily it all went well. Sometimes you just get a sense that something's going to be all right, but we wouldn't dream of taking this sort of risk now.

Nessie progressed steadily over the next couple of weeks, and Kelly's niece, Daisy, eventually came along to hack her out. The pony behaved beautifully, and went home at the beginning of March. Soon afterwards, Nicole and I went to Henley, to meet Monty and Kelly, and Daisy's mother Sandra, to show what we'd been doing with Nessie, and to see whether she'd be good to use in the demo. Monty flapped a large piece of tarpaulin over her back, and under her belly, and Nessie didn't move an inch. Daisy trotted her over a huge sheet of plastic, and led her under a clothes-line, and the only thing the pony did wrong all afternoon was to try to take a tiny little chunk out of Monty.

'Someone's been feeding this pony titbits!' he proclaimed, and looked accusingly at Nicole. No one said anything, and I didn't think too much of it, but I saw Nicole's face darken and her lips tighten. On the way home in the car she explained indignantly what had happened.

'Sandra and Daisy wanted to make sure Nessie followed them really well, so she'd go over the tarpaulin willingly. When they came up to ride her, they had a little Tupperware box full of treats that they'd rattle to get her attention. They've been feeding her treats, and Monty thinks it was me!' She nearly wailed this last bit.

The next time I saw Nessie she was at Addington, the prestigious equestrian centre where I had first seen Monty perform amazing feats with Dually. Nicole was buzzing because Kelly had arranged for her to do a join-up during the demo with a horse that had been on her ten-week course. She hadn't known about it until about half an hour beforehand, which was probably just as well for her nerves. Nessie behaved like a miniature police horse, walking under the clothes-line as if no horse could possibly find it spooky, and standing calmly on the see-saw bridge as it rocked under her feet. Daisy rode and handled her beautifully. Although I was becoming familiar with Monty's methods, I was still amazed to see how effective they had been, even when applied by virtual novices. This horse had been completely raw only six weeks previously, and was now virtually bombproof, ridden by a child in front of an audience of over a thousand. This was unimaginable progress to most trainers.

And then, less than a month later, we met Misty.

EIGHT

Misty
(Nicole)

Misty emerged from the trailer like a cork from a champagne bottle. Her eyes were bulging with fear, and her nostrils distended, snorting in a frantic attempt to gain information about her new surroundings. She wore a tatty leather headcollar, which hadn't been removed in over two years, still with a rotten piece of lead rope suspended from it. She followed her owner into the stable like a cat on hot coals, her whole body trembling, quivering with fear. When her owner, Tina, let her go, she shot to the back of the box, and stood cowering in a corner.

She was beautiful and wild, and I wanted to wrap my arms around her neck and tell her it would all be all right. I knew the most reassuring thing I could do, however, was leave her alone. We moved away from the stable, and Tina filled me in on her history.

She had bought Misty from a pony dealer somewhere in Wales. She could see the pony was very frightened, and felt that in a caring, loving environment she would grow more confident. She wasn't convinced when the dealer said that Misty was basically well handled, but she was wearing a headcollar, and Tina thought she probably wasn't too wild. The clincher was that Misty was in foal – and Tina very much wanted to breed a Welsh Mountain Pony foal.

When she got Misty home to Oxfordshire, however, Tina realised the full extent of her terror. For nearly a year, she was hardly able to get within ten yards of her. She and her daughter tried everything they could think of. Occasionally, after hours of very patient work, they could catch her, and she was slightly calmer once caught, but was prone to sudden panic attacks. At one stage, a well-meaning friend managed to grab hold of her, and tied her up while she combed her extremely tangled mane. Misty was terrified by this experience. It confirmed all her fears, and seemed to double her resolve to never let anyone get close enough to catch hold of her again. The patient work of months was eradicated in just one hour.

No one had ever managed to get onto Misty's off-(right)side, and since even from a distance she always made sure that she kept people on her near-side, the belief was that she was probably blind in her right eye. Whatever had happened to her had obviously been horrific, but there was no way Tina could find out the true story. It's rare to come across a former owner who says, 'Oh, yes. She was naughty, so I got her in the stable and beat her within an inch of her life. She always seemed a bit nervy after that.'

Tina would have been happy to give up her dream of Misty being ridden by her grandchildren, and might have considered leaving Misty alone (praying that she never needed any veterinary care), but the problem was the foal. Now almost a year old, she followed her mother's example, and never let anyone near her. Tina found herself with the prospect of owning two ponies she couldn't get near! Breeding *wild* Welsh Mountain Ponies in Oxfordshire had never been the plan.

So they had managed to herd Misty into the trailer, and brought her to me. I was naively confident that we'd quickly be able to make a big difference, and that starting her within six weeks ought not to be a problem, although I didn't guarantee she'd be safe for children by then. Luckily, the grandchildren were too young to be riding yet, anyway. Tina was wonderful, and said I could have as long as I needed. This was very generous, as even at the modest rate of £65 per week, we would quickly exceed Misty's market value. As meat she would go for just a few pounds; as a normal children's riding pony, she might be worth £500.

When her owner had left, I looked at Misty snuffling suspiciously in her 'stable' – this was a field shelter made secure by the addition of some zany spray-painted boards left over from a friend's rave – and reconsidered my plan. I had intended to fetch Cobweb, our trusty old schoolmaster, from another field to keep her company. In fact, I had even thought I'd turn her out in the small enclosure that the shelter was in, but I decided against it. If she had company, ample food, water, and shelter, what possible reason could she have for wanting to overcome her terror of humans? She would simply be able to avoid us indefinitely. I fetched a bucket of water and a large mound of hay, and, trying to make myself as small and inconspicuous as possible, carefully placed these in the corner of her stable. I did this by leaning over the board – I didn't want to invade her space and make her feel vulnerable by opening the door. As it was, she expressed great alarm at this intrusion, snorting and pacing and tossing her head. I retreated and sat nearby for a while. I wanted her to realise that I could be around her without her needing to feel troubled. The urge to try to reassure her was almost irresistible, but it was clear that, for the moment, there was nothing I could do that she would not find stressful. When I heard her begin to munch the hay, I quietly left to get ready for work.

Stepping into the Control Room at Thames Valley Police was like entering another world. It was a vast room, full of computer banks, screens, radio communications units, and recording devices. Located on the top floor of the police station, large windows looked out across the city. It reminded me of the set from *Star Trek*, and I always had to resist the temptation to say, 'That is illogical, Captain' to the shift Sergeant. Rows of uniformed operators with headsets, tapping information urgently into the computers, only reinforced the image. It could equally have been a scene from George Orwell's *1984*, as every phone and radio conversation was recorded, and it was even possible for the Sergeant or Inspector to 'eavesdrop' on computer screens, observing every word you typed while listening to the phone call you were receiving. This was reassuring when dealing with irate, abusive, or threatening callers, but could be unnerving the rest of the time.

Telephone operators received calls from the public, both routine and emergency, and then sent these details to the radio operators, who communicated directly with the police officers on the beat. Everyone took turns in these two roles, and no one could ever know if they were going to spend the shift dealing with armed sieges, violent assaults, and multiple-victim road traffic accidents, or disputes over noisy neighbours and complaints about unpaid car tax. More often it was a bizarre mixture of the two. It was a strange choice of a job, perhaps, but the hours suited me, being mostly after dark or very early morning, so I could make the most of the daylight hours to be with the horses.

The evening after Misty arrived, I worked 10 p.m. to 2 a.m. I was jumpy, irrationally expecting bad news. The thought that some thug might find Misty, cornered in the stable, and do her some unmentionable harm, would not leave me. Was this paranoia? At the time there were too many stories circulating locally of horses being stabbed, the sort of chilling cruelty that seems to occur in horrible, copy-cat cycles. It bothered me that I couldn't promise Misty that no one would ever hurt her again. After all the violence she had so clearly suffered, I wanted to protect her but ultimately I knew I couldn't.

So, when I finished work, I cycled through the deserted streets of Milton Keynes, straight down to her field. An eerie stillness pervaded the silent city. I skimmed past our flat, where I could see the lights were all out – Adam must be asleep.

She was just where I'd left her, seemingly none the worse for wear, just finishing off the last scraps of hay. I let myself into her stable, and she shot to the back, watching me warily. I sat down in the corner, and tried to make myself appear harmless. I hummed a little, and munched a snack bar, watching my breath as it floated like smoke across the cold stable. I wanted her to know that I had no intention of trying to touch her. As time went by, she relaxed: her head lowered a little, her tail wasn't clamped quite so tightly into her body. I was sitting near her last bits of hay – if she wanted them, she'd have to come near me. This was altogether too much for her to contemplate, but as I continued to sit still and do nothing, she began to let down her guard. After half an hour or so, she rested a back leg. Another half hour, and her ears began to droop. She'd had a tiring day – another half hour, and I think she would have dozed. But it isn't exactly warm in April at 3 a.m: my legs were cramping, and I'd lost all sensation in my feet. I got up, staggered along the side of the stable, and broke the spell.

Her head shot up with a start, and she sprang away. As I limped and hobbled backwards and forwards along 'my wall', she paced backwards and forwards against 'her wall' – the back wall – always staying diagonally opposite me, maximising the distance between us. I kept moving slowly back and forth along the same stretch of wall – I wanted my actions to be predictable for her, and to give her a space that she could be confident I wouldn't invade. As sensation began to return to my legs and feet, I decided to keep walking, noticing that her reaction was slowing down and becoming less violent. Then she did something that astonished me. She stopped moving.

I stopped too, holding my breath, unsure of what to do. Why had she done this? It couldn't have been a mistake – her spatial awareness was far too great for that. By staying in one corner as I moved back along my wall, she had deliberately chosen to allow me closer. I started trembling. Could this really mean what I thought it did? I moved a step or two away from her, desperate to reward her gesture in some way. She shuffled a half step in my direction.

I moved again, and she took a tiny, tentative step. I forced myself to breathe. I was sure she could hear my heart racing, even though she was still a good 10 feet away from me. She was putting her desperately fragile trust in me, and I knew I mustn't do anything to betray it. We kept up our slow, wary progress, and I came to the end of my wall. What to do? I knew I couldn't move back towards her, that would be much too frightening for her, but if I went along the next wall, I would be moving into what was previously 'her' space. I decided to risk it. She hesitated a moment, and then followed me.

At times like this, you wish you had eyes in the back of your head. I couldn't risk looking at her – the slightest eye contact might terrify her. I didn't even want to turn my head. But, as we crawled along the back wall, I realised we were silhouetted by the street light. She was now only about 6 feet away from my back. I watched our shadows creep closer as step by step she inched her way closer. When she was only 2 feet away, I made a huge mistake. I leaned back towards her, almost imperceptibly. She jumped back as if stung, and suddenly we were as far apart as we could be. I cursed myself for being so stupid – and greedy. That's the problem with humans, I muttered, always pushing it too far, asking for too much, never content with what they're given. I was stuck, now, too – I couldn't be further away from her because we were diagonally opposite each other again now. If I moved, I'd be closer to her, and she'd have to retreat to keep her distance. I moved anyway. She moved too. I stopped, and she didn't. I didn't deserve it, but she'd given me another chance: she was coming closer again.

We went around the stable three more times in this strange, shuffling dance. It was past four in the morning. I gave her more hay and water, and cycled wearily home to bed.

Adam is used to the fact that my feet defy the laws of thermodynamics – giving out unfeasible amounts of cold, unable to absorb heat – but even he was astonished (and awoken) by their impossible iciness. 'Everything all right?' he murmured drowsily.

'Oh yes,' I said, cuddling up to the warmth emanating from his body, 'very all right.'

When I woke up later that morning, I realised that my initial assumptions about Misty had been wrong. I had thought that we would spend a long time 'negotiating' about having people in her personal space. Her reward for allowing someone near her would be for that person to move away. It could take a week or more, working several hours a day, before she might even take a single step towards me. However, the events of the night before led me to a realisation: Misty wanted to overcome her fear as much as we wanted her to. She wanted human contact, too. But she was still terrified that someone might beat her again. I had made more progress in that first midnight session than I would have dreamt possible. Had I known how deep-rooted her problems were, however, I might not have felt so optimistic.

After a hasty breakfast, I cycled back down to the field. When I arrived at the gate, she looked up at me but didn't immediately back away. I tried to saunter casually up to her, moving slowly but hoping I didn't resemble a prowling cat. The noise as I opened the door to her stable was too much, and she moved away, but as I started my slow circling of her box, she started to follow me again. She had a burr in one ear, and something stuck to one of her eyelashes, but I knew it would be days, if not weeks, before I could remove these for her. Whatever else I did, I knew I had to keep my hands to myself.

I saw Misty several more times that day. I decided it would be a good idea if she saw lots of people, from a distance, and realised that she was still safe, and that they weren't all out to get her. So she met my mum and Adam, and meanwhile we continued circling slowly around the stable, building up more trust with each revolution.

My nocturnal visit that evening brought me one step closer to her. She let me stand by her near-side shoulder. Rather than trying to touch her with my hand, I leaned into her gently. She stepped back abruptly, but didn't break away. After a few more attempts, she let my body brush against hers. Trying to keep my pulse rate low, and my adrenaline down, thinking only friendly thoughts, I gently touched her shoulder with the back of my hand. Her whole body quivered. But she stayed still. Slowly, I started to scratch her neck. As I stroked her, she very gradually started to relax, finding safety in the presence of a human being for possibly the first time in her life.

The next morning, Adam checked her briefly on his way to work. I had arranged to go with another Monty student, called Gillian, to visit Windsor Castle, to look at a horse that she was thinking of buying from the Queen, called Never Question. She was a beautiful filly with a slight injury that would make her unsuitable for racing. Loyalty to an hereditary monarchy didn't feature highly on the ardent socialist agenda of my youth. But my respect for the Queen grew immeasurably when I discovered how much she'd done to promote Monty's work in this country. It was the Queen who had catapulted Monty to centre stage when, having seen some articles about his approach, she invited him from the US to demonstrate these methods. He started several of her horses for her at Windsor Castle. Deeply impressed, she insisted that he tour the UK, a journey that eventually led to him becoming one of the most famous horsemen in the world, and in turn to change my life, and bring Misty into it. So a day out at Windsor seemed appropriate.

The stables, of course, were immaculate. The tack room was an orderly vision of supple leather and polished steel, a time-warp, belonging to an era long gone for many, a time when taking care of such matters could be a daily priority. The Queen's Equerry had just finished showing us around one of the outside yards, when we heard a clattering of hooves behind us. Retreating quickly around the corner, we realised we had narrowly avoided meeting the Duke of Edinburgh, who was returning from a drive with his team of gorgeous Fell ponies. Our undignified rush for cover amused the Equerry, but we had no desire for a Royal encounter. Once we were sure the Duke had gone, we peered into the stables to see the Fells. Gleaming with sweat, flecked with foam, they stood gently steaming, their compact bodies bulging with power. With their long, flowing manes, and thick winter coats, they made a stark contrast to the elegant thoroughbred we had come to see, but to my eyes they were every bit as beautiful. Gillian finalised the details of the sale, and we set off for home.

This journey back to Milton Keynes was the start of a very annoying habit that continues to plague me – getting so engrossed in a conversation about horses that I stop paying attention to the road. It wasn't until we saw signs for Gatwick that we realised we were going the wrong way around the M25. Anxious to rectify our mistake, we left the motorway immediately – only to find ourselves on the M23, heading for the south coast! At least sitting in the rush-hour traffic gave us plenty of time to talk.

When we got back to Milton Keynes, I asked Gillian to come and meet Misty. Misty viewed her with her customary suspicion, but seemed to be resigning herself to the notion that her social calendar would now be filled with such encounters. We must have got too engrossed again. It wasn't until we were about to leave that we realised that someone had smashed Gillian's car window to grab some spare change off her dashboard. It had been parked about 20 feet away on the other side of a hedge. I should have been more sympathetic, as I gave her the number for the police station, but I was far too excited. Misty had just then allowed me to touch her head!

Over the next couple of days, I consolidated this work with Misty until I could touch her head and neck and shoulder on the near-side, and even attach a rope. I touched her headcollar, too, but was very careful not to put any pressure on her head – I didn't want her to feel at all restrained. It was very clear that her off-side was still a non-starter – I couldn't even move my hand over her neck to touch the other side without her panicking. On the fourth day, I let her out into the small paddock. I wasn't sure I'd be able to get near her again, but I couldn't bear keeping her cooped up any longer.

I needn't have worried. By using the mildest form of aggressive body language – simply looking in her direction – I could get her attention, and then by becoming passive and moving away, I could draw her to me. As long as I didn't move my hand too fast, I could even touch her. Best of all, she now saw her field shelter as her safety zone, and if ever she felt worried or confused, she would rush straight into it. I could simply follow her in and re-establish contact. This surprised me: horses are animals of the plains, and naturally tend to find security in wide open spaces. To be trapped in a confined space in the wild would mean certain death. I couldn't believe my luck the first time I saw her do it. I thought it must have been a mistake, but soon realised it was a deliberate choice. It was where she had been given a space of her own, after the terrifying ordeal of travelling, and it was where we had forged the beginnings of a bond together. As long as I didn't blow it by making her experience in the shelter an unpleasant one, I felt confident I'd always be able to get near her.

Ten days after Misty arrived I received my first phone call from a client asking for a home visit. She had got hold of my number through Kelly and had actually called and left a message several weeks earlier, but hadn't left a number. I had just about given up on her ever calling back, when she rang. I couldn't have known then how important Julia Scholes would become in my life.

She had a black, five-year-old, Welsh Cob mare, Dilly, who seemed to have appeared out of nowhere, with the express purpose of getting Julia back into horses after a several-year break. Julia had ridden throughout her childhood, and then worked with horses after leaving school, but like so many others she had become disillusioned with the horse 'establishment'. Dilly had definitely been broken to harness, but possibly not to ride, and Julia wanted some help restarting her from the beginning. She also had some ground-handling issues, as Dilly had very much her own views about who should be in charge of speed and direction while being led. Julia didn't want to send Dilly away anywhere, so I arranged to visit her at her home in Hertfordshire a fortnight later.

This was the earliest appointment we could make, largely due to my strange hours in the Control Room, and as she drove me out to the stables where the horse was kept, I was disappointed to hear that in the meantime she'd gone ahead and backed Dilly herself. She'd just hopped on bareback, and Dilly hadn't reacted at all. She'd probably been ridden as well as driven in the past. Julia assured me, however, that there would still be plenty to work on.

Dilly lived on a farm open to the public, and it had animals packed away in every odd corner. There were goats, pigs, cows, chickens, rabbits and guinea pigs, and a strange assortment of stable yards crammed into all the remaining spaces. There was a shop selling a strange selection of crafts and gifts, and, I was delighted to discover, a coffee shop. The idea of having hot food and drink available where your horse lived seemed exceptionally civilised. What seemed less sensible, as Dilly had pointed out to Julia on numerous occasions, was that to get to the fields you had to lead your horse through the tables and chairs scattered outside the coffee shop and around the paddling pool filled with screaming kids, while a gaggle of territorial geese did everything they could to impede your progress.

I didn't feel entirely comfortable in the role of 'expert', but Julia was lovely, and I began to feel more at ease. Slim and strong, almost wiry, she had the kind of long, fine fingers I've always considered artistic. An abundance of curly brown hair added a touch of softness, and her green eyes were friendly, honest and direct. Dilly, on the other hand, had an abundance of shaggy black hair, which did nothing to soften *her* look, and whichever angle you viewed her from, she couldn't be described as slim. Strong, definitely. She wasn't an aggressive mare, but she had the air of someone who wouldn't suffer fools gladly. I prayed she wouldn't consider me one.

Once I started working with Dilly in the school, all my worries evaporated. She responded to join-up like she'd read the book, and when I long-lined her she obliged by executing a wonderful, elevated, perfectly balanced trot. By this time I had an audience who, I later discovered, were astonished at how beautifully the horse was working. Like so many horse owners, they were obsessed with the idea of the horse being 'on the bit', and regularly invested in gadgets and lessons to achieve this end. In fact, Dilly was in such perfect self-carriage partly because her adrenaline was raised a little by the unfamiliarity of having the lines around her quarters, and partly because the lines themselves were causing her to tuck her quarters underneath her and 'engage' her hocks in time-honoured dressage fashion. Once she got used to the sensation, she didn't perform quite like that again, but for that afternoon at least, tongues were wagging.

Julia rode Dilly that afternoon, and we also worked on Dilly's leading. Dilly had always responded to a tight lead line by leaning backwards, and would almost sit down if she didn't want to go somewhere. After some work in the school, Julia was able to lead her successfully past some scary objects. The whole process of turning her out and leading her around the farm would become much easier.

Julia invited me back to her flat for dinner, and as we talked, the similarities in our lives began to seem almost spooky: exactly the same age, both vegetarian, in long-term relationships of (at the time) eight years, both our partners were also musicians (principally guitarists) and teachers … and we had very similar views on horses. In fact, it was astonishing that we could find anything to discuss at all, since we seemed to share the same opinion on everything, except tea, which, bizarrely, she does not drink at all. But from that moment we started a conversation that has never petered out, however much time we spend together.

Whenever she could, Julia came over to Milton Keynes and watched me work with Misty. We rode the other horses out together, and she gradually took over the Saturday teaching whenever I had to work. A fast learner, with a very precise and inquisitive mind, having her around was immensely helpful. She came out on several visits with me, and another long series of conversations in cars was started, along with the usual lack of attention to the route that resulted in many missed turnings as we raced to finish our thoughts before we arrived. The post-visit analysis would keep us going through the long drives home, and much beautiful English scenery passed unnoticed outside our bubble of thoughts, ideas and insights.

Although Misty remained very wary of Adam, she had instantly captured his heart. Since his working hours meant he was unable to see her that often, it took her a long time to overcome her fear, and approach him. Perhaps she also had greater reason to mistrust a man. She would reduce him almost to tears as she hovered at the edge of his space, unsure of him, torn by the dilemma of whether to trust him and come nearer and perhaps find a new safety zone, or to run away. It was particularly hard for him to get near her out in the enclosure. Often she would be unable to cope with the tension and rush back to her shelter. He kept himself between her and the stable door, making it less easy for her to break away. Eventually she would bring herself close enough so that he could just about touch her, and, knowing that even to move his hand slightly might send her reeling away, he would silently break into tears.

Misty was like a ball of tangled string; trying to unravel her seemed impossible because you couldn't find an end to start at, all the knots were so intertwined. She was particularly unnerved by having two people near her at once, so the option of one person holding her while the other worked around her was out of the question. She wasn't just worried at the prospect of having someone on her off-side – as far as she was concerned, that was non-negotiable. She could not tolerate having her legs even touched, much less her feet picked up and she would immediately run if any sharp movements were made near her. The tiniest step in the wrong direction could send her flying. She was terribly frightened of the lead rope, and would shy backwards if even an inch was hanging down. The idea of getting a roller or a saddle onto her back didn't seem particularly promising, let alone a rider. I had to quell a rising sense of panic. Would I fail the very first problem horse I had to deal with? All I could do was stay patient and gentle, and keep thinking.

One of the most difficult decisions to make when training horses is when to address something as an issue, and when to let it lie, in the often quite reasonable hope that when the horse has gained more trust, the original problem will simply disappear, or at least become easier to address. Only having access to one side of the horse isn't really the sort of issue you can ignore, however, and I knew I had to think of some way to overcome it. With a lot of gentle persistence, I had been able to touch her off-side neck when I was standing on the near-side, but she was not at all comfortable with that.

It simply wasn't possible to hold her head still and inch my way around to the off-side – if I tried that, she would shoot backwards and sideways in a panic, always keeping me on the near-side. Even had I been a lot stronger, I don't think this strategy would have worked – I sincerely believe she would have fought to the death. In any case, I needed her to *want* to let me into her off-side; any victory won through force would be hollow. Adam and I came up with two strategies, one quite clever and one unbelievably stupid. It was her reaction to the quite clever strategy that should have alerted me to how stupid the other one was.

We talked it through. 'You know, it's not actually impossible to get on Misty's off-side,' Adam pronounced. This was a definition of 'impossible' I hadn't previously come across.

'While you're on her near-side, there are people in the garden on the other side of the field who are on her off-side, they're just not very close.'

'Yeeesss,' I said, not even trying to conceal my scepticism. 'I can't see them being particularly helpful, though.'

'No, I know, but really we just have to work out how close she'll tolerate someone on that side, and even if it's three hundred yards, that's a start, and we can work on getting in closer. You know, keep working on the edge of her comfort zone, just using advance and retreat, with the emphasis on retreat.'

It was worth a try and we put the idea into practice later that day. I walked around with Misty following me in the stable, and Adam stayed outside, about 50 yards away. At a certain point in her circuit around the stable, she would have to let Adam be on her off-side. She made that moment as brief as possible, by hanging back for as long as she could, and then rushing past. She couldn't not go past him, otherwise she would be letting me walk up close behind her, an even less acceptable option. It was clear that the process caused her deep concern, even at such a distance, but we took care not to let her get too frightened. We let her get used to it bit by bit.

Along the same principles, we also worked with her outside the stable. I would hold her, and Adam would walk around her, at a distance of some 30 yards, and make his way to her off-side. She would keep him on her off-side for the briefest possible moment, pivoting to face him and put him back on her near-side as quickly as possible. It was slow, tedious work, not least for Adam who had to walk such large circles! In her frantic attempt to keep Adam on her near-side, Misty would often bash into me and startle herself in the process. She was like a small, rather hairy, unexploded bomb, always on the verge of going off.

We worked a lot in this manner, and made some significant progress. The problem was it required both of us. Our jobs in the Japanese school and Thames Valley Police meant that our paths simply didn't cross often enough, and supportive though he was, Adam wasn't prepared to meet me down in the paddock at two o'clock in the morning. I had to come up with a way to work on the problem on my own.

What would Monty do? I wondered. I hadn't seen him work on exactly this problem, but I had seen him work with several horses with phobias, and it seemed largely a case of demonstrating to the horse that there was nothing to be feared. There was always a tense moment while the horse confronted its demons, and then huge relief as it realised it wasn't so bad after all. If I could just get to her off-side, I reasoned, she'd realise it wasn't so bad. The fact that we'd been trying to convince her of this for several days already didn't daunt me. There was a degree of logic to this confidence: a horse that has been badly treated will often have the same sort of 'distance' issues. If you're far enough away that you can't hurt them, they're happy. If you're close and you haven't hurt them, it's possible you mean them no harm. If you're at about striking distance away, you're potentially very dangerous. Perhaps Misty was having trouble with us being in this 'hazard' zone, and allowing her to dwell on the anticipation of violence was the problem. It should have been abundantly clear to me, however, that Misty's problems with her off-side weren't suddenly going to dissolve with proximity. She was gradually getting happier about having me near her, but just realising that I was close enough to hurt her, but hadn't done so, wasn't good enough for her. I was going to have to prove my trustworthiness over an extended period of time.

In my mind's eye, I could see Monty dealing with the problem and arriving at a solution within minutes. I could see Misty with Monty on her off-side, tentative but trusting, her fear diminishing by the second. I decided to gently and slowly pass a long-line over her neck, from the near-side, of course, and attach it to the headcollar. Then I would simply step behind her, pull her head around to me, and for a moment as she turned, I would be on her off-side. I could repeat the process, and she would soon realise she had had nothing to fear all along. I couldn't think why I hadn't come up with this marvellous idea before. I decided to work in the larger field next to her small enclosure, so we'd have a bit more space.

One thing I hadn't taken into consideration was Monty's somewhat heavier build and greater strength. I knew that, even at 11.2 hands high Misty was too strong to hold, but I hadn't been prepared for the determination with which she pulled away. I wish I could say I held on to the line valiantly for a moment or two, but as soon as I stepped behind her, she shot off like a bullet and the line was instantly pulled out of my hand. I had just about been on her off-side, but only for a nanosecond. I watched helplessly as she took off hell for leather around the field, a terrible feeling of guilt creeping over me as I realised she was completely out of control and very likely to injure herself. She made several circuits, hotly pursued by the long-line. For a moment, she came out of her blind panic, saw her stable, and bolted straight into it. She stood there shaking and trembling. I got to the door and closed it behind me at the exact moment she realised that the 'snake' that had been chasing her was still attached. She tried to make a run for it, lost her footing on the bedding, and fell over. Scrambling to her feet, she desperately tried to jump out of the stable. The worst thing was that in her efforts to escape she was actually putting me on her off-side. This terrified her so much that she would spin around to put me back on the near-side, find herself facing the back of the stable, feel her legs being attacked by the snake, and spin back around to try to escape again. She made a desperate leap for freedom and got her forelegs over the front of the stable. It seemed that within seconds her flailing legs would break through the wood, or be broken in the process.

I knew decisive action was called for, but at the same time would have to be extremely careful not to get kicked, squashed, or trampled. Feeling strangely calm, but with my heart thumping loudly in my chest, I clambered over the door and got myself back on her near-side, outside the stable. From this position I was able to detach the long-line and take it out of the stable, and then push her feet back from where they were hooked over the barrier. Then I sat down and, now that the crisis was over, started shaking uncontrollably.

I couldn't believe I'd been so stupid. She'd been here just over a week, we'd made some good progress, and then I'd ruined it. I'd painstakingly built up a small amount of trust – which nevertheless had taken a huge leap of faith on her part – and now I'd betrayed her. In my haste to get a result, I'd taken a stupid risk, and now I knew I was going to pay the price.

Feeling thoroughly dejected, I let myself into her stable. I might as well get started on repairing the damage, I thought, that is if it can be repaired. Misty's eyes were still bulging with fear and she was still trembling a little, but as I walked in, something happened that I didn't expect. She began to relax. She edged a little closer to me, and I began stroking her neck. She leaned against me, and I started to cry. I didn't deserve it, but I was getting yet another chance.

I'm a great believer in silver linings and although I was devastated by my mistake, the silver lining to this otherwise very cloudy episode was simple: while Misty had been frantically trying to escape from her horrific ordeal in the stable, she had put me on to her off-side. It had been a brief, panic-drenched moment, but somehow we had both survived the trauma, just. There had to be an altogether calmer way around the problem. She would have to make the decision to allow me into that space.

The solution turned out to be very simple, and it fully engaged her willingness to work on the problem, while allowing her to take it at her own pace. I thought of a way to make it worth her while to confront this fear. We were both inside the stable, and I stood by the open door. She was loose, and could position herself wherever she liked. If she wanted to go through the door, however, she would have to let me onto her off-side while she went through, for I was standing on that side of the doorway. For a moment or two, it looked like she was eyeing up this option. It was clear that if she went for it, it was going to be at a considerable speed. But I reckoned that if we were able to repeat the process often enough, she would begin to slow down. She never did take the option of shooting out of the stable past me, but she felt drawn to the open door, and would repeatedly approach.

So what I did was to start scratching her neck on the near-side, standing pretty much in front of her. Before I worked out the attraction of the open door, it wasn't possible to be standing in front of her. The fact that it was spring and she was moulting made the scratching a particular pleasure for her. She was free to move away from me, or position herself so I was back on her near-side again. Every time she moved away, however, I stopped scratching her. Every time she moved back or allowed me to move into the position I wanted to be in, I started scratching her again. She very quickly learned that I would only do what she wanted me to do when she was standing where I wanted her to stand. Gradually, I moved my fingers under her neck until I actually had my hand on her off-side. I'd already been able to do this by putting my hand over her neck, but never when standing in front of her. I soon found myself standing just to the off-side of her, scratching the top of her neck. From time to time she would come to, realise where I was, and back away. If that was what she needed to do to feel safe, that was fine by me, but sooner or later the desire to be scratched would prevail, and she would come back to me.

This represented a major breakthrough in the whole issue. Little by little, day after day, she became happier with me on the off-side, and would let me further and further down her little body, until I could just about scratch the top of her tail from either side. Making headway in this one major area allowed the tangled string of her troubles to begin to unravel. In the course of this work, she also found a key to get me to pause any training session, giving her more control over the process, and added confidence. She taught me to hug her.

It first happened when I moved a little abruptly to get to her off-side. She swung her head around to put me back on her near-side, but didn't swing it far enough, and ended up with it on my shoulder. I immediately stopped what I was doing, and quietly put my arms around her neck. The Misty hug was born, and she soon discovered that I found it so endearing that she could get me to stop whatever I was doing if she simply put her head on my shoulder. On the few occasions when I would continue with my task, she would dig her jaw hard into my collarbone as if to say, 'Look, you idiot, I'm hugging you, so stop what you're doing right now!'

Misty wasn't just a sharp learning curve for me, she was an education. Picking up her feet, putting on a roller, saddle, bridle, riding her, leading her, especially from the off-side, taking her out for walks, and long-lining her all presented challenges at least as difficult as getting onto her off-side for the first time. We over-ran the projected duration of her stay by nearly three times, but in the end we achieved all the objectives, having long since stopped charging for her. The thought of her leaving us was simply unbearable, but Tina was thrilled with the changes we had made. Looking forward to having two ponies she could actually do things with, she also sent us Misty's foal, Pearl. Completely untouched, she was wary, but infinitely easier than Misty had been, only having to deal with fear of the unknown rather than fear of the known. She had never been caught, but within a matter of days was more relaxed around us than Misty. I tried not to think about the fact that Pearl's rapid progress meant that Misty would soon be leaving. As I updated Tina on the phone, I slipped in as casually as possible, a comment along the lines that, if she ever decided she didn't want Misty any more, we would gladly keep her.

Not long after she had started working for me, Julia had one of those experiences that you wouldn't wish on anyone. A visitor to the field had pulled the gate to as he left, but not closed the latch, and moments later Julia turned around just in time to see two grey tails disappearing around the corner. Misty and Pearl were in the front paddock so they could meet as many new people as possible, but clearly they felt it was time to extend their social circle. Not wishing to startle them, she followed them as quickly and quietly as she could, watching with dismay as they chose not to follow the under-pass that would take them safely under the main road, but, being Welsh Mountain Ponies, to clamber up the steep slope and onto the tarmac. It was a long, straight, fast road, and the only consolation was that it had recently been opened, and traffic wasn't yet heavy on it. At this point, Pearl, who had only been with us for a few days, had not yet had her first headcollar on, and Misty was not necessarily going to be easy to catch.

As Julia pondered what to do, a police car turned up. I was at work at the time, and her first thought was, Oh my God, Nicole can somehow see what I'm doing! She's spying on me.

Had I been working on the radios that morning I might well have received a startling message: 'Delta papa to delta alpha. Have just intercepted two loose ponies on H8 between Woolstone and Woughton. Will assist. Over.' Luckily, I knew nothing about it until they were safely back in their field.

'The police were fantastic,' Julia said. 'They stopped the traffic and that gave me a bit of space to work with Misty and Pearl. The best thing was they let me get on with it and didn't interfere, or rush me.

By this time, I think the ponies had decided that it wasn't so much fun up on the road after all, and with more and more cars stacking up behind the police vehicles, they were getting a bit worried. I put a bit of pressure on them, and just sort of herded them back to the field. Luckily, once they got back to the field, they chose to go through the open gate. You can't imagine how terrified I was, thinking I'd lost them. The prospect of phoning you up to tell you they were at large somewhere in Milton Keynes, rapidly reverting to their wild state, was not appealing!'

It was on 31 August 1997, the day Princess Diana died, that Misty and Pearl were due to go home. Tina came to pick them up in her trailer. Pearl bounced eagerly up the ramp, but Misty was very reluctant. I began half-heartedly to persuade her to load when Tina suddenly asked, 'Did you really mean what you said about there always being a home for her here if I ever don't want her any more?'

'Of course,' I replied, doubt creeping in as I remembered I hadn't really spoken to Adam about it. I knew he was heart-broken about the prospect of her leaving, but did that necessarily mean he wanted us to keep her? He was off in France anyway, at a wedding, so I couldn't get hold of him.

'Well, why don't you keep her here?' Tina suggested. 'I really wanted the foal more than anything, and I'm sure Misty would be a lot happier here with you.'

A surge of love welled up inside me as I looked at Misty. She stood looking dejected at the bottom of the ramp. I was sure that Tina and her family would look after her well and that she'd be happy. But the pony of my childhood dreams was mine for the asking and I couldn't turn her down. I waived the rest of Pearl's training fee, and Tina closed up the ramp and drove her away, leaving Misty and me hugging in the field.

Adam, of course, was delighted. And although she is never ridden,

Misty has an important job that no other pony could do. She hugs us whenever we need it, and she constantly reminds us that whenever we think a horse's problems are insurmountable, we only have to think them through and we'll come up with the answers in the end. She set us on the path of helping traumatised and abused horses. Her courage in dealing with her terror remains a source of inspiration, and, tiny though she is, she exudes a sense of quiet wisdom and dignity that makes her a pleasure to have around. Knowing that she's safe and happy now has made all those hours of painstaking work worthwhile.

NINE

Taking the plunge
(Adam)

Misty changed my life, too. It broke my heart to see that lovely little pony run to the back of her stable, shaking with fear, if I so much as stepped towards her from a distance of 30 feet. It would have been difficult to know where to start, if she hadn't been impossible to catch. To lead her, even just to move around her, however slowly, to pick up her feet, put on a saddle, or ride her, all seemed utterly out of the question. And yet, day by day, Nicole dispelled her fear, won her trust and eventually overcame all these massive problems in the most impressive feat of horsemanship I have ever witnessed.

Misty was fragile and timid, but full of character. Although she was petrified of humans, her special personality began to emerge as her fear subsided. She wanted so much just to be loved, to be safe, to be accepted. She soon found that being near Nicole was a place of safety. But it was another matter to persuade her that I was trustworthy too. I found myself reduced to tears time and again, when, although I stood as passively as I could, Misty would falter, unable to approach me for what seemed like hours. She would stand hesitantly about 10 feet away, struggling to muster the confidence to approach, her wish to be with me battling against her fear. But, even with my unsure grasp of her language, she understood what I was trying to say. In the end, she was won over. So was I. When we were given her in exchange for the work we did on her filly, I was astonished to find that Nicole's great childhood dream, of having a grey Welsh Mountain Pony called Misty, had become my own.

Monty came back to the UK several times, to meet every group taking the courses. This would generally be organised to coincide with a tour and Nicole was always on the UK touring team. I was left behind, then as now, to do the less glamorous jobs, such as cycling down to check horses at 11 p.m. But I took every opportunity to go and see Monty's demos, surprised to discover there was nothing I would rather be doing. This would be followed by a long, lonely drive back and then checking horses at some ridiculous hour of the morning, when I would often spend time just holding Misty, scratching Sensi or simply taking in the beauty of the peace of the night, into which the horses fitted so naturally.

If I had any doubt that Monty's methods worked, or that I could learn them and even adapt them, they were dispelled one day the next summer. By then I had done join-up with several horses, and had helped Nicole back Nessie and another youngster. But, at that point, I did not have much time to be with our horses, which was the main reason why our new pony, Finn, wouldn't let me catch him.

Finn is an Exmoor pony, the closest surviving relation to the only species of truly wild horse left in the world, Przewalski's horse, which come from Mongolia and look extraordinarily similar. Exmoors are incredibly compact and rugged, one of the very toughest breeds of horse, built to survive in the extreme conditions of the moor. Nicole had been hired to start him for someone's daughter, but the daughter had lost interest so we ended up buying him, and used him for lessons. Except that, not being able to catch him, this was not exactly easy. He didn't seem very scared, and Nicole could catch him easily.

But he didn't much like the look of me and used to saunter off, nonchalantly but deliberately, when I approached. It was as if he was sticking two fingers up as he went, emphasising the superiority of having four legs. This was a point I had to concede, especially in view of a double-barrelled kick I had seen him produce so readily for the other horses.

The way he interacted in the group made it clear he was a cheeky character. He would stand still and refuse to move when Sensi would tell him, with her most spectacular barracuda-face, to get lost. He wouldn't even move when she gnawed on his rump, which seemed to be made of rhino hide. When chased in the field he would turn and lift his bum into the air, ready to kick, but as soon as the larger horses had started to graze again he would turn around, come up and bite them. His attitude to people was not dissimilar. I didn't much like the fact that I was coming down in the middle of the night to check this little varmint of a pony and he wouldn't even let me catch him. But due to the fact that I never had enough time, I didn't do anything about it, and soon I was completely unable to get near the little bugger.

A couple of months after we'd bought him, I was on my summer holidays. One lovely morning, after breakfast, I went down to the field to see the horses and they were all happily grazing in the warm sun. I went up to each of them and gave them a scratch and check over. As I tried surreptitiously to edge my way closer to Finn, quietly working my way through the herd towards him, I could feel without looking that he already had his eye on me. I tried to pretend I was only interested in Sensi, who was standing next to him, but we both knew there was no way he would let me get near him. He started to meander over into the open, and when he felt at a safe distance, he went back to grazing, keeping his eye on me the whole time. I continued to tiptoe around for a time. But as soon as I made the slightest movement in his direction, he set off across the field.

The hell with this, I thought, I'm going to teach him a lesson. I changed my body stance completely and deliberately sent him further away from me. His head came up immediately, and he started to trot directly away from me, as I raised my hands and came after him, looking him squarely in the eye. He broke into a canter and started to wheel around to try to get on the other side of the herd. He was soon back in amongst the other horses, and got them running too, until I was sending all of them around the 4-acre field they shared. Realising that I would have to adapt what I'd seen Monty do in a pen, I remembered how he had learned to do join-up by observing the interactions of wild herds, in which the lead mare would exile the misbehaving youngsters from the group. So I kept my eye firmly on Finn, and did my best to single him out, getting between him and the group whenever possible. After a while, Sensi began to realise that it was Finn who was causing her to miss her brunch, and she began to lower her head and eat. The next time he got away from me, and ran towards her, hoping she would protect him, she turned on him with teeth bared. No longer so welcome in the group, Finn was running out of options. I tried again the softly-softly approach, keeping my eyes on the ground and approaching in as non-threatening a way as possible.

But he was still a long way from running out of steam, which could not be said for me. I was dripping with sweat, for the sun was by now really beating down, and my lungs were burning. I could not run any more, but I wasn't going to give up that easily. With a snort of triumph, Finn settled back to grazing with the herd again, ignoring Sensi's irritated flick of the tail as he disdainfully watched me walk back to the gate. Little did he know I was fetching my secret weapon.

When he saw me come back in with my mountain bike, however, his head came straight back up. Nostrils flaring, he looked across as I juddered along towards them. He was soon back off round the field with the others, but now I was able to keep up much better, and for what seemed like a very uncomfortable eternity, we went back round again. Although the field was not muddy, the impressions of the horses' feet had left it quite bumpy. Unable to sit on the seat for the vibrations, I sweated along, wondering if this was such a good idea after all, my shaky toil on the bike contrasting with the grace of the horses floating across the grass. In spite of being rather more elegant than myself, Finn was noticeably less well suited to this strategy of flight than the rest of the horses. The free movement of their legs were not matched by his choppy strides, and while they could simply trot, he was obliged to canter hard, his stubby legs hardly seeming to bend at the knees at all. When they were in the most bottle-necked area near the gate, I eased off a bit, hoping that they would settle there, but they kept running until I began to feel this join-up thing might not work with Exmoor ponies after all. And then, Finn did the last thing I expected. As the herd came to the bottleneck, he suddenly stopped.

I slammed on the brakes so hard that I nearly flew over the handle-bars. Somehow managing not to crash onto the ground and send them all running off again, I struggled to take up as passive a stance as one can when holding a bicycle. He stood like a rock. Panting, sweat seeping through his dun flanks, he kept stock still as I approached. He let me get really close, then I hesitated, thinking he was about to move. But he turned his head towards me. Lowering my eyes and retreating a step, I knew I was getting somewhere as I heard him run his jaws over each other. I reached out a hand to touch him, and heard him catch his breath as he tensed against my touch. I walked away in a circle and he began to follow-up, as I had seen him do with Nicole. I stopped, and he remained close enough for me to stroke him on the forehead. I scratched his withers and he began to relax. But then, as I stroked along his back, he decided to walk off again.

Lots of people tell me that their horse takes the mickey out of them, and it seems to me that they are often misinterpreting what is going on. When you think it's happening to you, though, it can be hard not to see it that way. I reminded myself that horses do what they are allowed to do, taking what they can get. There are so many mistakes we make, so many important things happen that we don't even notice. Had I given an unintended signal, moved too fast? I knew that by giving up so easily on other occasions, I had taught Finn that I was easy to get around. If he persisted, I would go away. Maybe he was just testing my resolve.

It was back to the bike and the juddering. But I knew I would get another chance, and sure enough, about the third time they came to the bottleneck, Finn put in another sudden halt. Again, I stopped immediately and took off all the pressure. He let me go straight up to him and put on his headcollar, and I have never had trouble catching him since.

He is now my favourite horse, and I get more of a kick out of riding him than any flashy Arab or thoroughbred. I just love being able to sling a headcollar on him, hop on, and bomb around bareback. And if you can ride Finn, you can ride almost anything, including a pneumatic drill.

Although this experience and many others convinced me of the power of Monty's methods, I had no particular thoughts of taking it any further. I went back to work that autumn, while Nicole continued to get more and more closely involved with the course.

So it was that on one rainy night in October 1997, I found myself driving back to Milton Keynes from Kent. Monty was on tour again and Nicole was with the team, rushing around the country in a motor home. It had been another astonishing demonstration, and I was ruminating on the contrast between my job and Nicole's work for Kelly and Monty. The latter was so inspiring, so rewarding, so full of possibilities, whereas just the thought of going in to work at the Japanese school filled me with anger and frustration.

I enjoyed teaching, having a great rapport with my students, who were all Japanese, aged sixteen to nineteen, and to whom I taught a total of six subjects (history, contemporary and British studies, economics, English language, guitar and, later, horse riding). I sympathised with the students in having to endure similar conditions to those I had hated so much at school and I tried to make my lessons as fun as I could. Given that the students had so little in the rest of their lives, I took them out as much as possible and tried to make them feel part of the community. I taught them about fashion, bad language, and the Beatles, often teaching them songs or watching videos with subtitles so they could get a grasp of real English, phrases they could actually use. I did a lot of extra private lessons in which I was able to get to know some students very well.

Life in a boarding school is indescribable to anyone who hasn't been through it, but is instantly and vividly memorable to anyone who has. The degree to which the institution dominates the lives of those within it is almost complete. It may not be possible to control your behaviour, but the school still dominates your every moment. You can't escape the system. You can be classed as a good student, or as a rebel, but you can't avoid being classed.

As a student you are not aware that the teacher is actually in a very weak position. When you find yourself standing in front of a class, however, and one of the students refuses to do something, you suddenly feel it. You are essentially powerless in the face of any direct refusal to co-operate. Yet the only real power you can have as a teacher is the respect of the students. And you have to earn that, just as you have to earn it from a horse.

I only once had a direct refusal to co-operate. It was in the video room. I wanted three students at the back to move further forward so they could read the subtitles. There was an empty row in the front so I asked them to move there. I had forgotten to take into account the obvious fact that sitting at the back is cool, whereas sitting at the front is very uncool. Too late, I realised I was not just asking them to move to the front to understand the lesson more, but to lose face in front of their peers. One of them said they didn't want to, and then said no, and all of a sudden, a hush descended.

This was a shock, as it was more usual for students not to express an opinion about anything, and I asked them politely again. But, although one of them shifted his weight, another one said something to him in Japanese, and then explained again that they didn't want to. Finally, they said they just wouldn't move, and didn't.

I felt the ego and adrenaline rising inside me as the battle line was drawn. They were obviously ready for a major showdown, but I wasn't going to blow up. I wasn't going to back down either. This was just like Wilberforce and the flooded bridleway. But the confrontation didn't need to happen. I decided to sit for a minute and think about it. I needed to find a compromise that we could all regard as some kind of victory. I knew that it was wrong to continue to raise the stakes. So I just didn't put the video on. Doing nothing kept the pressure on both parties, but also gave us some time to cool off. We all sat for some minutes, then I told everyone to go back to the classroom and we continued reading a textbook. This was obviously not the preferred class activity, so I had given the boys reason to regret being so rude to me, not least because their classmates were unimpressed at having to read rather than watch a film. The next time we went to the video room, I was careful to get the whole class to sit further forward and fill up all the gaps, as they came in. That was that, and the rebels never gave me any trouble again – in fact we got on particularly well, just as before.

Although I found it immensely rewarding to work with the students, I discovered that, as a 'foreigner', I had to accept some unpleasant facts. A lot of my politically correct, egalitarian philosophies had trouble standing up to the realities of life as an employee in what seemed to me the smallest of Japan's islands. For a variety of reasons, it was also clear that the school was a sinking ship. It had become very depressing to work there.

As I drove along the empty motorway to Milton Keynes that October night, rain lashing against the windscreen, it suddenly struck me. If there was no reason why Nicole couldn't be a 'horse whisperer', why couldn't I?

When I was seventeen, I decided to run away from school and get expelled. It was a decision I made in a flash, which led, almost inevitably, to disaster. But it was the best decision I had ever made. In a moment I found myself penniless, busking on the streets of Paris, but I also began to find my identity. In the next weeks and months I learned more about myself, and the world, than I had in all the years before, when I'd studied so much and yet been so insulated from real life. Having fourteen O Levels, I discovered, was not of much use on the street. I had to rely on my judgement, which was, unfortunately, not very reliable. I had gone to France largely because of a friend, who lied to me and betrayed me (and nearly kicked my head in too) before I decided to haul myself back across the Channel, having nearly been arrested yet again. All of a sudden I went from being at a top public school, heading for one of the best universities in the world, to washing dishes for £2.30 an hour. I found out what it is like to be at the bottom, exploited by the NHS, by taxpayers, by an employment agency that earned more than I did from my labour, and sometimes even by co-workers. But finally I was free. I was no longer over-privileged and unappreciative. I had learned something.

I wanted to work for myself. I wanted to work for horses. I decided then and there, driving through the rain on the M25, to give up my job, go on the course and get my Monty Roberts Preliminary Certificate of Horsemanship.

TEN

On the road with Monty
(Nicole)

'Nick, it's Kelly. Listen, I've got some news for you. I hope you won't be upset, but I've decided not to go on the tour this time.'

'Oh! Why not?'

'Well, there's just so much to do here. You'll all be fine without me. But you'll have to take my place – and introduce Monty.'

'No.' I don't often say no to Kelly, but then again she doesn't often make preposterous suggestions.

'Good, I'll take that as a yes.'

It was hard to imagine a tour without Kelly. She often joked that she didn't do anything on tour except drive Monty from venue to venue and keep him stocked up with Diet Coke, but in fact she was the driving force behind it, keeping everyone happy and holding the whole troupe together. It was going to be very hard without her. But either I was going to leave the country or I was going to have to stand in the middle of a round pen, speak into a microphone in front of hundreds of people, and introduce Monty Roberts.

The tour was starting in four weeks, and although I did get some sleep, whenever I woke up, I only had to think 'I'll be introducing

Monty' to be instantly wide awake. Kelly had looked over the wording of my very brief speech, and proclaimed it suitable, but I was still terrified that she was showing a profound lack of judgement in choosing me for the job. True, I could speak confidently to a roomful of students about the principles of join-up, but that didn't mean I wouldn't make a run for it when faced with numbers in excess of 1,200. There had to be someone else better suited to the task.

'No,' she reassured me, just the slightest hint of irritation in her voice, 'you'll be fine! Just don't mention the mane killer.'

We laughed at the memory of Kelly's horrendous gaffe. On a previous tour we had been promoting a gadget that could shorten and thin a mane painlessly, without the need of pulling the hair out by its roots. Many people were sceptical about its effectiveness, thinking it would damage the hair. Kelly meant to refer to it as a humane mane puller, but somehow managed to say humane mane killer. The manufacturers were less than pleased with this endorsement. Yet I was confident I had the potential to outdo Kelly's faux pas. I had certainly witnessed far worse. At the end of one of our more memorable university seminars, my Director of Studies stood up to express her appreciation for the guest lecturers, who had spoken on Freudian Feminist Psychoanalysis. 'I'd like to spank our speakers,' she said, before turning various shades of crimson as the auditorium erupted in laughter.

The first venue was Gleneagles, in Scotland, which meant driving up the day before. Julia, Hannah Rose (who helped with the books, videos, training aids and so on that people want to buy), and I were travelling in the motor home. On the way up, we stopped off in the Lake District to collect Simon Raynor, Monty's young English rider. I was feeling tense about my impending humiliation and the first thing I said to Simon when we picked him up was, 'You can only ask me ten questions between here and Scotland.'

By the time he'd said 'Why? Really? Only ten? Are you sure?' and was already down to six, I was confident I'd be able to concentrate on memorising my speech.

I've never seen the attraction of 'performing' in front of large groups of people. I'd stopped acting in plays at the age of five, for example, and never dreamed about being a singer (unless it meant I could meet David Bowie). Julia could understand where I was coming from, and was visibly relieved she hadn't been asked to do the job. Simon was sympathetic, but as a charming extrovert who adores being the centre of attention, he couldn't quite understand my concerns.

The exponential effect of four horse-obsessed people having in-depth conversations in the motor home meant that, again, we came off the motorway at the wrong junction, and headed in the opposite direction for at least fifteen miles.

'What is it with Scotland?' I queried petulantly. 'Why do none of the villages we're travelling through appear on this map?'

Once we'd solved the mystery I told the group about my experience of travelling the wrong way around the M25 and not noticing for 70 miles. They gasped incredulously, as we shot past the turning to Gleneagles.

Time behaves peculiarly on tour, sometimes going painfully slowly (when waiting to load up the last few things at one o'clock in the morning, so we can start driving to the next venue), but more commonly very quickly. A couple of hours will just slip away unnoticed, and then all of a sudden up to 2,000 people arrive all at once. On this particular evening, time marched consistently and deliberately on, ignoring my fervent wish that it would just stand still. To my dismay, I realised that a steady stream of people were turning up. That dashed my rather unrealistic hope that everyone would just decide to stay at home.

Niel (sic), the soundman, showed me how to use the microphone – a simple matter of switching it on and holding it in the right place, but he still had to go through it several times with me.

'You'd better check with Monty which end of the arena he's coming in from,' he said.

Monty was already surrounded by people wanting his autograph and asking him questions, but I pushed through to the front.

'Oh yeah, we'll go in from this side,' he smiled. I nodded numbly, and started to walk off.

'Hey, are you all right? Are you nervous at all?' He must have caught a glance of my ashen face and terrified eyes.

'Don't worry, you'll be all right. If you make a mistake, don't panic, just keep talking. It really doesn't matter, and anyway, most people won't be paying that much attention.' He patted me reassuringly on the back, and absurdly I felt a thousand times better.

I was immensely proud, standing next to Monty, waiting to go into the pen. 'Big Country' started playing, and Monty gave me a nudge, and then a moment later, a shove. As I marched into the pen, I remembered to smile, and tried to keep my voice low to minimise the tremors and avoid sounding squeaky.

'Good evening, ladies and gentlemen, and welcome to Gleneagles Equestrian centre. I'm Nicole Golding, and I teach with Kelly Marks on the Monty Roberts Intelligent Horsemanship courses held in Witney, Oxfordshire. On these courses, people often tell us how much seeing Monty work has changed their lives ...'

This is all right, I was thinking. I know this stuff. I'm proud to be associated with Kelly and Monty, and it's great to be able to say it. Now, mustn't miss out anyone I'm meant to thank, and don't even think of saying 'humane mane killer'.

Good, nearly home and dry. Just a little bit more and I'm out of here.

And, at that moment, my mind went blank. Nothing. Oh no! What was the last bit? I'd been joking all afternoon about how I'd just introduce Monty by saying 'and here's the man who needs no introduction'. Was it too late? Could I just say 'So without further ado', or had I left it too long already? What had Monty said to do if I got into trouble? Ah, yes, just keep talking. Oh.

Out of the corner of my eye, I could see Monty glance sharply at me. I thought I could hear all my friends holding their breath. I was pleased with myself for not saying 'um', but on the other hand I hadn't uttered a word for about seven seconds, which felt like a lifetime. Suddenly it all came back to me. I blurted out the last words, before I could forget them again.

Everyone clapped as Monty entered the pen, and I felt overwhelmed with relief.

Later that night, at the end of the 'round pen meeting' we customarily held to go over any problems and smooth them out for the next venue, Monty looked over and said, 'Nicole, did you—'

'Completely forget what I was going to say?' I cut in. 'Yes.'

'Oh,' he said kindly, 'I wouldn't admit to that. Let's just call it a dramatic pause.'

People often ask what it's like to tour with Monty, and it's astonishingly difficult to come up with a simple answer. Travelling around the UK with the team has been an incredible experience, with each tour being different, and every demonstration yielding new learning. Perhaps the early days were particularly special. Monty's seemingly sudden emergence onto the scene shook the foundations of the horse world to the core. Thousands and thousands of people who had become disillusioned with the prevailing methods and attitudes finally had someone who was offering another way. They streamed into draughty indoor arenas all over the country, packing them to the rafters. Young and old alike sat mesmerised, frozen with fascination and cold, as Monty worked his inimitable magic, a blend of common sense and genius, logic and intuition, and breathtaking skill. Night after night, the touring team saw horse after horse transformed, the change so radical it seemed almost miraculous, the miracles so commonplace they seemed almost mundane.

After every performance Monty was inundated with people. After years of rejection and ridicule, this acceptance was tremendously gratifying for him. There was the occasional sceptic, but overwhelmingly the crowd wanted to express their admiration and gratitude. To be told that they were right, that they didn't have to hit horses, didn't have to shout and 'show the horse who's boss', came as a big relief to many. At the same time, they were being shown ways of getting a pushy horse to regard them with a different level of respect. Many who had been out of horses for years because they couldn't stand the atmosphere returned to their old passion with the conviction and confidence to challenge the old notions.

Clearly, this was not an altogether comfortable experience for the people being challenged. Used to their role as the local experts, conventional horsemen all around the world were unaccustomed to being held to account over their methods. In particular, they found the assertion 'you have to hurt them before they hurt you' difficult to justify in the face of such obvious success with non-violent techniques. In countries such as Argentina, where macho methods of breaking horses can result in a 60 per cent death rate, Monty has even received death threats. There are still people who declaim the methods as a 'fix', believing that the spectacular results can't possibly be real. There were also the 'we were already doing it this way' people, who claimed they had been using the exact same methods for years, only had never brought it to anyone's attention. To be told simultaneously that his results were too astonishing to be believable and also too mundane to be note-worthy must have been a bewildering message for Monty, but criticism simply egged him on, making him still more determined.

In the early days, the team travelled around in motor homes, and the pen and merchandise travelled in a horsebox. Monty, Kelly and any book publicists stayed in local B and Bs or hotels. The sight of a horsebox fuelled the sceptics' suspicions that we brought horses around with us, but the logic of this always bemused me. If we had been bringing our own horses, how would we have trained them to perform as such convincing raw horses, buckers and rearers, kickers and biters and non-loaders? And then to become so compliant? And to do this consistently night after night? It would have been an achievement even more remarkable than the ones Monty performed each evening with the horses from the local area. And what about the people who came to more than one demonstration? Wouldn't they have noticed if we were using the same horses?

Some of my fondest memories are of my first tour, when we tended to drive during the day. We would sit around until the small hours of the morning, drinking tea, or wine if there was any, discussing the evening's demo, and gradually 'coming down' from the rush of activity that ended every night – packing up merchandise, chairs, and round pen. Then at about eight in the morning, we would receive a ten-minute warning for departure from the drivers on the team. Anyone who needed to would stumble out to the loos, still in their pyjamas, attracting strange looks from the yard staff at the venue. I always found it faintly astonishing how empty and ordinary the arenas looked in the mornings, with just the occasional chip mashed into the surface to indicate that anything unusual had happened the night before. Sometimes, we would emerge to find the arena had been transformed into a show ground, and we were suddenly surrounded by shiny horse-boxes and gleaming show jumpers.

The part of the operation that hasn't changed from tour to tour is the setting up in the afternoon. We would usually descend on the venue at around 2 p.m., check that the tiered seating was in the right place, and suss out any potential problems for the door later on. Some venues were arranged like rabbit warrens, and we quickly learnt that recruiting local helpers to prevent unauthorised entry was a bad idea. By 'unauthorised', we meant anyone without a ticket. They thought it meant anyone they didn't recognise ... Once the pen was set up, Monty could start viewing the horses. Each of the eight or ten horses brought by the general public would be introduced to the pen by Ian Vandenberghe, a top practitioner in Monty's methods, and moved around it for a couple of circuits to check for soundness. Monty, Kelly, and several others in the team, together with the owner, would be looking for signs of lameness, whether from being a little stiff after a long journey, or due to more chronic long-term problems. And although all the owners are required to have the horses checked out physically before they bring them to the demonstration, Ian would check for bad backs and sharp teeth as well. Monty wouldn't work on a horse that was in any physical discomfort. So often the behavioural problem would have its cause in some physical condition, and we needed to know that this was no longer an issue before the horse could be asked to work through its behavioural difficulties. Ian would also drape a rope over the horses' backs, and draw it up like a girth to check that the horse appeared 'raw'. Particularly in the early days we were worried about being set up. The last thing we wanted was for someone to present a horse for starting, and to then turn around and show us (or rather, the local press) a picture of the horse being ridden previously. If a horse appeared too quiet, it was rejected. Monty wanted the horse to be a good demonstration for the public and would almost always choose the most challenging of the horses presented.

At the end of the prepping, Ian and I would discuss the arrangement of the signing line. The idea behind this was that people who had bought books on the night could be 'fast-tracked' to Monty to get them signed, and people who just wanted their tickets signed would be in a separate queue. Apparently this was a popular set-up in every other country in the world that Monty was touring in. But not in Britain. Unless the queues were of approximately equal length, no one would consent to using the special line. We put up signs, explained the system to people as they bought their book, and even stationed team members on the queues to direct people appropriately. To no avail. People simply didn't want preferential treatment. Monty has never given up on this system, and we've never been able to satis-factorily enforce it.

Although the roles and jobs don't change at all from tour to tour, the people fulfilling them have varied over time, and when 'old regulars' have found themselves unable to attend a tour because of the dates clashing with other commitments, there's always been plenty of new blood to step in.

Two of the most entertaining new recruits were cowboys from the US, whom Monty had brought over to be his riders. I first met Zane and Matt at Kelly's. Shivering and hunched into their denim jackets, with their black, broad-rimmed hats pulled down over their eyes, they were muttering and moaning about the 'disgusting English weather', having just walked back from the pub during a light April shower. Used to the Californian sunshine, they were clearly disappointed by the climate. I couldn't help wondering how they'd react when they discovered how cold an indoor school can be at ten o'clock at night.

Zane was tall and slender, and unreasonably good-looking. He was the archetypal image of a cowboy except that, being a fervent Mormon, he didn't do any of the things you might expect a cowboy to do, except rope cattle and ride bucking horses. He didn't even spit, let alone swear or drink, and was a devoted husband, a source of great disappointment to many in the audience. A gentle soul, he was easily shocked, and would blush if he heard a woman swear. He was a fantastic rider, sensitive and kind, and able to stay on virtually any horse, whatever it threw at him.

Matt was also unreasonably good-looking and a superb rider, but with quite a lot less experience on the rodeo circuit. Being shorter than Zane, he tended to ride the smaller starters. He had the most astonishing blue eyes, with the thickest, black lashes, and almost none of Zane's scruples. He was a lot harder to shock, but he looked on with horror the first time he saw baked beans being eaten for breakfast.

'But you're cowboys,' we reminded him, our illusions lying in tatters. 'You eat these things straight from the tin, don't you?'

'Yes,' he replied with an affronted dignity, 'but not in the morning. That's just disgusting.'

Matt and Zane caused a stir wherever they went. They almost never removed their hats, which was probably just as well as the straight line etched in their hair by the rim of their stetsons was not particularly fetching. Whenever we went into a pub they'd be greeted with 'Yee-haw, ride 'em, cowboy!' or 'Howdy, pardner'. They always seemed surprised by this attention, and would respond with quizzical looks, and a polite hello. It was as if they couldn't work out how anyone knew they weren't from 'around these parts', wherever 'these parts' happened to be.

One of the biggest challenges on one of Monty's early tours was to hold a demonstration at London Arena. With a huge capacity, this could be a fantastic opportunity. On the other hand, with no purpose-built facilities, and no stabling, the logistical problems were considerable. Horses would have to stay in their own lorries or trailers on site, and somehow have to be decanted into the round pen, for which we would have to provide our own surface. And being located in the East End of London, with an entirely urban local population, there was a definite possibility that if we couldn't sell enough tickets, we would be making a considerable loss. But if we could even approach a full house, it would be the biggest event of its kind ever held in the UK. Kelly took this challenge on with typical zeal and determination, but even so from the moment she decided to undertake the task until the night itself, some twelve weeks or so later, she never had a good night's sleep.

The cavernous arena was like a huge metal box, lined with high stands of seating on all sides, facing a square of grey painted concrete floor. Dean, a student on the course, had assured Kelly that he would be able to make a suitable surface for the pen. It simply involved ship-

Sensi. 'She peered at me from under her forelock and I fell in love.'

*Linda riding Rupert bareback over what had
been his greatest fear. (Photo: Colin Vane)*

Opposite:
Sensi, proprietress of the smallest riding school in the world.

Sensi and Wilberforce on the ridgeway.

*Adam receives his Monty Roberts Preliminary
Certificate of Horsemanship from Kelly Marks.*

Off-side at last – and the 'Misty hug' is born.

Finn showing the Chief who's boss, Long Street, 1998.

'To lead her, put on a saddle, or ride her seemed out of the question.'

'Yard to let – Cotswolds. Idyllic location. Ten minutes Cirencester.'

'Even to my unbiased eyes, Karma looked very peculiar.'

Maybee, the first pony we trained at Moorwood.

Adam and Karma sunbathing by the round pen.

Amber with Jo, Brian and Adam.

Opposite
Nicole exploring the best spots to scratch Karma.

With Monty and Kelly.

Opposite:
Joe.

Finn demonstrates the correct way to canter.

Moor Wood in the snow.

Sky being long-lined by one of his devoted fans.

The gang relaxing in their pasture.

ping in tons of dirt, placed on a temporary chipboard floor, and then topping this with several more tons of sand. 'Rake it smooth, and Bob's your uncle.'

'And afterwards?' Kelly asked dubiously.

'We simply put it back in the lorries and take it away. No worries.' Kelly was still a little unconvinced. If the premises weren't completely cleared and vacated by 1 a.m., there would be a £10,000 fine.

In the event, a record four and a half thousand tickets were sold, the horses were a tremendous success, and Monty said the surface was amongst the best he'd ever worked on. What he did next, then, was perhaps a little unkind.

Kelly, Monty, Dean and Dido (another student and later a teacher on the courses) were just relaxing for a moment at the end of the demonstration, waiting for the lorries and diggers to come into the arena to start clearing the surface.

'Have you given any thought as to how you're going to separate the sand from the soil?' Monty asked Kelly conversationally.

The colour drained from Kelly's face as she asked, 'What do you mean?'

'Well, the soil arrived in a different truck from the sand, didn't it? Obviously they need to be separated out before being taken back. I was just wondering how you planned to do it.'

Kelly looked beseechingly at Dean, who was nodding matter-of-factly. 'Yeah, they won't take it away if it's been mixed up.'

Kelly looked at the surface, with clumps of soil appearing through the sand, looked at her watch, and then looked at the team, clearly wondering if we had enough spades. Then she looked at Dido, who was taking Monty firmly by the arm, saying 'Monty, no, that's not fair, don't be so unkind …'

Monty retreated quickly. Trying unsuccessfully to hide from Kelly behind Dido, he protested, 'Now, now, violence is never the answer.'

ELEVEN

Long Street to Moor Wood
(Adam)

By the beginning of 1998, it had become obvious to us that the little paddock in Milton Keynes where we had already spent so many hours training Misty, and several other horses, and where we had taught many a riding lesson, was not going to be suitable for the volume of work we were now getting. We had already looked into surfacing an area for the riding school, but as we were only renting the land from the Milton Keynes Parks Trust, we were unwilling to invest much money. A round pen in a field overlooked by a number of rather expensive houses was unlikely to be popular with the council. The prospect of having more horses prompted us to look for somewhere else to use as a training yard.

Scanning through the local equestrian magazines, we came across an advertisement regarding a medium-sized yard in a village called Hanslope, on the outskirts of Milton Keynes. 'Long Street' seemed ideal. Having just been taken over by new managers, it only had a couple of liveries in as yet, and the chances were we would be able to take on as many extra boxes as we liked, at least in the early days, on an 'as and when' basis. It had an outdoor school, which, although it was built on quite a significant slope, and had a less than perfect surface, seemed like luxury after so long doing without a school at all. Best of all, it was large enough to accommodate a round pen and still have room to ride around, so Leslie and Karen, the couple managing it, were happy for us to install one there when we eventually got one. The yard was also located just about a mile away from the Milton Keynes Eventing Centre, which meant we would be able to hire their indoor school and other facilities if the need arose. With the optimistic view that Nicole would be spending all day every day training horses, it made sense for our lot – Sensi, Misty, Finn and Cobweb, and our friend Jenny's ex-Police horse, Major, to be on site. Jane, our friend who knew Lucy Rees, and who kept her horse, Jasper, near ours, decided to come too. What really clinched the deal was that there was a large barn available for our horses to stay in, so they wouldn't have to be stabled.

When we worked out the sums, it turned out not to be much more expensive than the cost of the paddocks we were already renting. I still had one more term to finish at the Japanese school, so at least we had a steady income for a few months. Even so, it was a worrying commitment, particularly as Nicole had just given up her job with the police at Christmas. Knowing that she needed to concentrate fully on the business and not spread her energies too thinly, the decision felt right, but January is a notoriously bad time of year for many businesses, and perhaps particularly so for horse trainers. Everyone feels the pinch after an extravagant Christmas, but with months of mud and rain ahead, the average horse owner tends to shrink into survival mode. 'Doing' the horses every evening becomes some sort of endurance, assault trial. Head down, battling against the elements, knee-deep in mud, hands red and raw and deeply lined with dirt, feet frozen and numb, they search a rain-sodden field for their mud-drenched equine by the light of a torch, carefully checking that the horse is warm enough under its state-of-the-art, arctic, breathable, self-righting, lightweight rug. Risking life and limb, they lead their four-legged friend through the wellie-snatching, slithering mire, extricating it from the gnashing teeth and flying hooves of the hungry mob at the gate, to a stable knee-deep in straw, haynets and feed waiting, water buckets filled to the brim, all having been prepared at some bone-chillingly cold, dark hour of the morning, before the owner rushed home to change for work in order to be able to pay for all this pleasure. Occasionally, inspiration will strike, and the wise will pack off their horse, and its numerous rugs, lotions and potions and feed supplements, with careful instructions for hay soaking, feet scrubbing, and feed mixing, to someone like us, while booking themselves a fortnight's holiday in the sun, re-mortgaging the house if necessary.

Misty's former owner put us in touch with a new client called Marianne. I'm not sure if her decision to send us her beautiful chestnut Trakehner stallion had anything to do with the mud. More likely it was about getting him up and running for the summer season. In any case, we were encouraged by the prospect that she had other horses she would want starting, and also by the fact that we had a couple of small ponies arriving for training too. Emboldened, we decided to invest some money that Nicole's dad had recently given her in a round pen. He had suggested that she might like to put this down as a deposit on our right-to-buy council flat, but she had somehow managed to argue that a round pen would be more useful than a roof over our heads, and he had resigned himself to this fate for his hard-earned money.

So one fine Saturday in mid-January, Jane, Jenny, Julia, Nicole and I moved our five horses the twelve miles to Long Street, taking it in turns to ride Sensi, Major and Cobweb, and to lead Misty and Finn. A bridleway led right from our field to Hanslope, with only the last mile or so on roads. Misty was slightly worried by this part, being anxious about vehicles approaching from her off-side, but sandwiched in the middle of the string, she coped admirably. Julia and Nicole had spent the day before bedding down the barn with forty bales of straw, and our horses viewed the sight with approval, seemingly particularly impressed by the huge wooden hay racks stuffed to overflowing with good quality hay. They appeared unperturbed by the move, and settled in immediately. Jane rode Jasper over a few days later. He had a stable in the main yard, and seemed happy. I suppose alarm bells should have rung, however, when we discovered we couldn't turn our horses into a field as a group, as had been discussed when we'd looked round the place with Leslie. 'That ought to be all right' had suddenly become 'out of the question'. Our horses would have to go in with the others, mares in one field and geldings in another, whether we liked it or not.

The reaction to the round pen was less than favourable, too. An imposing metal structure, it looked enormous in the outdoor school. If it hadn't been for the fact that Leslie was having a lot of difficulty breaking in an Arab he'd bought, I think he might have asked us to take it down, and only assemble it when we used it. As it was, he discovered just how useful a small enclosed space can be when riding a difficult horse, although it didn't help him much when his horse threw himself to the ground with Leslie on board!

So Marianne's chestnut stallion duly arrived at the end of January, accompanied on his journey by two Dartmoor fillies from the same part of Oxfordshire. Being two-year-olds, they were coming for some general handling. In fact, one of them, Kim, had been with us the summer before. Nicole had put on her first headcollar and taught her to lead for her owner, who had rescued her from being exported to France for meat. A dockers' strike had delayed her departure for two weeks, and she had spent all that time locked in a crate. Let loose in a field, she had understandably decided it was probably best to avoid humans, and her new owner had been unable to get anywhere near her. She had been lured into a trailer to visit us the first time by following a handsome Shetland gelding. She was doing really well back at home, and her owner just wanted her to be exposed to traffic and brought on a little. Her companion, Kit, would accept having a headcollar put on, but was otherwise fairly wild, not leadable, and very averse to having her feet handled.

It was quite a sight watching the three of them come off the horsebox. The ponies stomped down the ramp, looked around them, gave a shrill neigh, and then tried to go in search of grass. Leslie, who had fetched the horses in his lorry, was holding Kit, and looked astonished when he gave a little pull on the rope and she responded by locking her neck against him and carting him across the yard. We managed to get her into her stable by having her follow Kim. The ponies moved in that straight-legged, economical way so typical of Exmoors and Dartmoors. The stallion, by contrast, bounced down the ramp, as if powered by enormous springs, and trumpeted his greeting to the yard in a most proprietorial way, immediately earning him the nickname 'The Chief', although Tigger would have been just as appropriate. Installed next to Jasper in the barn, he settled down immediately, completely unfazed by the fact that the horse on the other side of him was a mare.

The Chief was all horse. At 16.2 hands high and growing, he could be quite a handful. When he went into Tigger mode, he seemed to grow a hand, and Nicole often looked rather small beside him, or on top of him. We put him out in the round pen with Finn, and they would tussle endlessly, with Finn giving at least as good as he got. The stallion would chase Finn and mount him, taking chunks out of his mane and coat, and you'd be just on the point of going to rescue Finn when the Chief would get distracted by a mare in the field and then the cheeky bugger would turn around and nip him hard on the knees (which were more or less at Finn's nose height). Another round of chasing and rearing would ensue. Allowed this free expression for his natural exuberance, the Chief was better able to contain himself and concentrate when asked to. We were so fortunate that Marianne was happy with this arrangement, and not worried by the odd bite mark. On the thankfully rare occasions that Leslie decided no horses were allowed out (on account of the weather), the Chief would be climbing the walls. On other occasions, when he was out on his own, he would try to play with us. He was inevitably always disappointed that we wouldn't rough-house with him.

The Chief's training went smoothly enough, and Nicole was delighted to have such a quality horse to work with. Being a stallion, he muscled up extremely easily. The second time he cantered under saddle, even coping with the slope of the school, he was already far better balanced than Sensi was after five years of riding.

Then Pinky, another of Marianne's Trakehners, arrived. She was 17 hands high, and seven years old, and had never been started. She'd bred a couple of foals, and had been saddled and long-lined, but Marianne had never had a rider for her at the right time. Becoming a mother can often make a mare have more of a mind of her own, with different priorities. Also, with a couple of what we saw as 'false starts', where she'd been prepared for backing, but had never gone through with it, she could have been quite difficult, but, in fact, she was surprisingly easy. She was also fully mature, strong and straight, so she could easily handle the weight of a rider. I was surprised when I heard people talking about starting them young, before they got too big and strong. It was so much easier to work with her than an immature three-year-old, and the fact is, if we'd been trying to start her using brute strength, she would have already been too strong by the time she was one.

It was around this time that we worked out a fantastic arrangement with the Japanese school. They wanted to extend the curriculum and offer interesting alternative activities, and decided that horse riding would be a good option. The arrangement was good for us in that it meant steady money, and although we were only charging the going rate, the number of students involved meant that it was, to us, very lucrative. Even better, it didn't involve weekends, and so didn't interfere with the normal riding teaching that Nicole was doing. By now, Sensi's School was no longer the smallest riding school in the world, but we still only had a few horses we could teach on, so we suggested to the school that they might like us to include horse care and management in the curriculum. This was very popular with them as it made the activity seem much less frivolous. We already had the licence, the insurance, and now that we'd moved to Long Street, the facilities. We were set to go.

So it was that I took the first group of students up to the yard to introduce them to the horses one day in April 1998. Nicole was away on tour with Monty at the time, so I faced the prospect of dealing with the first days without her. It was raining very hard when I drove down to the school, which was not the plan, as I knew well the fortitude of this generation of Japanese. Rather than '*Samurai*', the first word of Japanese I picked up was '*Samui*', 'I'm cold'. It was pointless to even consider working a horse outside in rain like this, but I had in my rucksack a box of doughnuts. Putting on a headcollar or picking up a foot would be about the limit of what we could do, but there would at least be something to fall back on, to make the first horse activity special. The six students – five girls and an extremely brave boy, all sixteen years old and fresh from Japan just two days before – met me in the lobby. They were accompanied by a Japanese teacher called Nori, a jovial and friendly man of about thirty-five, with very good English. As he also taught history, we had worked together for several years on a unique Second World War reconciliation project. Now, as the school was falling apart around his ears, he was being promoted into the void left by the best members of staff, and put in charge of redesigning the school curriculum to make it more attractive for parents. One of his main proposals had been to introduce several non-academic activities, of which horse riding was a star attraction, being a very exclusive activity in Japan due to the incredibly high cost of land. I knew a lot of his credibility was riding on this.

So I was not overjoyed when I discovered that the kids hanging around in the lobby in school uniform were actually my riding club. Several of them did not have any kind of coat, and none had outdoor footwear. I sent them off to get better equipped, knowing this would take ages, and went off to find some umbrellas. When the kids finally reappeared, they were still woefully ill protected, for the rain was still bucketing down outside. We clambered into the school minibus, which rapidly filled with steam as we drove the 10 miles or so to the yard. The students started out with a lively chatter, until one of them asked, 'Does it always rain like this?'

I made light of it, but it wasn't until we started to get out of Milton Keynes that I realised there was actually something pretty serious going on with the weather. The roads in MK were all so new and well made that you hardly noticed the volume of water on them. Once we got off the main road into the countryside, it was clear this was going to be a flood. Roadside ditches were already overflowing, and torrents of water were gushing out of gaps in the hedges and from gateways on the side of the road. The only time I had ever seen rain like this was in Africa. It was thumping down on the roof in great blobs, and the windscreen wipers, working at full throttle, could not cope. We descended into a wide valley, and found ourselves going along a narrow raised causeway between fields usually full of sheep, already completely flooded. By the next day the road itself would be submerged in more than 2 feet of water, and impassable for over a week.

We made it to the yard, however, and Jane met us in the car park. She had kindly volunteered for the job of assistant tutor, and as soon as the kids saw her smile, I knew they would get on well. But she couldn't hide the anxiety in her voice as she told me, 'You'd better drive down to the barn. You couldn't walk it. The track's under water.'

So, rather than stop in the car park, I drove down the flooded track to the barn where I knew the horses would be. As we drew round the corner, however, I couldn't believe my eyes. The area outside their barn had turned into a fast-flowing stream about a metre wide. The students would have to leap across this to get into the barn, unless I carried them. Wails of protests and exclamations of '*Samui*!' greeted me when I explained what they would have to do. They hardly noticed Sensi and Major, standing behind the waterfall pitching off the roof between us. Putting up my hood, I stepped out into the rain.

I found the horses warm and dry. With a deep bed of straw throughout the barn, and mangers all round stuffed with hay, they had little to complain about. But they seemed to have an air of dejection about them, which I could not put a finger on. Surely for once, they must be grateful not to have been out in the rain. I beckoned to the students. 'Look, all you have to do is jump over this,' I said, pointing at the torrent of water that ran between me and the barn, on a normally dry path. 'As soon as you get inside, there's dry straw.' It was a big jump but I leaped forward confidently towards a big hummock of straw just inside the entrance.

As I landed on it, it was all I could do not to fall unceremoniously onto my backside, for the hummock turned out to be an island floating on a bed of water about 4 inches deep. No wonder the horses were looking so miserable. The entire barn was flooded. The students, complaining every inch of the way, shrieked and exclaimed as they negotiated the short distance between the van and the barn, while Misty cowered in the corner, terrified of the noise they were making. But as soon as they were inside, trying to find a lump of straw big enough on which to stand without being immersed in the water, the magic of horses took over, and their shouts and cries gave way to hushed tones and expressions of wonder. '*Cho kakoee*! *Misty wa ee desho*! I love Misty!' I looked at Nori, who was smiling for the first time all day.

It wasn't long, however, before the thrill of standing in a dark, flooded barn began to wear off, and it was clear my bag of doughnuts was going to prove invaluable. Leslie had assured us he had plans to build a proper tack room, but for the moment there was only an old shipping container, a long, windowless steel box with a naked light bulb suspended in it, and more importantly, a kettle. This was not exactly a quality venue for a school excursion, but it would have to do, and the mention of coffee and hot chocolate perked the children up immediately. We said *sayonara* to the horses and jumped back across the stream as best we could, and I drove back to the top of the yard.

There wasn't a great deal of room, or a sufficient number of mugs, and all the kids were cold and wet, but as I had anticipated, the sight of a fresh doughnut made it all much better. I began an impromptu vocab lesson, in my most enthusiastic manner, trying to explain to them the difference between hay and straw, when Leslie suddenly appeared around the doorway. Interrupting me, with a face transparent with rage, he asked if he could have a word with me, and it was clear he meant to do so without delay. I stepped outside, leaving Jane and Nori to fill the silence as best they could.

We stepped around the corner, under cover of an old carport whose foundations were peppered with large rat-holes. It was obvious that Leslie was furious, for his face was a seething purple. He turned around and raised his fist, and I really thought he was going to hit me. Barely able to stop himself from screaming, he managed, 'Who the f*** are these Japs and what the f*** are they doing here on my yard?'

I was for once glad that the tack room was a large steel box, because I hoped the noise of the rain hammering on the roof would be loud enough to drown out our conversation so that the kids would not realise what was going on. Feeling the anger rise in me, I began to explain my position, but there was no telling Leslie he had made an agreement that we would be able to teach our clients at the yard.

'It's not that I'm racist,' he began with that time-honoured lie, 'but nobody told me anything about loads of kids,' he said. 'Get them off my yard right now. You'll have to find somewhere else for them.'

I found myself shaking with rage, which I was barely able to suppress. After the first few days of our being at Long Street, during which Leslie was reasonably polite, his demeanour had begun to degenerate until none of the liveries liked or respected him, and he had become a constant source of irritation. A number of incidents around the yard, as well as a constant stream of childish notes stuck up around the place to remind people to do this and not do that, had alienated everyone. But this was beyond the limit. We were paying for the use of his facilities, we had agreed the terms, and now, all of a sudden, he was banning my clients from using them, on the basis of their race. With a supreme effort, I managed not to tell him what I thought of him, his horsemanship and his yard, as I just couldn't risk the hassle of finding my five horses wandering outside in the road that evening, up to their knees in flood water. I wouldn't have put it past him.

Taking a moment to compose myself, I pretended everything was all right as I breezed back into the tack room. Trying not to seem in too much of a hurry, I got the kids back into the minibus, and waved goodbye to Jane, promising to come and pick her up as soon as I had dropped the kids off, and collected my own car, as she needed a lift back home. She set about the arduous job of trying to sort out a dry area for the horses in the barn, by spreading about twenty bales of straw out at the back, which was a bit higher than the rest, until eventually they had a patch they could stand on. Still close to exploding every time I thought of Leslie, I hardly noticed that the rain was still coming down as hard as ever, and it was now nearing rush-hour.

Having deposited the kids and their minibus, and arranged to meet them the next day, I got in my car and headed straight back to the yard. I got almost to the edge of Milton Keynes, before finding myself in a traffic jam. It wasn't long before I realised that this was not an ordinary traffic jam, but there was nothing I could do. The car did not move at all for about an hour. The M1 had been closed and all the traffic had been diverted onto the A5, which had now become blocked. I only needed to get about a mile further before I could turn off towards Long Street, but it took me more than an hour and a half to get that far.

By the time I finally did get back to Long Street, Jane had long reached the point where her sense of humour had failed. She exploded into a tirade until I managed to get a word in about the traffic. But as her anger receded, she was suddenly gripped by a panic. 'We've got to get back to my place as soon as possible. Last time it rained like this, the river broke its banks and the house was under a foot of water!' I remembered her boyfriend Patrick, whose recording studio was on the ground floor, as she lamented the fact that, after the last flood, they had been unable to get any insurance.

Knowing that to go back the way I had come would mean waiting for hours to get past the A5 roundabout, we opted for a cross-country route. This was not easy, for in several places there were lines of cars stranded where they had flooded their engines through bad luck, bad judgement or through staying on the left-hand side of the road instead of driving through the shallowest part of the river that once had been the road. The emergency services and AA were overwhelmed, as this was the worst flood we had seen for many decades. We came to a place where the road curved around the edge of a hill, leaving a wide dip that would normally have coped with any runoff, but was now a lake overflowing with muddy water that filled the road. A queue of cars had built up on the other side, and several were lying broken down in between. I took off my shoes and socks, and waded through it, to find it came above my knees. It was obvious that if we tried to go through we would break down. There was nothing else for it. On one side was the lake; on the other, a large wall gave notice of a fancy country house, its gateway bracketed by stone pillars topped with ornamental carvings. Sensibly, the wall had been well set back from the road, to allow a clear view to either side when emerging from the driveway. The space between this and the road was filled with a fine lawn, edged with a small white chain-link fence. Reaching down, I found that the posts were easily pulled out. Without pausing to consult my conscience, I removed them, rolled up the fence and put it neatly to one side, before getting in the car and driving over the lawn.

So we managed to get back to Jane's, where we found to our amazement that the river had not burst its banks. Nevertheless, Nicole being on tour, I took up Jane's offer to stay for the night, in case they needed to make a sudden evacuation of the contents of their ground floor. I spent most of the evening on the phone vainly trying to contact Nicole, to see if she could talk to Leslie and negotiate a stay of execution for a few days so that we would have time to make an arrangement with Milton Keynes Eventing Centre, to hire their facilities for the Japanese students. This would cost extra, and would require riding and leading the horses along the road every day, but at least we would be able to fulfil our contract. In the event, the road in the valley on the way was so badly flooded that it was impossible to get near Long Street for almost a week, without a boat or a tractor.

And all the water in that valley had to go past Jane's house, or else right through it, which, in the end, it did. We went to bed that night with a sense of distinct unease, leaving wellies at the top of the stairs, rather than the bottom as they had done the last time, only to find they had floated away in the morning. Patrick got up every hour to check the state of the river. Suddenly, at about 6.30, he woke us up with a shout. 'This is it, it's coming in the yard!'

We stumbled outside to find water advancing at a rate of several feet a minute into the cobbled yard outside the house. Frantically we set about rescuing Patrick's artwork, motorbikes and assorted equipment from an outhouse, before racing into the house to stuff the contents of the ground floor up the stairs. Computers, keyboards, guitars and amps underarm, we ran up and down while Jane desperately battled to delay the water with a rampart of sandbags. The last item was impossible to move, a full-size Hammond organ weighing about as much as a small car. Setting two stools at either end, we lifted it up as best we could and placed it on the stools and turned off the electricity supply just in time, as the first water broke over the sandbags, inundating the house to a depth of one foot.

Around this time Jane's mobile phone rang. It was Nicole, who had finally got the messages I had left. 'How are things?' she enquired routinely. I hardly knew where to start. 'Yeah, I suppose it has been raining a bit,' she said absently. 'We're up in Lancashire at the moment, fantastic demo last night …'

Although my involvement with the riding club continued, it was time to leave the Japanese school.

It was sad to go because I felt I was making a real contribution to the lives of many young people. I particularly enjoyed teaching them about the war (which remains almost a taboo subject in Japan and has been deliberately misrepresented for years in official Japanese textbooks). It brought a sense of the reality and presence of history in our lives, to be teaching the granddaughters of Hiroshima victims. With Nori, I initiated visits by Second World War veterans, from both sides, involved in reconciliation efforts. These are truly remarkable men who have somehow managed to find it in their hearts to forgive, while making great efforts to ensure we do not forget. It was very moving to see the positive response of the students and several members of the Japanese staff. But there was no hope of survival for the school, which had been chronically mismanaged for years. Soon afterwards, many equally frustrated teachers also decided to leave. The school closed in 2002.

It was also becoming increasingly clear that we needed our own place. I was about to go on the Monty course at West Oxfordshire College, and just before the latest tour had begun, Nicole had been offered the assistant tutor's job on the course. The hour-long drive each way, to do just two and a half hours' teaching every afternoon, didn't seem sensible. It was time to move on. We succeeded in renting facilities from MK Eventing Centre for the Japanese students, and I managed not to come to blows with Leslie, but it was far from convenient. As soon as Nicole got back from the tour, she had a meeting with Leslie and Karen. They were amicable enough, but the message was clear: We won't turn you out on your ear tomorrow, but the sooner you can find another place, the better.

If life hadn't been so hectic, we might have had time to dwell on the problem and feel really desperate. As it was, our lives were so complicated and fast, we were struggling to keep up almost every second of the day. Nicole's job on the course came as a complete surprise, the departure of the previous assistant tutor being rather unexpected. Additionally, the course was scheduled to begin just two days after the end of a tour and started early every morning except Monday, when I would entertain the Japanese, but as Nicole was only teaching in the afternoons, we couldn't even drive in together. So I had to buy another car and spent a few nights a week with some friends who live close to Witney, to cut down on travelling.

Back in MK, there were several horses in for training, and the usual endless mucking out, and with Julia also on the course, no one to help out. Jane had taken over the role as main tutor to the Japanese students, so she had her hands full. At the same time, Nicole and I were doing an evening course at Bedford College, working towards a qualification in teaching adults in further education. This was a condition of Nicole's job on the course, but I decided to go for it as well, as the skills were bound to come in useful, and this way at least we got to spend one evening a week together! With all this going on, it was not exactly easy to find time to search for a new yard nearer to Witney.

Yards to rent are in short supply. In particular, small yards are very hard to come by. We had asked a few people and their responses had been very uninspiring. It seemed everywhere was taken and that prices were high. Buying somewhere was out of the question. We had looked in the classified adverts of a few horse magazines, but there weren't any yards to rent.

The decision to leave Long Street was made on a Thursday evening, and on the Friday, Nicole thought she had better buy a copy of *Horse and Hound* to see what was on offer.

'Not much in this one,' she said, flicking through the classified section. 'But this one might be a possibility, if it's not too far. "Small yard to rent in idyllic Cotswold countryside, ten minutes from Cirencester."' She looked at the map on the wall. Cirencester looked almost as far away as Milton Keynes, but other than this yard there was nothing. 'Shall I ring up and at least find out which side of Cirencester it is?'

A few moments later, Nicole put down the phone, a hint of guarded optimism in her voice. 'Well, it's the Witney side of Cirencester, so it might be close enough. I've arranged for us to go and have a look on Sunday afternoon. There's also some self-contained accommodation available, although it sounds very small.'

The yard was called Moor Wood Stables, in the small village of Woodmancote.

It was mid-afternoon on Saturday, and we'd just come home from the morning's chores at the stables, turning out the horses, mucking out, watering, preparing haynets, training the couple of horses that we had in (almost an incidental task after the repetitive, tiring, but to Nicole, 'great fun' daily jobs), and we had a couple of hours' respite before we had to go back and do the afternoon tasks of bringing the horses in for the night, sorting out evening feeds, et cetera.

Nicole looked up from her steaming tankard of tea, munching thoughtfully on a chocolate biscuit. 'The thing is,' she said, 'these yards don't come up very often. If it's suitable, we should put down a deposit straight away. I think we should bring a cheque book.' This is possibly one of the most sensible things Nicole has ever said.

For the last couple of years that I'd been working at the Japanese school, and Nicole had been doing two or three jobs at once, we had seen so little of each other that we hardly had time together at all. The transition from job-free idleness to workaholism had happened so imperceptibly that somehow we had both come to regard working non-stop as quite normal. We'd never been exactly house-proud, but the busier we got, the more our flat slid into chaos. It wasn't just that we were lazy, but we genuinely didn't have the time to tidy up, or wash the dishes, certainly not with the sort of regularity that most people consider hygienic. Every now and then, a visit from someone who might feel 'uncomfortable' with (or revolted by) the level of mess would force us into action, and we'd blitz the place, even if it meant staying up even later than usual to do so. Within a day or so, however, recently cleared surfaces would become lightly mulched with dirty dishes, unanswered letters, bills, documents requiring immediate attention (which they never received), unfinished marking, slowly rotting vegetables harvested from the allotment, cats and bits of fur, and discarded items of clothing. Luckily we were both more or less blind to this unsavoury view, unless there was absolutely nowhere to sit when we came home. A burglar coming in to ransack the place might have left disappointed, thinking that someone else had got there before him. A Feng Shui adviser would probably have dropped down dead on the spot.

All through this, however, we at least got to spend the nights together, to fall asleep or wake up in each other's arms. Now I was away for days at a time. My absence was hard for us, although I suspected that Nicole secretly enjoyed the space. The fact that she acclimatised so quickly to occupying the entire bed by herself, stretching out diagonally with the cats, confirmed my concerns.

That Sunday, as we set off to check out this prospective yard, we felt a sense of release, almost like we were going on holiday. Having seen to the horses in the morning, we arranged for Jane to do the evening chores. We had what amounted to an afternoon off! It was a bright spring day and as we passed Witney and set off into new territory, the countryside seemed to become even more beautiful, with low, weed-infested hedges giving way to thick belts of mature trees, lined with long stone walls and sheltering an under storey of yew and holly. Meandering rivers emerged from the rolling hills, their cosy valleys dotted with picture-postcard settlements. Even the sign saying 'Welcome to Gloucestershire' seemed reassuring. Catching up on all our news, we made an unusual mistake. Engrossed in discussion, we found ourselves at a pub at the bottom of a hill, as described in the directions, and turned right, several miles *before* the turning we were supposed to take.

Being lost, however, was a pleasure. As we left the Fosse Way, the Roman road built to allow the legions to move around their conquered land in the days when Cirencester, now a small market town, was the capital of England, the scenery became even more spectacular.

'Ooh look, a cross-country course,' cooed Nicole.

'Ooh look, lovely big trees,' I answered.

We finally worked out where we were and rejoined our intended route to Woodmancote. The directions were very specific, but as we turned through unmarked stone gates and drove slowly down the long driveway to Moor Wood Stables, we were sure there must be some mistake. It seemed too beautiful to be real. Descending through a cluster of huge trees, we seemed to leave the world behind, and come out into a land like a dream.

Back in Milton Keynes we had become very fond of an oak tree next to one of Sensi's many fields, whose gnarled, twisting branches seemed almost to claw at the orange night sky, reflecting the millions of street lights in the city. I once climbed up it, as the branches were perfectly placed.

What we found ourselves facing now was quite impossible to contemplate climbing. In front of a grand house was an enormous Cedar of Lebanon, in almost perfect condition, looking out over a beautiful valley, in which nestled a number of old cottages.

'I don't think it's going to be difficult to choose our favourite tree,' I blurted out before our view opened out across the estate to reveal a large wood down the side of the valley. At the time I could only identify about five types of tree, but it was obvious at a glance that this was a collection that would rival many arboreta. The great spread of mature oaks and chestnuts, their branches edged with a tinge of light green, leaves just peeking out of their buds, was broken by the sharp spires of black pines. Towering at the foot of the wood were two huge Wellingtonias, the taller of which had a broken tip, having been struck by lightning, but it was still about twice the height of the large native hardwoods around it. Later, as I learned to recognise more of them, I would realise that standing in the yard you can see about thirty-five different species, almost every one a near perfect example of a type of exotic or native tree.

We drove down beyond the cedar, past old stone walls encrusted with moss and bizarrely colourful patches of lichen, from which dangled an array of climbing roses (which turned out to be the National Collection of rambler roses), until we came between two L-shaped yards and a house. We drew up in front of a huge old granary barn and got out. As our ears accustomed themselves to the calm, which closed around us as I switched off the car engine, we realised there was another sound, not merely the wind in the trees or the birds.

'A stream?' We looked at each other. Sure enough, there at the back of the car park was a perfect little babbling brook, its clear water looking clean enough to drink.

A couple greeted us with a friendly smile, introducing themselves as Sarah and Peter. Recently married, they were not in fact the owners, as everything in sight belonged to one Henry Robinson. He lived with his family in the big house, which in spite of the conspicuous lack of piles of old tyres, rusting machinery and dilapidated buildings, was called Moor Wood Farm. They showed us around the fields, which they explained were four hundred years old pasture, designated ESA (an Environmentally Sensitive Area) under an EEC directive to preserve them. However, many years of continuous grazing by horses had left the land in a pretty sorry state, poached by hooves and dotted with patches of weeds. It was quite steep, too, and exposed to the west wind, which roared across a huge open field on the other side of the valley and seemed to blow right through our clothing. But as soon as we stepped through the gate into the squelching mud, I noticed a flat area, just big enough for the round pen. Nicole's eyes met mine, and I knew she was thinking the same.

The fields they were offering amounted to about 8 acres, together with one of the yards, containing six stables made from Cotswold stone. One of the stables was huge, at least twice the size of the others. Sensi wouldn't mind this, I thought, especially with the view out onto the woods.

It was perfect, and although even one month's rent would seem like a fortune, we knew the chances of finding somewhere cheaper were minimal. But the accommodation was not ideal. Used as we were to living in a one-bedroom flat, the annexe was much smaller, and had no internal doors except into the tiny bathroom, which would have been impossible to step inside if it had actually contained a bath instead of a shower. If we were going to live here, we would have to make sure we never had an argument, as there would be nowhere to storm off to. We would also have to throw away a large number of our books and other possessions, as there would be nowhere to keep them.

Fortunately, Sarah and Peter had a suggestion. For an extra 'peppercorn', they could rent us a room in the granary across the car park. The moment I stepped inside, I knew it was the perfect place for my musical equipment – a barn with walls two feet thick. There was, however, a major drawback. Half of the roof was full of holes big enough to let in shards of light, and there were already several swallows making their nests among the beams. I hoped we would not disturb each other too much, because my mind was already made up. A bit of tarpaulin nailed to the ceiling, and this would be the music studio I had always craved.

We looked at each other without needing to say a word.

'We'd like to take it. Can we leave you a deposit?'

Sarah and Peter looked slightly taken aback, and said, 'There's just one problem.' Seeing our faces fall, they added, 'Nothing terrible. It's just that there are some holiday bookings for the annexe. It won't be available until the end of May at the soonest, even if we cancel some of the later ones.'

This was less than a fortnight away, and as we had yet to pack, arrange transport for the horses, and sort out our stuff, the wait wasn't too much of a problem.

In fact, during the next fortnight, there were two weekend courses at Witney, which Nicole was teaching on, as well as the course from Tuesdays to Fridays, so we only had two days, two Mondays, to arrange everything. Nicole had ambitions of sorting through the flat, recycling or throwing out things that we didn't need, and only packing and bringing useful items. In the event, we didn't even have time to gather together sufficient boxes, and ended up just throwing the chaos of our flat, rubbish and all, into, appropriately enough, bin bags. Even then, we ran out of bags.

We hired a 7.5-tonne curtain-sided van to transport all of our stuff, but we weren't too confident about driving it. Nicole called her Australian friend and karate instructor, Rohan, and dropped hints until he offered to drive the van for us. A typical Aussie, prone to bad-taste humour, extravagant tales and with more than a hint of arrogance, he is nevertheless a real gentleman, the sort that would always help a friend in need, give generously of his time, and gladly give up his bed and sleep on the sofa if you needed to stay the night. Tall and strong, he was also bound to be helpful with the heavy items.

The first of the heavy items we had to deal with was the round pen, which we went to collect from Long Street. Twenty panels of eight by six galvanised steel mesh, and a gate, which Nicole and I were already very familiar with loading and unloading on tours. Usually, however, there are hordes of helpers. With only three of us, it was a back-breaking task.

It's possible that when Rohan asked whether the stuff from the flat was all packed up and ready to go, and Nicole said 'more or less', he may have had rather different expectations of the situation than the scene that greeted his eyes when we got back to the flat.

'Ah,' he said testily, surveying the wreckage, 'a definition of packing that I hadn't previously come across.' He added, 'It helps if you put the stuff in boxes.'

'We have!' Nicole exclaimed indignantly. 'Look!' And she pointed to the half dozen or so boxes crammed full with the sort of stuff that even we didn't consider suitable for plastic bags – crockery, glasses, knives. 'It won't take long,' she said, with the sort of misguided optimism that would be endearing if it didn't so often mean me getting roped into impossibly big tasks with ridiculously little time to do them. To prove her point, she picked up two large bin bags and an armful of books, and set off down the stairs to the lorry. Sighing, Rohan effortlessly hoisted up a couple of the largest boxes and set off after her.

Innumerable trips later, and we were beginning to make an impression. Surfaces were becoming visible, the piles of bags were diminishing, the boxes and most of the big items were already in the van, and although we were getting hot and fed up with the job, we could see an end in sight. I was just about to follow Rohan and Nicole out of the flat yet another time, when the phone rang. Glad of the excuse to sit down for a moment, I picked it up.

TWELVE

New beginnings
(Nicole)

And that's how we found him, sitting on an amp, looking like all of the air had been punched out of him. I had been about to chide him for slacking, but one look at his face, and I knew something was wrong.

'That was my mum on the phone. Dad's been taken into hospital. I've got to go to London. I don't know how long I'll be there. Mum's told me to bring a suit.'

The significance of this last remark didn't bear thinking about. For years, Adam's father had been struggling against the inevitable decline of Alzheimer's disease, but recently it had become painfully obvious that he was going to lose the battle. I felt useless, not knowing what to do to make the situation better. As I hugged him, he said, 'I'm so sorry to be burdening you both with the packing and moving, but I really can't stay. I must get down to London as soon as possible …'

Rohan said, 'Of course, don't worry, we'll be fine.' He really can be very lovely sometimes. 'We'll probably do it faster without you anyway.' If a little insensitive occasionally.

It had already become clear that we were going to have to make two trips in the van, so it was decided that we should set off sooner rather than later, grab a quick lunch, and then go our separate ways. Sitting in the Little Chef at Old Stratford we ate a miserable meal (in more ways than one). I couldn't believe that I wouldn't be going with Adam to London. The thought of not being with him in such a time of need was terrible. But to abandon the move and have to do it another time would have been horrible too, not to mention more expensive than we could afford if we had to hire the van again. I consoled myself with the thought that by going ahead and moving our stuff to our new home, I was doing something positive for our future, and saving him an onerous task as well.

But it felt strange, sitting in the van next to Rohan, instead of Adam. We were moving to our dream spot in the countryside, and we weren't together. I tried to chat cheerily to Rohan to take my mind off it, and the 70 or so miles passed quickly enough.

We stayed at Moor Wood just long enough to unload the round pen. ('Don't worry, Adam and I will put it up later,' I said to Rohan, who answered with a look that said, 'Of course you bloody will.') We threw the horse equipment into the tack room and, after a cup of tea, headed straight back for round two.

It was past 9 p.m. when we had finally decanted the last of the loose objects from the lorry into the studio. I'm still not sure how we managed to drag the phenomenally heavy deep freezer up the steep stone steps, but I imagine it had more to do with Rohan's muscles than mine. Before the day was out, Rohan would have driven the best part of 300 miles and have handled more bin bags than a rubbish collector on the 27th of December. I decided to take him to the pub and buy him a drink (non-alcoholic, of course, as he still had to drive me and the van back to Milton Keynes). As I sipped my pint of beer, I looked around at the typical country pub décor, and wondered if this would become my local. The people seemed friendly enough, and

I found myself explaining to the bar owner who I was, where I'd come from, and what we did with horses.

The journey back to Milton Keynes went surprisingly quickly, considering how tired we were, and the fact that we had already done the route once that day. Perhaps we had hit that level of tired-beyond-tired, a sort of automated exhaustion, where you just keep going in a vacuous, unthinking sort of way, a feeling I was familiar with from touring, and that any parent will recognise instantly. In any case, I was grateful to get back to the flat and the two indignant, disgruntled felines who were demanding to know what had happened to their comfortable furniture.

Adam had phoned me on Rohan's mobile earlier, and we were relieved to hear that his dad's condition was not quite as serious as was originally feared, and he was 'comfortable'. Adam was going to spend the next day, Monday, in London, then drive up to Moor Wood in the evening, and from there go to the course on Tuesday morning. I had confidently assured him that I would be fine loading the horses on my own, but as I lay in bed, I wondered. It had been hard work loading so many heavy inanimate objects all day, but would live horses be any easier?

In the event, my fears proved entirely justified.

Of the six horses that were in our care at the time, Major (our friend Jenny's horse that we had been looking after for some time and were soon to own) and Cobweb were 100 per cent reliable loaders. Cobweb, however, was staying behind for a few weeks to teach the kids at the Japanese school. The other four all had question marks over them. Sensi was notoriously bad. Finn had been so bad loading that once when I hired a box to take Wilberforce to the vet, the driver mentioned him in passing as the worst pony he had ever had to load. He hadn't realised that I knew Finn at the time (we hadn't yet taken him on), and just referred to him as that '****ing stubborn little Exmoor git from Newport Pagnell', naming the yard where Finn used to live. The Chief, whose owner wanted us to continue his training, had only once been in a box, and Misty, after all, had become ours only after she had refused to go home in a trailer. When we moved them all to Long Street it had been easier, more fun, and cheaper to ride or walk than hire a box. In an ideal world, I would have worked on getting them all really good to load before the day I had to move them, but as well as being just a bit busy, I simply didn't have a box or trailer to practise with, and Leslie, who had agreed to transport them, had been unwilling to let me use his.

Julia had come over to lend moral and practical support, for which I was profoundly grateful. I'd decided that, in view of the stallion's hormones and Sensi's displeasure, the best way for them to travel was for the Chief, Finn and Major to be in the horsebox, driven by Leslie, and for Misty and Sensi to travel in a trailer that belonged to a student from a previous course, Cathy, who had very kindly offered to drive the horses over to Moor Wood. Leslie backed the lorry up to a loading bay. This meant that the ramp was horizontal, which made it a lot easier. The box was open and inviting, and I felt sure the Chief would follow Leslie straight in, as I went off to make preparations for the other horses in the trailer. But I was interrupted by Julia just a few minutes later.

'I'm not sure it's such a good idea for Leslie to be loading the Chief. He seems to be getting a little frightened.'

For some reason, I had assumed Julia had meant that the stallion was getting worried. One look at the situation revealed her meaning immediately, however. The Chief was getting angry. It was Leslie who was getting frightened. His face had turned an ashen shade of grey, and although he was sternly saying things like, 'Come on now and stop messing around,' there was a tremor in his voice.

Oddly enough, Finn, now that he didn't have to climb a ramp, was strolling in and out of the box quite merrily, as if he'd been doing it all his life. That Finn was inside only seemed to agitate the Chief further. It was as if he was annoyed with Finn for undermining his protest. His ears were flat back, his eyes were rolling, and he was pawing the ground furiously with a foreleg.

'Shall I have a go?' I asked, as tactfully as possible. 'I shouldn't really be giving you my dirty work, after all.'

'Just be careful,' warned Leslie, 'he's a vicious brute. He nearly got me with his feet a couple of times.'

The Chief was seriously annoyed, but after I'd stroked his hot, damp, neck for a while, his irritation seemed to dissolve a little. I moved him backwards and forwards a few times, just a few steps, and rewarded him extravagantly every time he complied. I asked him to step onto the ramp, and he resisted angrily, leaning back against the pressure, and jerking his head from side to side. I met his resistance with one concerted pull, leaning all my body weight back against him, but as always ready to release should he rear up. He stamped his foot hard on the ramp, once, and then shot into the box, nearly bowling me over in the process. By the time Finn was ensconced beside him, he was happily munching his hay, playfully taking bites out of those parts of Finn that he could reach over the partition. Major tucked himself in beside Finn, like a perfect Police horse.

Sensi was another story. Cathy had offered to load her, and I had gladly agreed, feeling it would be easier for someone who wasn't emotionally involved. Sensi eventually agreed to go in, after she'd exhausted every other option, and we'd shut down every possible escape route.

We'd put Sensi in first, being the larger horse, so that we could swing the partitions across and give her a bit more space initially, but this meant that the space for Misty didn't look very inviting, particularly as Sensi was swishing her tail in a most unwelcoming way. The trailer was in the corner of the school, with a fence along one side, and straw bales stacked up on the other. I was at a loss as to how to get Misty to step up the ramp. I had never used any kind of force with her, and even getting her to back up and come forward felt a bit strong. In the end, Cathy suggested holding a line behind her – not touching her with it at all – and without any better suggestions, I agreed. Misty saw the line, backed up towards it, felt it against her quarters, panicked, and pulled back. I let go, and Misty set off frantically around the school, hotly pursued by the lead rope. She stopped in a corner and stood trembling. I gently gathered up the rope and led her slowly back to the box, wondering what on earth we could try next. To my astonishment, as I led her up to the ramp one more time, she leapt straight on. I guess she was more frightened by the ropes than the trailer.

With everyone on board, it was time for one last quick check around to make sure I hadn't forgotten anything, a quick squeeze with Julia, whom I'd be seeing the next day on the course, and then I set off in the car to try to catch up with Leslie and the other horses, who'd left about twenty minutes before us.

I managed to get to Moor Wood in time to unload the horses. The stallion leapt out of the box, neighing loudly, and passaged impressively across the yard. Finn, who couldn't passage to save his life, ambled across the yard like he'd been there all his life, and following his example, the stallion soon settled down. Major looked around, probably wondering where the football match was.

As Leslie drank his tea in the annexe, I was glad we were parting on good terms. He seemed very genuine when he said, 'I wish you well. Good luck.'

Months later I saw an ad in *Horse and Rider*. I was looking idly through the 'Horses for Sale' section, and my eye was caught by a photo of a horse that looked very familiar, a striking grey Arab. I looked at the phone number, and realised with a shock that it was indeed Leslie's number. It was the horse that he'd been trying unsuccessfully for several months to break in, misrepresented as a genuine, unstarted youngster. We'd had our differences, but I'd always thought he was a decent, if somewhat unfriendly and awkward person. I just couldn't believe that he would pull such a deception, and try to sell such a horse knowing not only that someone could get hurt, but almost certainly *would* get hurt, and that the horse was likely to be destroyed as an untrainable and dangerous animal. I know it's common practice in the horse world to send difficult horses to the sales, on the understanding of 'buyer beware', and some people consider this honourable enough, but to me this deceit was a step too far. I looked at the front of the magazine, and realised the edition was already well out of date. There was no point phoning up and telling the editor. Months later I found out from Jane that someone had indeed bought the horse, a mother and daughter team, who were intending to break the horse in themselves and do endurance riding with him. We never heard if they survived the experience or not.

Leslie had just left when Cathy arrived with Sensi and Misty, who were delighted with their new space, and charged around it several times, causing chaos in the adjoining fields, before settling down to eat.

When Adam arrived later that evening, we put up the round pen. The light was fading, and bats were flickering around us. We looked out across the valley to where the glow of the setting sun could be seen dimly through the trees. Adam looked harried and care-worn, but as we worked on, the colour returned to his cheeks, and the systematic, repetitive work seemed to revive his spirits. By the time we were pushing in the last holding pin, the moon was high, and the stars were glittering through the fast-clearing cloud. Adam hugged me and we both stared up at the heavens, fascinated to see a night sky that was never visible in Milton Keynes, unable to pierce through the nightly blanket of light-pollution.

Finn was visibly unimpressed the next morning when we turned him out, not into the fields, but into the round pen with the stallion. We had placed the pen on the site of an old cow byre, and it was all hard-standing, with just a thin smattering of short grass to occupy them. Finn usually accepts his role as playmate to the big-and-burly with good grace, but occasionally he feels the restraints of the job quite keenly. He got the position as a result of three major attributes: he's made out of rhinoceros hide; he isn't intimidated by anyone (except, oddly enough, Misty, the only one who's smaller than him); and he'll play for hours at a time. This makes him worth his weight in gold to us, and although we don't have to call on his services all that often, when we do, he's invaluable. After an hour or two of being with Finn, the Chief was so calm, willing and manageable, that no one would have guessed he was a stallion at all. I don't know if all Exmoor ponies are as bold and cheeky as Finn, but I suspect many would make excellent companions for stallions.

To appease him, I set about putting up some electric fencing so that they could have a portion of the field to themselves. This worked well and the Chief seemed to respect it until, predictably enough, we went away for a few days.

On the Friday after we arrived at Moor Wood, Monty came over to England to do a mini-tour. Really, one of us should have stayed behind, but our landlady Sarah kindly offered to look after the horses for us. It didn't seem fair for Adam to miss the tour that was part of his course, and Kelly wanted me to go along to do the merchandise. While we were away we received a call to say that the stallion had broken out, got in with our other horses, and generally caused chaos. Luckily he hadn't got in with Sarah's lot, or things could have got very ugly. As it was, he had sustained a nasty kick to the inside of one of his forelegs, which Sarah was taking care of. It had taken them hours to catch all the horses and separate them out again, and to repair the damage to the fence. In our hearts, we knew we should have just had the stallion stay in the pen, but it would have meant more mucking out and hay-fetching, and we wanted to give Sarah and Peter as little extra work as possible. Besides, in the first few days that he'd been in the field he had shown no sign at all of wanting to break out. They were very good about it, but we felt terrible. It didn't seem like the best start to our tenancy. And it confirmed in my mind the suspicion started by the flood during the April tour: whenever I went away, something bad happened.

It was the evening after the tour, and the stallion's wound was beginning to heal nicely. Our new farrier was in the yard, putting some shoes on the horses, when Adam said, 'Perhaps we should ask him to take Sensi's back shoes off, so we can get the Chief to cover her. I think she's in season. And we won't have him for all that much longer.'

'Oh, I don't know!' I said crossly. We hadn't got back until the early hours of the morning, and I didn't want to have to think about anything. 'I don't think she's in season, anyway.'

Sensi chose that moment to spread her back legs and urinate copiously, producing a stream of hormone drenched fluid. The acrid smell left no doubt as to her reproductive receptivity.

'Although I suppose he might as well remove the shoes anyway,' I conceded.

The conception was an unorthodox mating, watched with fascination by the neighbour's two young children. We didn't want to interfere too much, yet we weren't quite confident enough to leave them to their own devices. But aside from one worrying moment when the stallion nearly strangled himself with Sensi's lead rope, it went fairly smoothly. When it was over, we led a rather smug-looking Sensi away. For some reason, Adam and I both felt certain that she had conceived, and I think Sensi knew too. She had no further need of the stallion, and when he whinnied plaintively across the field to her later, she didn't even flick an ear in his direction.

Two weeks later she ran straight through a metal gate and broke her nose in twenty-five places.

I found her and Major munching the long sweet grass on the triangle outside their field when I went to do the morning check. At first glance, they looked fine, perhaps just a little guilty. Sensi is a brilliant escapologist, and I thought perhaps she'd worked out how to open the catch on one of the gates. She looked like she had a slight graze on her nose, but closer inspection revealed that quite a large portion of her face was caved in, and that every time she exhaled, blood bubbled from two deep puncture wounds to her sinus. It was definitely time to call the vet.

It may have been the lack of breakfast, or it may have been the way the vet diligently pointed out the various cracks and breaks and holes as she carefully probed the wound, but either way I felt quite faint as I held the saline wash for her. A nagging thought pushed itself to the front of my mind:

'Do you think this could affect her foal? We think she conceived a fortnight ago ...'

The vet's face said it all. Horses tend to abort or reabsorb the foetus when they undergo severe shocks. We would just have to wait and see. The ultrasound scan was booked in for a week or so.

'Don't worry if she seems a bit depressed, she'll probably be in a lot of pain. She's likely to have one hell of a headache. I don't want to give her too much for it, in case she does keep the foal. The biggest worry is that she gets some kind of bone infection. That could be very serious. We really have to put her on antibiotics, because an infection on this sort of site could be fatal. I'll give her the first injection now. Will you be all right to give her the others?'

I agreed, possibly too readily, as she subsequently proved very hard to inject. It turned out that we'd been given the wrong needles, ones too fine for the thick penicillin, and it took about a minute to get the damned stuff into her muscle. This must have been very uncomfortable for poor old Sensi.

'The other thing is, we must keep the flies off the wound. She'll have to stay in for at least a week.'

That posed more of a problem. Most horses don't take to box

rest like humans take to bed rest. They take to it like humans take to prison.

Sensi watched me intently as I busied around, making a stable comfortable for her. Her eyes were bright, her ears were forward, and she seemed to be wondering what all the fuss was about. As I settled her in her box, I was suddenly overcome with a blinding headache. She started munching her haynet contentedly as I staggered back to the annexe, hardly able to see. I felt very much like I'd just run head first through a metal gate. She obviously felt fine.

When I got to work that afternoon, the shock of it all suddenly hit me. I could barely fill Adam in on the details, so close was I to falling apart, and Julia later told me that looking at my face she had to fear the worst.

When Adam and I got home that evening, I showed him the accident scene. What had happened was clear. Sensi and Major had been on opposite sides of the electric fence. Major had for some reason charged through it, and Sensi had found herself surrounded by the fence, and had to run to escape it. When they got to the field boundary, Major (more or less) jumped the metal fence, buckling it completely out of shape, but causing only a minor injury to his leg. The end of the electric tape was still draped over the top bar. Sensi, on the other hand, heading for the gate, had tried to stop. There were skid marks nine feet long leading up to and straight through the gateway, and no sign at all that she had attempted to jump it. Indeed, she must have had her head right down, balancing herself in her attempt to halt. She had burst the antique wrought-iron gate open, bending it dramatically in the process. She could have killed herself.

Sensi took to box rest surprisingly well. It could have had something to do with the numerous small treats we took her, the hours spent grooming and massaging her, the fresh grass we picked, and the night-time walks we took her on to avoid the ravaging flies. If she'd had a bell, she would have rung it incessantly. As it was, she didn't need one. If we spent too long indoors, or walked through the yard without stopping at her box, she would neigh imperiously. She even started insisting that we got up earlier in the morning, and on one occasion I was convinced she had surprised me into dropping my toast so that she could have it.

So all in all, it was perhaps not the smoothest possible start to life in our 'picturesque country idyll'. We loved the place, but, having two sets of landlords – Sarah and Peter, and Henry – we always felt like we had to creep around, and were perpetually worried about saying or doing the wrong thing. We needed to surface the round pen, and do something about the leaky roof in the studio, but Sarah and Peter had been adamant that as sub-tenants, we weren't to bother Henry directly. 'He's categorically stated that he'll only deal with us,' they told us. So not only was the surfacing of the round pen not a foregone conclusion, but even the right of this large, metal, not so picturesque structure to be there was under question. They seemed loath to bring anything up with him, and clearly felt that they were using up favours to address any of our issues.

In addition, there was the small problem of money. We didn't have any. The rent was £750 per month, plus £75 per month for the studio. This was not exactly the sort of sum we had in mind as a 'peppercorn', but without the studio we couldn't have lived in the annexe. Not that it would have been a bit cramped, we simply wouldn't have fitted, not unless we put most of our stuff into storage. I was being paid about £12 per hour by the college, which seemed reasonable, but at only ten hours per week it didn't add up to much. Kelly was paying me generously for the weekend courses, but again, there weren't that many. Adam, as a student on the course, had an income of exactly zero. We were still receiving a little money for the courses we had designed for the Japanese school, but the person we had franchised them out to had driven a very hard bargain. So when we were offered an unrideable pony to train, we jumped at the chance, even though the terms were not at all favourable.

Although she was the first horse we took in at Moor Wood, Maybee's story was quite typical of the horses we've trained. Her owners, a woman called Doris and her ten-year-old daughter, had started to break her in themselves, and all went well the first couple of times she was ridden. Then on the third occasion she simply exploded, bucking off her young rider, and careering across the field in a mad panic. They tried sitting on her a few more times, but she was getting worse and worse. They decided to leave it for a while, and breed a foal from her, but when they tried to ride her again, eighteen months later, she was just as bad. They tried getting professional jockeys to ride her, but Maybee managed to get through three of them before they decided to call it a day with that particular option. She'd had a few months off, but her owners were anxious to do something with her. She was a bright, friendly pony, perfect in every other way, and still quite young, at seven years old. They'd broken in many Arabs, and were by no means inexperienced, but Maybee had them stumped.

In spite of the fact that we were offering a money-back guarantee, and only charging our increased but still modest rate of £80 per week, Doris was only prepared to let us have the pony for two weeks. She told me later that she really didn't think I'd be able to help, and that even though she was prepared to give the pony one more chance, she didn't want me to waste any more time than that, or risk traumatising Maybee further.

She was only about 13 hands high, but no less dangerous for that. In addition, when she arrived, she was covered in show sheen, a silicon-based substance that made her extraordinarily slippery. Round as a barrel, she needed no help on that score. She was kind-hearted and generous, however, and although she was clearly terrified at the prospect of being mounted, she worked hard to overcome her fear. As she was so small, I didn't need anyone to give me a leg-up, and so I was able to practise jumping up and down beside her, and leaning across her, without having to do all the sessions in the evenings after the course with Adam.

Maybee progressed brilliantly, and the only thing she ever did under saddle was to once do a helicopter impression – spinning around several times on the spot. I may not be able to sit more than a few jumps of a bucking horse, but years of Sensi's shying had improved my ability to deal with very sudden turns. After that, Maybee never really had another issue under saddle again. Knowing that, against our advice, she hadn't yet had her teeth checked, we took the precaution of only ever riding her in a headcollar, which certainly contributed to our success, for the owner discovered later that she had a cracked wolf-tooth that would have caused her considerable pain, had it been knocked by a bit. When Doris came to see her, she was overjoyed with her progress, and let us have her for another week so that her daughter would be able to ride her confidently when they took her home. She said something that provided a useful insight into a very frustrating phenomenon. Owners often say to us that their horses are unrideable, dangerous, only worth a bullet, and that this is their last chance. Then when the horse is 'fixed', they say it wasn't so bad in the first place, and complain that the canter isn't very collected, for instance. (I heard this said by someone at a Monty demonstration who had brought a bucking horse that no one had successfully ridden for five years. He was cantering around smoothly and happily after half an hour, having bucked like a rodeo horse initially, and she said, 'But look at how loose those reins are, he's not trying to collect the horse at all. No wonder it's not bucking.') Doris said something that made me realise this sort of comment isn't mean-spiritedness. She said, 'If I hadn't seen her be so bad, I would almost believe I was making it up, or exaggerating. Seeing her this good makes it really hard to believe she was ever difficult. I really would doubt my memory, if I didn't have the photos to prove it.'

That single comment has always made it easier for me to deal with owners moving the goal-posts.

Maybee arrived mid-June, and ten days afterwards we had Sonny, a comparatively straightforward starter that we'd met through Julia. A month after that, Harry arrived, a lovely, talented, but quite difficult Arab starter. We had one horse on short-term grass livery. A slow trickle of work for which we were very grateful, but hardly enough to pay the rent, let alone the other numerous expenses involved in keeping horses, or ourselves. The ten-week course was ending, and although there were plenty of five-day and weekend courses, we were stumped. But we had one trick up our sleeves, one event we were pinning all our hopes on. Adam was hoping for a settlement from his former employers, the details of which cannot be divulged. It came through in November, just in time to pay the rent, which otherwise we couldn't have covered. It was enough to surface the round pen properly with quality materials, buy an ill-fated horsebox, some seriously good winter clothing, and our future. For a short while, we were safe to build up our business, free from the anxiety of falling into debt.

The best news of all was that Sensi managed a remarkable recovery – astonishing the vets with her ability to deal with necrotising fragments of bone, which were simply reabsorbed into her rumpled face – and she kept the foal. We couldn't have been more excited if we'd been expecting the baby ourselves when we saw the image on the ultrasound. And in spite of her somewhat altered profile, Sensi maintained an air of dignity and grace that seemed to prove beauty really is only skin-deep.

THIRTEEN

Always know the direction of true north (Adam)

I was more than halfway through my course and despite the obvious potential for my high expectations to be unfulfilled, I had enjoyed every minute of it. As well as getting practice in the pen, it was good to feel that I was filling in a lot of holes in my knowledge.

The group I was with got on really well and there were several truly exceptional people among them, such as David Grodek, born on a farm in Argentina, whose grandfather had strapped him onto an unhandled horse at the age of six and left him to break it in. David had later served in the Israeli army, called by some the Israeli Defence Force, when it invaded neighbouring Lebanon. Not surprisingly, the violence he had experienced and meted out made it difficult to fit into society afterwards and he had spent years working with horses in a remote area of Israel, having little contact with people. He had learned to hate violent horsemanship as a child, but his response to seeing it had not always been non-violent. He had, for example, once broken a man's arm for beating his horse with a whip. David had then met and married a British woman, which was how he had arrived in the UK, as well as coming to terms with his past.

For him as for all of us, it seemed that the horsemanship and our shared sense of mission brought out the best in us, and there was a general air of camaraderie. We all shared a distrust of the equestrian gadgets man has invented to force his will upon the horse – starting with the rope, and continuing with devices like whips, side reins and spurs. At the end of the twentieth century, after so many techno-logical advances, devices and aids, here we were, studying a training system that starts with taking off every last bit of tack and using the original tools to connect with the horse more strongly than any gadget ever will.

Unlike David, for whom English is his fourth language, I didn't find it hard to learn all the medical and technical information we were taught in the morning classes, although it wasn't quite as enthralling to me as it had been to Nicole. The afternoons were brilliant, being spent working with horses, and on projects. I worked with David and others, comparing different techniques of 'spookbusting', which has been very useful since. But the best thing about the course was Kelly's horse psychology classes. Everything she talked about made me realise how little I had really understood about how a horse thinks and expe-riences life – and how this is the key to effective training.

One hot morning, we eagerly assembled around small tables in a stuffy little room. Kelly handed out a paper with several sentences typed on it, each separated by an expanse of blank page. I immediately recognised several of Monty's stock phrases, those little nuggets of wisdom, which make it so much easier to remember his ideas. Kelly began to assign one of the sayings to each group of three or four students. We had to interpret its meaning and find three examples of how it could be applied in horsemanship. Most of these phrases were already familiar to me, but my confidence suddenly evaporated when Kelly gave our group a question.

'Explain three reasons why you should always know the direction of true north. I'll give you all a few minutes to discuss it before we begin.'

I looked at my three table-mates. Julia looked a bit bemused, and Tim, a lovely but very shy young Scot who had endeavoured to say as little as possible in every public forum since we began, didn't seem likely to chose this moment to blossom into a confident contributor to the debate. David kept asking me to explain the question, certain that he couldn't have understood what Kelly meant. But I didn't, either.

I asked David about his army training. 'Surely they tell you the answer to that before you can get to be in the Israeli special forces, Rambo.'

David grimaced and made as if he was going to spit, perhaps remembering long days and nights trudging all over Israel as he learned how to use a compass. Or the ones in Lebanon where it really mattered whether he had learned his lessons well. 'No, they only told us to know the direction where to point the bazooka. But of course, I know how you can tell where north is without a compass.'

I waved my hand. 'You look at the sun. It rises in the east and sets in the west.'

'Even if it's cloudy or night-time and you don't know what time it is?'

That shut me up.

'You look on the trees or rocks. No direct sunlight reaches the north side. Moss can grow there.'

I thanked him for this helpful tip and told him I'd remember it if I was ever stuck, lost in the wilderness, without a compass. Around the parts of England I was intending to be, even if you were completely lost, you never had more than a few miles to go in any direction before coming across a perfect little village with a phone box and a pub at which to wait for your taxi.

This was all very interesting, but it wasn't actually helping us find even the first of our three reasons why we should always know the direction of true north.

'Well, you might get lost on a hack and not have a compass,' piped Tim.

We stared at him. All along he had been hiding it, but he was a genius. In spite of the fact that a compass wouldn't be very much use without a map, and you were unlikely to have one of those if you'd forgotten your compass, you couldn't argue with his logic. It was a solid start. But beyond this reasonably obvious scenario, we could only come up with variations on the theme – getting lost on a long-distance endurance ride, getting lost driving to the stables ...

'I know,' Julia suggested. 'It means you shouldn't have to rely on technology. You should be self-reliant.'

Great. So we had two compelling reasons why we should know the direction of true north. I was even starting to convince myself that I should make sure I actually did, by getting a compass. I still didn't really trust the moss method.

As I looked down at the sheet, I had a nagging thought. 'What if it doesn't mean only what it says? What if true north isn't the physical direction towards the pole, but the direction towards a goal, the truth, some sort of holy grail?'

David looked at me as if I had lost my mind. 'Holy gril, what is holy groiled?'

'It's what a holy man seeks. True north, maybe it isn't just the actual direction north, maybe it's like a metaphor for a perfect existence, the best way to live, or train horses and share your life with them or whatever. Like making a Garden of Eden, finding the holy grail of horsemanship.'

Tim and Julia looked like they thought this might be halfway credible, but of course David had to stick a spoke in the wheel.

'OK, so you know the direction of true north, that still doesn't mean you know where you are. Or where you want to be. So it doesn't help you get there.'

I hadn't bluffed my way through all those supervisions at

Cambridge for nothing. I had learned that if you say something positively enough, you just might come to find meaning in it.

'Yes, but if you don't have anything to refer to, you can't even find a destination,' I replied. 'Perhaps it means, always seek to know where you are, where you want to be, how to get there. You may not be heading directly north, you may not be able to, but you can know whether you should turn left or right – maybe you could have more of an idea of where to go.'

Julia added, 'Maybe true north is perfection, or the perfect horse. Always seek to make the perfect horse. Anyway, if you don't know where north is, how are you going to ever find your place? The horses do, they know their place, although they may not have words for it, or notice the moss on the trees unless it gets in the way of the grass.'

By now I was really warming to the idea. If only horsemanship – and life – had such clear, reliable, easy pointers as a compass, or even the moss on a tree. It would be so easy to know whether what you were doing was taking you closer to where you wanted to be, or further away. Too many people are aware that they have made huge compromises in their lives, that time is running out and that the left-overs from their history will never let their slate be wiped clean. I'd hate to be thinking, I know my life shouldn't be like this, as I drifted from day to day in the sort of career in which I could so easily have found myself. But it's hard at times to imagine what could make it better. Always easy to see what's wrong in someone else's picture, it's so hard to see what's wrong in your own. Perhaps we each decide the direction of our own true north, and make that the destination we seek in life. For the world around us has so clearly lost its direction. What David was involved with in Lebanon is testament to that. It is easy to see why people seek answers in religion, and why extremist religious and political views are on the increase all around the world. For we all seek to live with a sense of 'true north'. Everyone needs an ethical framework. And I believe, whatever your religious belief, the most important thing to do is to get violence out of our lives. If we do not, we will destroy ourselves and probably, all other life on earth.

David screwed up his mouth sceptically. 'Sounds like bullshit to me. Anyway, if you think you can explain that to anyone, go ahead.'

I tried, at least.

In our discussion afterwards, Kelly confessed she had always ribbed Monty about how it wasn't the Wild West any more, nobody really needs to know that kind of thing these days and it's more important to be able to read a road sign. I guess Monty had told her stories about how his compass got broken when he was out in the wilderness catching mustangs.

A year later, in the midst of the Kosovo campaign, when the roar of B-52 engines burst the air over Moor Wood as they flew in to nearby RAF Fairford, I was surprised to hear Monty publicly criticising the bombing. He is, after all, American, and very patriotic. 'Violence is never the answer,' he repeated every night to the audiences in cold English barns, while in the Balkans American bombs exploded.

But I had to question whether it was right never to fight. What else could those victims of ethnic hatred and violence do? And should we not support them in their efforts to be accepted? Is it not right for a horse, if it is pushed beyond the limit, to kick out? I was glad I never got into a political discussion with him over it. Because, as usual, I found out more by pondering the answer myself. Violence may seem, it may even be, the only alternative – but it is never the answer. The horse that fights back – the 'vicious', 'aggressive' animal that, pushed too far, injures its owner – is the horse that gets a bullet in his head. Towards peace, surely that is the direction of true north. And horses, in their manner and nature, can help to point the way.

FOURTEEN

Riding doctors
(Nicole)

When Kelly mentioned that she'd like me to run riding clinics as an optional extra to the Preliminary Certificate, I was astonished. She said it in such a matter-of-fact way, and as if we'd discussed it already, but it was a complete surprise. 'Put together a syllabus,' Kelly said, 'and I'll add it to the course details. Let's just see what sort of interest there is.'

It was a particularly busy month, May 1999, when we held the first clinic. We'd been at Moor Wood for just one year, and everything was going well.

We had several challenging horses in for training, including Duncan, a bottle-reared colt. I'd gone all the way to Grimsby to meet him, just to see if we'd be able to help him at all, since he sounded so unruly and dangerous when his owner, Judith, whom I'd met at a demonstration in Market Rasen, described him to me.

He'd been a twin, and rejected by his mother, and the odds on his surviving were considered poor. Judith hadn't put a headcollar on him for years, and used to bring him in from the field by opening all the gates from the field to the stable, putting his feed in the box, then calling him and scarpering. To get him back into his field, she simply did the reverse. The last time she'd tried to lead him anywhere, he'd knocked her over and broken her hip. Underneath it all, he was good-natured and affectionate but still very difficult to handle, all teeth and hooves and tossing head. Like so many orphan horses, he was also prone to tantrums, and more than once resorted to throwing himself on the ground (occasionally with me on top) when he couldn't get his own way. He arrived a tight bundle of hard muscles and jangled nerves, and when he went home, he was soft as butter. Adam drove him back and stayed for a day to make sure he remembered his manners, and spent some time teaching Judith how to handle him. He was immensely gratified to watch Judith's young granddaughter ride him in perfect safety, like a reliable old family pony who'd been doing this for years.

We also had in an enormous cob called Elliott, who objected, perhaps reasonably enough, to having his poll clipped, but as he was hogged out (his mane completely shaved) this represented quite a problem. His neck was enormous, you could hardly circle it with your arms, even at the top, and it joined on to a set of shoulders that put you in mind of a rhinoceros. He had learnt that he could easily go wherever he liked, with or without a human in tow. He was perfectly good-natured about it: he would never dream of kicking you, for example, if you ended up being in the slipstream of his back end as he went about his explorations, but he didn't see why he should pander to someone else's whims about where he went. I'll never forget the sight of Adam waterskiing along behind him on the day he arrived, as Elliott gave him a thorough but quite unnecessary tour of Moor Wood. I was so helpless with laughter I couldn't have given him a hand, but I don't think having two of us on the end of the line would have slowed Elliott down. Teaching him to lead was just an added extra to his training, 'money for old rope', as his owner put it, but it didn't feel like that when Elliott tried to take off. The prospect of persuading this huge horse to stand still enough to clip his poll without accidentally taking his ears off at the same time was daunting to say the least. I don't think it could have been done without the use of a pressure halter, but what probably made the most difference was teaching him that if he got worried, he could back away, and we would give him breathing space. This was by far a preferable alternative to his previous tactic, of going straight over the top of you and out through the door, whether it was bolted or not.

Chesley could not have been more different. A slightly built Arab, badly scarred both physically and mentally from years of neglect and abuse, she was so sensitive that even the merest pressure on her headcollar would stop her dead in her tracks, and if she had found herself towing someone along behind her, she would probably have had a heart attack! Scared of her own shadow, she was completely unsuitable for her two novice owners, one of whom was far too heavy to ride her, particularly as Chesley was so badly put together that her back barely looked strong enough to carry a saddle. The best we could really do was to teach them how to handle her, and build up her trust. In the end, they were rewarded with a friend who really enjoyed their company and was a credit to their patience.

Forrest was a comparatively straightforward starter, a big bay four-year-old whose only real foible was Elliott-like tendencies. Several times he had got away from his owner when she'd been leading him on the road, and what had particularly unnerved her was that he'd done this when she'd been leading him off the bit, too. She had honestly believed it wasn't physically possible for him to do this, and was quite shocked when he showed her it was.

Polly, the other resident in training at the time, was a gorgeous Highland mare who had gradually become more and more worried about being ridden, to the point where she regularly bucked people off. Her owners came and rode her at Moor Wood, and were delighted with her progress. Weeks later, we were dismayed to hear that she'd thrown someone off again, but not surprised when we heard the circumstances. Due to problems acquiring a new saddle, they'd given her three weeks off when they got her home, and then chosen a blustery day to get on her – bareback. The person leading her had her on such a loose rope that she got it caught around her front feet and panicked. Although we didn't feel this was our fault, we were so upset that we gave the owners back a significant portion of the training fee.

So we had our hands full. But by far the most exciting thing about May was that Sensi was due to give birth. By my calculations, she was due on the tenth. When she didn't deliver that night, I thought perhaps she was holding out for my birthday, the twelfth. When that came and went, I began to get worried. I was going on a ten-day Monty tour that started on the seventeenth – what if she didn't foal before then? The idea of leaving her at such a time was heartrending, to say the least. I was trying to work out the practicalities of commuting to the venues so I could return home and sit up with her, but it wouldn't be particularly easy. I'd been checking her every night since the eighth or so, but I didn't get the feeling she was particularly imminent. But on the night of the thirteenth, things started to look more promising.

I was in two minds about how to handle the foaling. I had a strong sense that she'd prefer to foal outside, particularly as she was used to living out. On the other hand I was, of course, terribly anxious lest anything go wrong. Horses have so little margin for error when giving birth, and I didn't think any vet would fancy the prospect of trying to sort out any complications whilst she was lying in the mud in a dark field. I knew I probably shouldn't wait up with her. Many mares wait until they're on their own before giving birth – in fact, in the teaching stud colleges, there's an astonishing number of horses that give birth at nine o'clock in the morning, after the night watching shift has finished! In the end, I decided to compromise – I'd leave her in the huge foaling box, check her every forty-five minutes or so, and let her out as soon as it got light.

Sensi was unsettled that night, looking at her belly, and pacing around the stable. Her teats were waxed up, and every time I went out to check her, I wondered if there would be eight legs instead of four in the box. But each time there was just Sensi, looking enormous and gorgeous, but definitely alone. When the first light of dawn crept into the stable, I decided to let her out: we would be able to find her in the field now, and she'd either give birth imminently or leave it until the next night. I went back to bed.

Less than two hours later, we were awoken by one of Sarah and Peter's liveries banging on the door. 'The sac's showing! I'd get out there soon if I were you, or you'll miss it!'

We arrived just in time to see two forelegs and a head poking out, quickly followed by the rest of the foal's body. She was born on a hill, in a pool of mud, and by the time she'd worked out which way was up and where her legs were, she'd tumbled quite a way from Sensi, who was looking over at this scrawny creature with fascination. We decided to call her Karma.

It was a cold morning, and Karma was shaking and shivering. Sensi ambled over and licked her, and we gathered round, cleaning off bits of mucus and amniotic sac. Although Karma was still too weak to stand, we decided we should try to get her inside as it was starting to rain. As per the usual foaling instructions, I tried to tie up the placenta, but discovered it was extraordinarily slippery and deftly managed to untie itself no matter what I tried. In the end, I simply carried it behind her somewhat like a bridal train while, under Sensi's watchful eye, Adam gathered up the foal, and found she was just light enough to carry. Staggering slightly, he brought her back to her stable, where he sat down and leaned against the wall. After she had suckled a few times, Karma joined him on the floor. She lay next to him, and he hugged and stroked her all over, moving her little feet around until she was happy to accept him handling them. Finally she put her head on his lap, and they fell asleep together.

It was Monty's birthday, 14 May 1999.

I'd like to say that Karma was the most beautiful foal I'd ever seen, but even to my biased eyes she looked very peculiar. Her face was extraordinarily long and thin, and her sticky, scrawny body hardly fitted the fluffy vision I was expecting. Her legs looked like a spider's, ridiculous in their comical length. However, almost by the minute, she began to look more normal, until, just one day after her birth, she was so completely gorgeous I almost couldn't bear to leave her to go on tour.

In the end I compromised and missed one demonstration near the end of the tour that had a day off either side of it, and thereby was able to spend an extra three days at home with Sensi and her foal. This also gave me more time to prepare for the imminent riding clinic.

So on a Friday evening, one year almost to the day that we'd moved to Moor Wood, six horses and their riders descended on our yard for the weekend. With our six stables thus filled, we arranged with Sarah and Peter to move the horses we had in for training into their yard. We worked out a rigid timetable so that we wouldn't be hogging the school all weekend, and managed to squeeze all the cars into our yard. We did our best to turn the studio into a lecture room. The bright blue tarpaulin hanging down from the roof with the weight of the water it had collected looked quite festive. It was clear that six students and three tutors (Adam, Julia and myself) wouldn't physically fit in the annexe, so we set up a couple of kettles in the studio, setting by several large containers of water, and an ample supply of chocolate biscuits.

Having overall responsibility for the entire clinic was nerve-racking, and during the introductions and first lecture on Saturday morning, I was acutely aware of how important it was that everything went really well. The nerves, however, melted within the first few minutes of having the first pair riding in the pen. It was a sultry, sunny day, and the horses were all settled and steady, helped I think by the fact that the pen, only recently surfaced, was still rather deep, in spite of hours of rolling to try to firm it up. Adam was filming, Julia and I were teaching, and almost before we knew it, we were through all three pairs, and it was time for lunch.

In the afternoon, we had scheduled long-lining. We included this on the course because we feel it's such an incredibly useful skill, very much 'riding from the ground', so much more educational than lungeing, and yet so rarely practised in this country. The first horse and rider combination, Suzanne Marshall with her horse Trojan, were in the pen, and about to start when Adam looked out across to the west and said, 'There's a storm approaching. I think perhaps we should take cover.'

I looked up at the sky immediately above me, which was blue and clear. Then I cast my eyes across the valley from where the wind was rising, to the ominous wall of thick, dark cloud he was indicating, and stated confidently, 'Oh, I'm sure it will blow over.'

'Yes, it will blow *us* over. Don't you think we should go in *before* we get wet?'

'Oh, we'll be fine,' I said, and started teaching. I had been reading quite a lot of self-help, positive thinking books at the time, and felt that if only Adam wouldn't keep drawing everyone's attention to the imminent hurricane, it would simply go away.

About three minutes later the sky blackened, the wind whipped up and the heavens opened. Trojan immediately dropped his head to his knees, turned his backside to the wind, and resolutely refused to move. The watching group stood poised, uncertain whether to obey their instincts and run for cover, possibly causing offence, or to stay and watch and get soaked. I was still clinging firmly to the belief that it was only a shower and would stop at any minute. But the drops of rain were as large as golf balls, and falling thicker and faster than most waterfalls.

Finally Adam came up with a compelling argument. 'Think of the horse, you can't ask him to work in conditions like this,' he begged, at which I relented and allowed him and the rest of the soaked participants to flee to the studio.

We got Trojan rugged up and back in his stable just in time to hear the first claps of thunder booming out across the valley.

With most of the group now thoroughly drenched, Adam handed around some towels and plugged in the electric heater. Shivering, we settled down to watch a Mary Wanless video, and I put the kettles on. Three seconds later, this excessive load on what turned out to be a botched electrical supply, shorted out the circuit, and we were left in darkness. 'It'll just be a fuse,' we reassured each other, but when we examined the fuse box, by the light of a handy torch, we found fuses that looked nothing like what we were used to. Luckily, Peter turned up about ten minutes later, and happened to have a spare. We were back in business.

At the end of the next day, we piled back into the studio and studied the video of the lessons. Everyone, without exception, had improved enormously, and here was the proof right in front of their eyes. We handed out student evaluation forms, and everyone was really positive, the only negative comments being about the rain. Studying the forms later, over a glass of chilled champagne, we realised we had organised a good course and were immensely proud. But we were acutely aware that without the pioneering work of Monty Roberts and Mary Wanless, we would have had almost nothing to offer. In particular, it was Mary's research into how to actually teach that made the biggest difference. Her years of work in decoding and defining the fundamental, underlying principles of riding were the sole reason we could enable such rapid transformations in other people's riding. The first time I heard someone say, 'I've learned more about riding on this weekend than I have in the last ten years,' it took my breath away. But then I thought back to that first assessment I'd received from Mary when she lectured on my ten-week Monty course, and how I'd learned more in that thirty minutes than I ever had before. It is a privilege to be able to pass on this knowledge. In particular, I was delighted that Suzanne Marshall, who is a BHSAI, was so intrigued with this 'new approach' that she signed up to the next available Mary Wanless course and also the Monty Roberts Preliminary Certificate of Horsemanship. She is now a credited Ride With Your Mind coach, was one of the first Intelligent Horsemanship Recommended Associates, and runs a successful teaching and training yard in Kent.

Suzanne was a real pleasure to have around – always smiling and enthusiastic, and a very fast learner. Her parents had come up with her, towing Trojan with their brand new Subaru people carrier, to take advantage of a few days in the Cotswolds, and they were just as lovely. So much so that they didn't even complain when we set fire to their car.

It wasn't deliberate, of course. It's just that at the time we were the frustrated owners of a monster green horsebox, which had decided, not for the first time, that the conditions were not optimal for it to start. We think it had strong astrological tendencies, and would only burst into life when Aries was ascending, or something. Sadly, the particular cosmic conditions it required seemed to coincide lamentably rarely. In addition, if there was any suggestion of cold or damp in the air it would need to dry in the sun for several weeks before it could cope. Unfortunately, in the Cotswolds, these weather conditions only happen once a century or so. I guess the downpour on Saturday had depressed it too much, and the fact that it had had a couple of days off meant that it couldn't possibly hold the charge in its battery.

The upshot was that it wouldn't start, the Subaru was just sitting there, and we happened to have a pair of jump leads handy. Suzanne's dad, being knowledgeable about these matters, confidently volunteered for the job.

We set them up and Suzanne's dad switched on his car, and then revved the engine. From time to time, Adam turned the ignition switch, and although the noises coming out of the box were slightly more encouraging, it still wasn't firing up. Instead, small flames and a lot of smoke were appearing from under the bonnet of the Subaru. With the engine switched off and the flames subsiding, we stepped over to inspect the damage.

The hole the fire had produced was quite small, considering, and as he pointed out, only in the battery. 'That'll be all right, I should think a small piece of gum or something would seal that up.' So saying, he produced a small wad from his mouth, but when he placed it over the hole in the battery, it promptly fell through and sizzled quietly in the battery acid. 'Perhaps I'll need two sticks,' he said, beginning to chew again.

The car was so new it was more or less still in its wrapper, but they wouldn't hear of us buying them a new battery. In fact, they kept apologising to us about the fact that their car had failed to start the box! We should already have known by then that it wasn't a question of mechanics. The vehicle we had bought was perfectly mechanically sound. It just had an attitude problem, and if it didn't want to start, it wasn't going to be forced to by some upstart trailer-towing vehicle.

We ran seven clinics that summer, including two in Kent. Julia, who was by now teaching regularly on Kelly's courses, had more or less moved onto the sofa in the annexe. If we'd thought the annexe was small for two people, it was astonishing that all three of us managed to squeeze in. Perhaps more surprising was that we still had so much to say to each other, and on the drive to the course, Julia and I continued to talk incessantly.

Towards the end of the summer, we sensed something was in the air with Sarah and Peter. For one reason or another, they'd had a pretty rough time since they'd been at Moor Wood. We thought perhaps they wanted to leave, but we couldn't work out how it could possibly make sense for them to do so. We knew we were already paying more than half the rent, and this together with the money they received from another tenant and their livery clients meant that they were living in this fantastic place, and keeping their horses and ponies here, for about the same cost as a one-bedroom flat in Milton Keynes.

At the same time, we weren't sure if it would be good or bad news if they left. On the one hand, it would be fantastic to have the place to ourselves. On the other, we didn't know if we would be able to afford it. It wasn't even clear that we would have the opportunity to take the lease on, since we weren't direct tenants of the landlord, Henry, only sub-tenants. We pondered the situation for several weeks, trying to work out what was going on.

So when one evening towards the end of August they asked if they could see us both, we weren't sure quite what to expect. And even though we'd been considering the possibility for some time, it still came as a shock when they told us that they'd already informed Henry that they were going to leave. Sarah had signed a five-year lease when she had moved here with her previous husband, and it still had more than twelve months to run. Henry was well within his rights to demand that they either sit out their commitment, or pay him the rent for the remaining time, but he let them off. The biggest shock was that they were leaving as soon as the current month's rent ran out. They had already signed a lease on another property. This meant that in just a fortnight we would either be moving out of the annexe and into the bigger part of the house, or we would have to leave Moor Wood and find another place for us, our two cats and by now seven horses, the round pen (and its 100 tonnes of surface) and horsebox (if it would start) to live.

It was one of those decisions that wasn't really a decision. The chances of finding a similar place locally – or at least, within reasonable distance of Witney – in two weeks were unlikely to say the least.

We couldn't simply stick around and see if the next tenants would want sub-tenants. The prospect of going back to our little flat on an estate in Milton Keynes was not enticing. There was still the problem of finding somewhere suitable in Milton Keynes to train the horses we would take on, let alone the issue of what we would do with the training horses we currently had in at Moor Wood.

We hardly had to discuss the matter. We were staying. We would just have to find a way to make it work.

The most frightening aspect was that the rent was such that we couldn't simply borrow some money from either of our families to cover it if we were stuck one month. It wasn't the sort of money that anyone we knew could simply draw out of their current account and not really notice. In fact, even if one of us were to get a reasonably well-paid full-time job, it probably wouldn't cover the whole amount. We would simply have to be successful. We calculated that if we had x liveries at y pounds per week, and z number of horses in for training, we should be all right, but we were still acutely aware of the fine line that existed between success and failure. I kept thinking of that well-known joke: 'How do you make a small fortune in horses? Start with a large one!' It didn't seem so funny any more.

Sarah and Peter informed Henry of our decision to stay, and he came down to the annexe to discuss the details. We'd only really been on waving terms before, and we were curious to find out what he was actually like. Sarah and Peter had given us the impression that Henry and his wife were rather snooty, that they lived the high life of the propertied classes, hardly having to work, income just rolling in from every direction. This image fitted in nicely with our preconceptions, but we'd already noticed that for someone who lived a life of leisure, Henry Robinson appeared to be working extremely hard. I often saw him out on his tractor in the fields, on my way to work in the early mornings, and at certain times of year we could hear the drone of the combine harvester at all times of the night and day. Henry and his right-hand-man Les, the only full-time employee on a farm of 1,500 acres, worked almost constantly to hold the farm together in a climate of great uncertainty. Even the income from renting a number of cottages in and around the estate was not without its drawbacks, for with this seeming bonanza came the huge responsibility that every last Cotswold stone used to build it was listed at grade two or higher, meaning Henry had no option but to keep all the buildings in a state of good repair using antique materials, regardless of their financial viability. We began to realise that owning a lot of property could be as much a liability as an asset, and didn't necessarily guarantee a lot of spare income.

But even so we were shocked when Henry, politely removing his wellies when he stepped into the annexe, revealed socks full of holes. He looked at his feet as if they didn't belong to him, and we realised it was probably just an oversight. Obviously he could afford a new pair of socks. But all of a sudden we realised he wasn't snooty at all.

Henry was apologetic about the way we had suddenly been thrust into this major decision, but he said he knew from past experience that once people wanted to leave, there was no point in holding them back. He was clearly unimpressed with Sarah and Peter reneging on their commitment, but he didn't want the bad will of pursuing them about it.

As we discussed the practicalities – the payment arrangements, the solicitors, the lease, the various ways of bringing income into the business – we discovered something quite shocking. 'If the worst comes to the worst,' I said, 'we can always do what Sarah and Peter did, and rent out one yard, half the land, and the annexe.'

Henry's face darkened momentarily. 'You could,' he said, 'but that's another area in which they didn't fulfil their lease agreement. It says quite specifically that you have to inform me of any arrangements of that sort that you make.'

Adam and I looked at each other, comprehension dawning slowly.

'Do you mean to say that Sarah and Peter didn't ask permission to sub-let?' we asked.

'Not just didn't ask permission. Didn't even tell me they'd done it. The only reason I knew you'd moved in was that your car stayed around a lot longer than a holiday booking would.'

'That explains a lot …' Adam's voice trailed off, and I knew what he was remembering. The bemused expression on Henry's face when we'd introduced ourselves to him about a month after we'd moved in. The way Sarah and Peter had made us promise not to speak to Henry directly. The fact that they never wanted to bring up any of our issues with him, such as the leaking studio roof or the surfacing of the round pen … The round pen! Henry's help with his JCB in spreading out the gravel and sand of the pen was all the more generous considering we weren't even meant to be there, and no one had asked him about the pen in the first place. It also explained Adam's first encounter with Henry's wife, Susie.

It was one summer afternoon soon after we arrived that she came down the drive with a group of children on ponies, who picnicked in the orchard by the school. On her way past, Susie peered through the annexe window, as if looking for someone. Adam, who was doing the dishes at the time, stuck his head around the door, and asked if he could help. He had no idea who Susie was.

'I'm looking for Sarah,' she said.

'You want the other part of the house,' Adam replied helpfully, 'the door's just through that yard.'

'Yes, I know,' she said.

Adam was confused. If she knew that Sarah lived in the other house, why was she looking for her here? To clarify the situation further he said, 'We live in the annexe now. We rent it from Sarah and Peter.'

'I think I may have made a bit of a gaffe,' Adam told me later. 'I didn't realise she was Henry's wife, I thought perhaps she was a client or something. But I can't think why she looked so startled when I said we were living here now.'

Henry laughed when we told him this story. With the formalities out of the way, we suggested a glass of bubbly to celebrate. 'Although it's not very special,' we warned him, suddenly embarrassed at the ordinariness of what we were about to offer him.

'No,' he said firmly, 'as long as it's cold and bubbly, that's fine by me.'

The meeting with Henry set our minds at rest. We could get excited now about the prospect of living at Moor Wood on our own. Or rather, not quite on our own. Surely it made sense for Julia and her husband Danny to move into the annexe? Julia was more or less living with us anyway with the number of courses we were both teaching on, and this way she and Danny would see more of each other. At least, that's how we tried to sell the idea to Danny. The persuasion worked, and to our intense delight, Danny and Julia moved into the annexe about a month after we moved into the 'big house'. The only downside was that now they were much further away from London than they had been, which meant that Danny, rather than commuting, ended up staying a few days a week in London.

Adam was particularly thrilled that we would have the place to ourselves. In recent months he had been assembling a band, having met a number of local musicians through a girl who had kept her horse with Sarah and Peter. But, in spite of having the perfect practice room in the studio, they had been forced to hire a room miles away, which severely detracted from the pleasure of 'letting rip' twice a week with his incredibly loud amplifier. Even the thick stone walls of the studio could not contain the noise and he hadn't even bothered to ask Sarah and Peter for permission to rehearse there, knowing what the answer would be. 'It's the best band I've ever been in,' he said categorically, which I found easy to believe.

Now, to my delight, SCSI would be able to practise just across the yard. This, he attempted to convince me, would be good for the horses as it would desensitise them to loud noises, and educate them regarding the beauty of 'quality feedback', in which he specialises. Generally, this seemed to be the case, but there was one notable exception. This horse had come from the stud owned by Charlie Watts, of the Rolling Stones. She was perhaps used to a higher calibre of performance.

To cap this period of momentous change, Adam received a phone call from someone with a brilliant suggestion. I came into the house just as he was finishing the call. 'Hang on a minute, I'll ask Nicole,' he said, cupping his hand over the phone and explaining the situation. It was a young woman looking for work. 'She just called up and said she wanted a job and did we have one for her,' he said apologetically, as if this meant we were obliged to take her on. Certainly, anyone brave enough to do that was worth considering. As I had just come home from the course to find the yard not swept, the dishes not done, and the water buckets not filled, this struck me as a particularly good idea. I nodded enthusiastically, and Adam set up a time for Jo to come and have an interview.

Jo had seen Monty back in 1989 when he had first come over, when she was eleven. She and her mum had been instant 'believers', because the horses he had used had come from a neighbouring yard, so she knew they were genuinely un-started youngsters. She saw him again on a later tour, and that was where she had picked up the information about Kelly's courses. Our riding clinics were outlined on the course details, and she had looked Woodmancote up on the map, and decided to drive out to have a look. She didn't find our yard, hidden as it is, but thought that Woodmancote looked like an all right place to work. She had recently graduated and didn't give it much more thought until she returned back from a summer trip to Bali and Australia. With a BSc in combined Geography and Psychology, what was more obvious than a career working as a groom in an Intelligent Horsemanship yard?

Jo worked part-time to start with, five days a week, for three hours a day. We gave her a week's trial, and never looked back. In the early days I used to think that someone was tickling her, so often did we hear her laugh. Her role expanded when we took her on full-time, and she graduated to riding the starters and remedial horses, which took a lot of pressure off me, and meant I didn't have to ride in the evenings after I'd been at work on the courses. Everyone should have a Jo.

But she isn't altogether perfect. Adam, for example, has always felt she should grow taller by a foot or so. Despite his frequent suggestions that she should do so, she has remained stubbornly small. And for such a bright, cheerful, and overwhelmingly caring person, she can occasionally say things with a spectacular lack of tact. On one occasion a newly-arrived client was struggling around the yard, her husband in the car, trying to quickly unload all her horse's stuff and inform us of all his foibles before, as she put it, 'My husband gets too stressed out with waiting.'

Jo picked up a saddle and a sack of feed and said, 'Well, why doesn't he get out and help? He's got legs, hasn't he?'

The lady looked at Jo sadly and said quietly, 'No, I'm afraid he hasn't. Well, not ones that work, anyway. He's disabled.'

Jo told me the story later, still mortified.

But apart from the odd faux pas, we sensed we were right on track. Having Jo around meant we could spend more time concentrating on the business of training horses, and the trickle of work we'd started with had turned into a steady stream. Having the place to ourselves was very exciting and, free to do our own work, we began to feel we really belonged.

FIFTEEN

Getting on
(Adam)

Loading horses into horseboxes is one of the most common problems we deal with. Everyone knows horses are sociable, outdoors animals, but, nevertheless, we isolate horses in stables far more than they would choose, perhaps being unable to separate our own needs – a quiet, warm, dry den and a bowl of concentrated food – from those of the horse – space, a herd, grass. We can sometimes be blind to the ways in which we regularly flout these most basic rules of horse behaviour. Rare is the owner who really appreciates what they are expecting from their horse in many everyday situations. We take for granted things like tying up a horse, picking up their feet, taking them away from the herd and field, into a stable, or through a doorway. Most people, however, do have some awareness of why horses have 50 million years of reasons not to load. Every instinct tells them not to step on an unstable surface and not to be in a small enclosed space. Short of sunbathing in front of a lion's den there are few more cardinal rules for a flight animal. In addition to going into the horsebox and being cooped up there, he has to cope with your driving, and the fact that you are taking him to whatever destination you choose – his life is literally in your hands. But how many owners – myself included – have cursed a 'stupid' horse that wouldn't load?

It seems quite normal for any person who happens to be in the vicinity, at a show for example, to feel it is their duty to come up with a different method to get your horse in the horsebox, each of which is tried in turn for a short time before the next person 'helps'. After they have done so, the job is often still not done and the prospects of success are usually somewhat worse. I'm sure many people offer to help out of very genuine concern for your predicament. They're hoping they can get the horse in quickly for you, but they can't devote their whole day to it. They do their best and then have to move on. Sometimes they'll succeed and then it's smiles and relief all round. Once when Nicole was patiently struggling to get Sensi on the trailer in Cambridge, an old man she didn't recognise came up and quietly offered to help. He said he was a plumber from the neighbouring building site, but he seemed to have stepped out of another world. He appeared kind and gentle, so Nicole agreed. Sensi seemed intrigued by him, and after he had stroked her neck and placed one of her forefeet on the ramp, she followed him in. 'Never be in a hurry,' was his advice.

On other occasions, we weren't so lucky with outside help. I vividly remember one occasion when we were moving Sensi from a yard near Milton Keynes, to take her back to Cambridge. We had been trying for about twenty minutes, parked in the middle of the yard, attempting to bribe her with food. We coaxed her onto the ramp but couldn't get her any further. Feeling powerless, we were already embarrassed and under pressure, because Nicole's dad was waiting to start driving. The yard owner's husband then appeared and said he needed us to get on with it so he could take a truck through the yard. The logical thing, of course, would have been to just move out of the way and let him through, so as not to put ourselves and Sensi under even more pressure. But having spent what felt like so much time to get her just on the ramp, we couldn't bear to let her off. We tried to get on with it.

The harder we tried, the more stressed Sensi became. Eventually the husband reappeared and started 'helping'. I don't remember the details, only how much we all disliked him, and that he was definitely in a hurry. The more he hassled her, standing behind, the more focused she was on the people outside, the less on the space in front of her. She was getting more and more uptight and resistant. Eventually (after about a minute), he said we should put a long-line around her quarters, and went to get one while Nicole and I looked at each other, feeling uneasy and impotent.

I was standing behind Sensi, telling her to move on, while he attached the lunge line to one side of the trailer, then passed it through the other, and dropped it down over her tail. 'Go on, girl!' he shouted, pulling sharply on the line as it tightened above her hocks. I watched her tuck her legs beneath her as she looked back with white in her eyes and, through the noise and commotion, I had a sudden and powerful intuition that I ought not to be standing just there. I took a deliberate step back, and a second later, the space where my head had just been was punched by Sensi's back hooves. I saw the dull gleam of the metal of her shoes, frozen in the air for an instant, less than a foot from my face.

I'm not saying that a lunge line around the quarters doesn't work, and applied well, I don't see anything wrong with it. But we didn't get her in, needless to say, until the man stopped helping and went away in his truck.

Possibly the most shocking intervention happened when Nicole took Sensi to the vet, to have a kicked leg X-rayed in case it had a star fracture. Sensi loaded perfectly on the way there, but having been sedated so that she wouldn't trash the X-ray machine, she was not really very with it when it came to loading her to go home. The vet was keen to lock up the yard before going out on her rounds, so she didn't want to leave Nicole to wait for Sensi to wake up more. With a 'Come along, old girl', she slapped her cheerily on the backside a couple of times (the vet, that is, slapped Sensi), and gave her a few concerted heave-hos, but when that had no effect, went off to fetch a whip and a Chiffney.

'I felt so helpless,' Nicole told me later that evening. 'I knew she'd be all right if we could just give her half an hour, but the vet wouldn't let us wait. I've no idea why they call it an anti-rearing device, because the first thing Sensi did when she felt the pressure in her mouth was to rear straight up. She tried to run through the tiny gap between the trailer and the fence, and nearly crushed me in the process.' Nicole rolled up her sleeve to show off an impressive bruise. 'She scratched her face, too. The vet was standing behind her with a whip. She didn't hit her really hard, but she did hit her. I've never seen Sensi like that, she was terrified. But also, because of the sedative, sort of far off, too. She kept rearing, and barging past me, and her mouth was all open and twisted. I didn't know what I was supposed to be doing with the Chiffney, and all I could think of was how she would blame me for it. Her mouth's cut and bruised and sore.'

Her leg, as it turned out, was absolutely fine.

I knew from the beginning that if I was to work with problem horses I would come across many bad loaders. But, despite having seen Monty and Kelly working with umpteen cases, and having done several at home under supervision from Nicole, I still was not fully prepared for my first real solo job in the summer of 1999. I had never worked alone, away from home, before.

The loader in question was a beautiful young 16.2 hands high chestnut mare called Cassie. As I took the details over the phone, she didn't sound too bad – the owner could eventually get her onto a lorry, but if anyone tried to put a trailer ramp up, she would fly out backwards. She sounded pretty easy so I decided to go alone. As I was doing join-up, I was told a very disturbing story about some partitions falling down and trapping her in the box and also a harrowing account of how she had been beaten into the trailer when the owner had bought her, not long before. 'Oh,' I said, a little daunted, 'so she's actually quite badly traumatised.'

'You don't need to tell me, I know!' the owner replied.

I resisted the urge to ask why she hadn't told me on the phone.

I didn't notice anything unusual until I was leaving the indoor school, having completed join-up and the usual halter training. As we passed through a wide door, Cassie flew through it at an incredible pace, barging me out of the way. I don't know why I hadn't picked this up on the way in, but she definitely had a problem with going through even quite a large gap. Worried that something was going to hurt her, she belted through as quickly as possible. Of course, this would only increase her chances of being hurt, making her more likely, for example, to bash her hip on the doorframe. It took over an hour, before she could stop and stand still in any part of the doorway, calmly enough not to rush. Eventually I got her to the point where I could reverse her through in both directions. It was a massive phobia for her, but the owner hadn't mentioned it, perhaps not thinking it was relevant to her loading problem. When I felt she had got over her phobia of the doorway, I phoned home.

'How's it going?' Nicole asked, a little anxiously.

'Great! We're doing really well. I'm about to take her to the horsebox now.'

There was a tactful silence at the other end of the line. I'd already been there for two and a half hours.

Having come so far already with such a major phobia, and having built a bond in the process, I was confident that the box would pose few problems, but when Cassie came round the corner and saw it she panicked. Unable to contain herself, she started trotting on the spot, literally shaking with fear. So I moved her away from it, and worked her on the halter again, asking her to move backwards and forwards many times, rewarding her for every effort, until she was calmer and more focused. Eventually I worked her round to the bottom of the ramp, where I spent even more time moving her around. By now, the wind was blowing briskly, and the doors flanking the entrance of the horsebox were flapping loudly against the sides of the ramp, in spite of our efforts to secure them with string. She was managing to cope, but the stress of the beating she anticipated was clearly visible in her eyes. As calmly as I could, I walked up to the ramp and stepped on it.

She snorted and backed away, while I held on to the lead rope for all I was worth. At first she lifted me up and pulled me towards her, but when I held on she came forward as I had taught her, so I immediately released the pressure. I was still asking too much, so I got off the ramp and asked her to keep backing up and coming forward some more. As the space opened up between her and the ramp, she became calmer and more concerned about having to respond to me and come forward off the pressure, than she was of the idea of loading. I asked her to go on the ramp again.

She couldn't have made a better effort, for she leaped up and put both front feet squarely on the ramp, and stood, heaving, obviously expecting that I would insist that she continue to come forward and finish the job. Instead, I loosened the halter, rubbed her forehead and then asked her to step back off again. We walked around for a moment to give her time to think about it. The next time I asked she came a lot further up the ramp. I rewarded her again by asking her to step back off, and you could practically see the cogs turning in her head.

The next time I approached, she did not hesitate and got all her feet on the ramp, so her head was in the doorway. I hesitated, unsure whether to ask her to come forward. If she pulled back and hit her head, protected by a poll guard as it was, she would frighten herself and confirm all her worst fears about me. Tentatively I put a tiny amount of tension on the line, then released it and moved to the side, making a big space for her to move into. She walked straight in. I felt a flood of relief, gratitude and joy as I stood and gently stroked her neck.

She could hardly believe it when I immediately asked her to unload again, instead of the ramp being slammed shut as quickly as possible. She gave me her all after that, and within minutes was following me in with no lead rope on her at all. She seemed extremely pleased with herself, proud of overcoming her trauma, and it felt as if her whole attitude towards humans had changed too, no longer based on distrust and resentment. Within an hour the owner could load her with ease, put the partitions up, with or without other horses, close up the ramp and turn on the engine. I had spent over three hours preparing her and it had taken no more than four minutes to get her in.

Loading jobs never seem to be as straightforward as you might expect, and I learn something new from every one. An interesting horse I trained was an extremely posh Andalusian, owned by the Duchess of Richmond and Gordon, who lives at Goodwood near the south coast. It was easy to find, since it was clearly marked on my road map, as well as at every junction for miles. But when I arrived, I began to regret not paying more attention to the directions she gave me for what to do after I reached the estate, for I promptly got lost somewhere between the golf course, the motor racing circuit, the enormous palace, the woods and several huge stable blocks. I eventually was sent about a mile up a road in the opposite direction, past another large stable yard, school and house, to a wonderful little mansion set in a picturesque rolling valley. This dip had saved the cedar trees in this area from the worst of the 1987 hurricane, which had destroyed 30,000 trees on the estate, and left many of the huge old cedars that dominate the grounds as shattered hulks, scarred by the loss of massive boughs and often with no tops left at all. I was filled with dread at the prospect of what a similar storm could do to Moor Wood. But it was still a magnificent setting and the Duchess, who was very friendly and asked me to call her Sue, had a horse to match. Wisps of creamy mane curled down his handsome face and neck, and he was in superb shape, gleaming with health.

When I went to do join-up in her round pen, though, I immediately noticed that he didn't think a great deal of humans. He kicked out several times to make sure I wasn't going to get too close, and was difficult to join-up with. After I got follow-up, he broke away several times, and he did a great line in pretending I wasn't there. I knew that the Duchess and her stable staff were very kind and took good care of him, but I had the feeling that whatever I managed to achieve that day, it might be a long time, if ever, before humans would appear to him as anything better than a necessary evil. The loading issue was only the most obvious manifestation of a deeper lack of trust. It was not as if he flinched or expected to be hit. But somehow, it seemed that perhaps his upbringing was not all it could have been. An example of this was his previous boxing experiences. The last time he'd been on a horsebox had been when he came to Goodwood from Leicester – a journey of eight hours. But he had been bred in Spain, and so it's quite likely that his introduction to loading was being hustled onto a vehicle and subjected to a journey of many hundreds of miles by road and ferry. In his experience, going up the ramp did not just involve trusting people sufficiently to go into a very confined space. It also meant travelling for between eight and up to about forty hours. Why would any horse, having been through that, ever consent to go in a box again? Why would any human expect not to have created a bad loader by the end of a journey like that?

I got him to load pretty easily but couldn't bear to take the risk that he might not follow me in without the lead rope. Even though the nearest open road was miles away, the estate was so huge we would have been searching for weeks if he'd gone AWOL, and this horse was probably worth more than my insurance company. We took him for some short drives, stopping to reload him a number of times, in the hope that he would gain confidence when his average journey time went down so dramatically.

I was exhausted but elated when I got back home and showed Nicole the cheque I had earned. I was particularly glad that it had been me who went, given the potential for disaster generated by Nicole's subsequent question: 'It says here the cheque's from the Duchess of Richmond and Gordon. Who's Gordon? Her husband? Doesn't he even have his own cheque book?'

I had met the Duke briefly in the corridor and been unable to think what I should call him, but at last I managed to stammer out, 'Are you Sue's husband?', which was probably not quite the appropriate etiquette but at least would not have disgraced me quite as much as asking him whether he was Gordon!

Funnily enough, although I have now succeeded in curing every other one of dozens of extremely bad loaders for other people, the last horse I could not load was our own Sensi. Looking back on it, it was probably a very good thing that I didn't, as it quite possibly saved her life.

This was about a year before I visited the Duchess, for I had just recently finished my ten-week course. It was about two months after Sensi had given birth to Karma, and Nicole had gone to Kent, with Julia, to do a riding clinic. Sensi decided to do her usual trick and protest against this great injustice by making the vet come and attend to yet another medical emergency.

Now Sensi is well known to most of the vets in North Gloucestershire, and every other part of the country she has ever lived in. Although she has a very strong constitution, heals miraculously quickly and has hardly had a single day's lameness in her whole life, she seems to have systematically worked her way through most of the veterinary textbooks. I can't understand how her insurance company remains financially solvent, and would like to take this opportunity to apologise to any members who might have found their premiums going up in recent years.

Just in the eleven months when she was pregnant with Karma, she had broken her nose by running through the metal gate in the middle of the night, had laminitis, and then cut a four-inch gash in a hind leg while climbing down the muck-heap in a midnight escape from the stable yard. This last injury, while not quite in the right place to cause permanent lameness, nevertheless meant spending the last three weeks of her pregnancy standing on three legs, which seriously compromised the straightness of her spine and pelvis, as well as badly damaging several ligaments, which were softening in preparation for the birth. But despite the seriousness of all these incidents, she was in a far worse condition when she went down with a severe colic that summer evening.

It was about 10 p.m. when I went out to the field to get Sensi and Karma and bring them in for the night. I soon knew something was wrong. Sensi was sweating and agitated, turning and nudging her flanks. I put her in the round pen and ran to get Sarah, for a second opinion. She quickly agreed with my diagnosis and went to call the vet.

Sensi had lain down in the sand of the round pen, panting. She would groan periodically and roll on her back, a glazed expression coming over her eyes. I stroked her face, trying to calm her as a sudden rush of panic gripped me. She was dying. The thought of what this would do to Nicole, whose own father had died just two weeks before, was almost unbearable. After what seemed an eternity, the vet arrived. He administered a strong painkiller and anti-spasmodic drug, but it didn't seem to work. Sarah told me I should stand back, for although I wanted so much to help, Sensi was now having convulsions. Her legs flailed wildly, her head writhed in the sand. The vet had called the nearest equine hospital capable of doing the major surgical procedure that was the only medical action that could be taken. The operating theatre was being prepared. It seemed a big gamble, being about forty minutes' drive away. The first thing we needed to do was to get her standing. When there was a lull in her exertions, I pulled her lead rope with insistent urgency while everyone pushed her on and, on the second effort, she made it to her feet. Sarah very kindly went and got Peter and their trailer.

It was not an ideal situation. It was very dark up by the round pen, being past midnight. There was one weak bulb at the front but other than that there was no light except the brake lights on the trailer, which was painted dark both inside and out. It could not have been much less inviting, and in addition to having Karma behind her, charging around the pen in a panic at seeing her mum being led away, Sensi was also heavily sedated. She breathed laboriously and swayed on her feet as I tried to get her moving backwards and forwards. But even a pressure halter was ineffective, due to the sedative, and Sensi remained inert. I could hardly get her moving when she was away from the trailer, and as soon as she resisted the pressure, locking her head and body against it with a stubborn determination that still glinted in her hazy, faraway eyes, I was unable to shift her no matter how hard I pulled.

I tried to load her until my arms felt like they were about to fall off. The others also tried. Having waited patiently for a considerable time, holding back from giving me advice, they must have been itching to have a go. But they soon found that nothing would shift her. She would go to the edge of the doorway but no further. We continued for over an hour, and then the vet and I suddenly were struck by the same thought. Our eyes met. 'Why are we bothering?' we said to each other. 'She doesn't have colic any more.'

Sensi had pulled it off again, in some style, keeping the four of us up half the night. She was fine. It seemed as though the struggle she had put up might have helped take her mind off the pain. Karma was even more relieved than I was, even though she was not aware that it would have meant weeks of us feeding her every few hours if Sensi hadn't made it.

In the end I never did teach Sensi to load. Instead I watched as my working pupil, a quiet strong man from Denmark called Brian Mortensen, did it for practice. She behaved exactly as one would expect, in fact she was not very hard at all, and within twenty minutes of him starting to work with her, she was loading without a lead rope, as if she had done so all her life. Even though I had cured many worse loaders by then, I was still surprised, like so many owners I have worked for. To see my own horse, such an established bad loader, whom I had never seen walk confidently up a ramp, going up inside my horsebox as if she had never done any differently, was simply unbelievable. I had a real insight into the feelings owners must often have when I work for them. It can be very hard to let go and accept that things have changed.

SIXTEEN

A noble visitor
(Nicole)

Joe didn't sound promising when his owner, Sally, described him on the phone. His grandfather had won the Grand National, which meant that from the moment he was conceived, Joe was in danger of being regarded primarily as a form of investment rather than a sentient being. Now retired, he was twelve years old, a 16.2 hand high thoroughbred with a major napping problem and a phobia of pigs. As he lived on a pig farm, this fear was a big problem, and his napping was so bad that he couldn't even be ridden the 100 yards or so to a neighbour's outdoor arena so his owner, Sally, could school him. 'He's had quite a long time off,' Sally said, 'while my broken leg's been recovering.'

It's never very comforting when owners refer to their broken limbs in connection with a horse. It reminds you what a risky business it all is. Of course, the difference between a nasty break and a few bruises can simply lie in the way you land. As they say, it's not the falling that's the problem, it's the hitting the ground at the end of it.

In this case, as it turned out, the owner had hit the ground having slipped while feeding her chickens!

Sally wanted to do the best for her horse. She'd had his back checked, a new saddle fitted, and his teeth done. She'd had riding lessons. Confident that his problems weren't physical, she'd 'tried everything' when riding him. By now I'd worked out what this was code for. 'So what does he do when you hit him?' I asked her, when we met.

'Oh, that makes him far worse. He gets angry, rears, swishes his tail. And when I tried riding him in spurs, he just bucked me straight off. I didn't try that again.'

I tried to stop myself from grinning. Horses put up with a lot, but they all have their limits. Joe clearly didn't consider having bits of metal stuck into his ribs acceptable.

I stepped back and had a good look at him. He was in some ways a very beautiful horse, but he had an air of despair about him. He had an extraordinarily long, fine, elegant face, but his body looked like it had been through the wringer a few times. There were deep hollows along his back where years of ill-fitting saddles had dug into his flesh. He had thirteen lines of white hair seared into his skin on both front legs, a legacy of line firing, which used to be common practice in the treatment of tendon injuries. Hot irons or a blistering agent are applied to the tendons, in the expectation that the inflammation this causes will help the tendon to heal, by building up scar tissue. Although applied under anaesthetic, the treatment results in the horse being unable to move without pain for a considerable time. This is believed by some to be the only benefit of firing, as it means the horse has to be on box rest, and cannot be worked for a long time, even by the most over-zealous trainer. Even so, box rest is now considered of dubious benefit for most injuries.

Not surprisingly, he hated vets. He could sniff one out at a hundred paces, and Sally's had become adept at long-range diagnosis as soon as he realised the perils of close inspection. Scars rippled his hindquarters where he'd been hit by a bus when he'd panicked while being long-lined, and had broken through a fence onto a road.

Overall, he had an 'upside down' look, where all the muscles along the top of his neck and back were virtually non-existent, and all the muscles on the underside of his body were bulging and tight from the effort of moving while resisting the discomfort of a rider on his back. No wonder he didn't want to go anywhere.

He shifted uncomfortably under my gaze, and I had the feeling that he knew he was in a mess, and that he knew it wasn't fair to have had that inflicted on him. A horse of natural grace and splendour, it was degrading for him to look such a wreck. If I've ever seen disappointment in a horse, I saw it in Joe; he'd given everything that had ever been asked of him, but it hadn't got him anywhere. Now he'd given up. He expected nothing of anyone, and it would be easier all round if no one expected anything of him.

When I placed his new saddle on his back to check its fit, he stamped his foot and swished his tail. As I gently did the girth up, he not so gently tried to take a chunk out of me.

'He's always like that,' Sally said.

It was easy to see why: his saddle was so narrow it was pinching his withers.

'I did wonder about that, but my master saddler said it was fine. But it didn't seem right that he should have such a violent reaction to it. I wondered if perhaps it was remembered pain?'

There's some logic in this; if a horse is caused pain by, say, an ill-fitting saddle, they can have a negative association with any saddle, however comfortable it is. The reaction can fade over time, but you can still see some of the anticipation or the memory of the discomfort. However, Joe's reaction was raw and current. He was telling Sally loudly and clearly that the saddle wasn't right. Like so many people in her position, she had trusted the 'experts' rather than herself and her horse. Most owners could work out what their horses are telling them if they allow themselves to listen.

It was particularly uncomfortable for him to be mounted, as the weight in the stirrup caused the saddle to dig into his back even more on the other side. He tried to communicate this by moving away from the mounting block unless he was held by someone on the ground. Once the rider was on board, he was gentlemanly enough not to try to dislodge them, but he was determined he wasn't going to go anywhere. I was not about to make him.

Joe came to Moor Wood for several weeks. Sensitive and intelligent, he went through the usual processes with a sort of disdainful good grace. Tarpaulin work was a little beneath him, and long-lining, after his horrific accident, clearly worried him, but introduced to it slowly, he overcame his fear. Sally and I led him up and down the steep Cotswold hills, and he gradually began to take an interest in his surroundings. His reluctance to go forward melted with the miles and soon we found our legs unable to match his enormous stride. Pennie Hooper, our massage therapist, began to smooth out the knots accumulated over years of tension, and he visibly softened. There was still a long way to go, but he was starting on the road to recovery.

'You know, this horse has hurdled,' Pennie said the first time she assessed him.

Pennie can look at a horse from 50 yards and the body will tell her the horse's story. Her fingers fill in the details. She's petite and slim, but her hands are like iron, and she's got muscles like Popeye. With a shock of cropped blond hair and an assortment of trendy jewellery, when she pulls into a stable yard in her sky blue Porsche, she hardly comes across as a typical horsewoman. The establishment accepts her, however, because of the incredible depth of her knowledge of horse anatomy and movement. Most of her clients are competition riders who use her skills to get the best performance from their horses. We use her with almost every remedial horse we have in, to gain as much insight into the horse's history and physical state as possible.

'Oh, no, I don't think so,' I told her confidently. 'He was a flat race horse.'

'Maybe so, but he's also definitely hurdled.'

Sally later confirmed what Pennie had known for certain. Joe had hurdled, but only for one season, several years ago. Because hurdling involves jumping at speed, the horse moves his forelimbs in a particular way, throwing them forward, as in a gallop stride, rather than tucking them under his chest, as in showjumping. This movement pattern is written in the muscles, and unless something is done to remove it, it stays there.

It's not that I think there's anything intrinsically wrong with hurdling. It's just that any horse needs well-fitting tack, a careful fitness regime, support and maintenance, and the more intense the activity, the more help their bodies need to be restored to their healthy state after such stressful activity. Some of what we ask horses to do, on the other hand, does compromise them unnecessarily. We once did a lecture-demo at a riding club, and Pennie came along to assess the horses for us. One horse we were asked to work with was notoriously aggressive. Pennie took one look at him and said, 'This horse is jumped with a tight martingale.'

This also turned out to be true. Unable to stretch his head and neck properly over fences, the horse was forced to use his body in a completely unnatural way. As a result, his muscles were like rock from head to toe. He was in constant pain. This horse, who greeted anyone he met with a flurry of teeth and hooves, stood quietly while Pennie eased his aching muscles, only shooting her the odd warning look when she went in deeper than he could bear.

Joe also told Pennie what he could cope with, and every time she saw him he was able to heal a little more.

With his body more comfortable, and a saddle that didn't pinch, Joe began to reconsider his views on being ridden out. The early rides involved a lot of standing still and going backwards, but within a week or so he would quite happily ride out on his own or in company. We used an item of equipment called a 'wip-wop'. This is just a piece of soft rope that you flick at the horse, touching him behind your leg on either side. Unlike a whip, it doesn't hurt at all, but it's an unpleasant, possibly annoying sensation, and also works in the horse's visual field; the sight of something moving swiftly behind their head will often encourage forward movement. The trick to using the wip-wop lies in the timing. As soon as the horse moves forward, you have to stop using it, and in this way they learn how to 'switch it off'. With Joe, however, there was an additional factor. If you used just slightly too strong an aid, it seemed to offend him, and he would point-blank refuse to move until he had recovered from his sense of wounded dignity. You had to ask him politely, not tell him what to do. I had some fantastic rides on him. His trot felt like he left you up in the air for minutes at a time, and in canter he seemed to cover 20 yards in one stride. The power coming up through him, even in his still far-from-perfect physical state, was breathtaking, and I longed for a race track to really let him loose on.

Sally successfully rode him at Moor Wood and also at home, but he was never really happy about the pigs, and she began to feel he wasn't the right horse for her. Julia, however, had fallen for this noble, damaged creature, from the very first moment she set eyes on him, and it was decided that she should loan him from Sally, and continue to bring him on.

Julia spent all her hard-earned money and spare time trying to restore Joe to the horse he should have been or, at the very least, to make him comfortable in his own body again. It was a difficult healing process for him, and he seemed to find it hard to let go, as if it was only his tension that was holding him together. Julia longed to gallop him, but wouldn't have minded if she never rode him again, so long as he was happy.

When Pennie wasn't available, he was worked on by a Shiatsu practitioner, a rather abrasive woman of the 'stand still and be healed!' variety. She once pinched Joe on the lips when he tried to bite her (having warned her several times that he was unhappy with what she was doing) and even slapped him on the rump when he didn't want to let her into the scarred part of his body that had been hit by a bus. I thought Julia was going to deck the woman, but she managed a restrained 'I'd appreciate it if you wouldn't hit my horse!'

Even so, Joe changed. He had a lot more energy and 'presence', and even began prancing around and showing off to the mares. His personality began to shine through, and he started to exhibit a real joie de vivre. Julia started riding him again, and they began to have fun together.

It was a cold, dark, windy night in February, and we had just finished for the day. Down in the field, Julia and Jo were checking our horses before the last light faded. I was looking forward to going inside for a cup of tea, when Jo came up from the field.

'Julia's having a bit of trouble with Joe. She can't get him to move. She's wondering if you could go down and have a look, and bring a headcollar.'

I hurried down to the field. In the gloom, I could make out Julia standing next to Joe, who was resting a hind leg near the fence. I felt something drop inside me as her frightened eyes met mine.

'I noticed he didn't come over for his hay when I put it out for them, and it looks as though he can't move. I think he might have been kicked.'

As soon as I saw the leg, I knew in my heart it was no good, but my head refused to believe it. It was puffy and swollen, and he wasn't putting any weight on it.

'Perhaps he's pulled a tendon,' I suggested hopefully. 'Let's get him inside, and then call the vet out.'

We tugged politely on the rope and he started to move forward obligingly. As soon as he tried to put that hind foot on the ground, however, it was clear that he simply couldn't.

'Or, on the other hand, let's leave him here and the vet can look at him in the field.'

As I raced up the track to the house to call the vet, I couldn't stop myself from crying, for I feared the worst. But I tried to be matter-of-fact as I told Danny and Adam about it, and when I called the vet I was able to speak quite calmly. By the time I got back down to the field to Julia, I was composed again.

'I think it's probably broken,' she said. 'Will you stay here with him while I go and get him some food while we wait for the vet?'

Alone with Joe, I put my arm around his neck, a gesture he would normally shrug off. He turned and nuzzled me.

'I don't think you're going to make it,' I told him.

He already knew.

Joe seemed pleased to be brought an impromptu feed and chewed calmly and thoughtfully. Not normally a demonstrative horse, he seemed glad of the company, and accepted having his neck stroked and his mane smoothed most graciously. When Danny arrived he acknowledged him with a 'how nice of you to come' sort of expression.

Adam arrived with the vet, Greg, shortly afterwards. By now it was dark, and he had to park in the gateway and shine his lights, full beam, into the field, where we stood with Joe and some of our horses, who were milling around, unaware of what was happening. A quiet man with a soft Australian accent, Greg introduced himself to Julia and said hello to Joe before walking around to have a look at his leg. He felt it gently, and then straightened up and looked at Julia.

'I'd like to sedate him so I can have a proper look and assess the damage. Is that all right?'

Julia nodded her assent, and Greg scrambled through the mud to his car to collect his equipment. Joe watched him leave and return with a calm interest.

Sedated, he showed no concern as Greg palpated his leg.

'I'm afraid it's no good. It's completely fractured, and not at all likely to be fixable. I don't think he'd ever be free from pain.'

Julia's eyes brimmed with tears, but her voice remained steady. One hand stroking Joe's neck, she looked Greg straight in the eyes.

'All right. Tell me what we do next then.'

As Greg talked her through the procedure, she listened intently, questioning him from time to time. Protective to the end, she wasn't going to let Joe suffer if she could possibly help it. Satisfied that he would die painlessly, she nodded. 'Just give us all a minute to say goodbye.'

I felt utterly helpless. Without the adrenaline that comes from being directly responsible in a situation, there was nothing holding me together. I couldn't believe what was happening. The thought of Joe's life being so abruptly terminated was almost unbearable. Worse was the grief and pain that Julia was feeling, and there was nothing I could do about it. Stepping forward to say goodbye, I knew I was in the presence of a great spirit.

As the drugs coursed through his veins, he looked surprised for a moment and then sank gently to the ground. Julia knelt beside him in the mud, stroking his long nose again and again. After a minute or two, Greg crouched down and gently pressed his stethoscope to his chest. He looked up and nodded. 'He's gone.'

We all felt a strange sense of gratitude to Greg, whom we had only just met. He had made a terrible situation bearable, and had treated Joe with so much care and respect. He said gently, 'He seemed a very noble horse. He died with true grace.'

Julia and I fetched a tarpaulin to protect Joe from the buzzards. We hung the lantern torch on the fence next to him. The warm glow made it seem a less desolate place for him to be lying as the frost began to crystallise on the grass around his body. He was finally free from all the pain he had carried around for so many years. Feeling numb, we walked back to the house.

Over a whisky, we all talked and remembered. There was a shared sense of having witnessed something truly remarkable, and we all felt honoured to have been part of it, to have shared Joe's last moments. Joy, gratitude and love mixed with grief, sadness, and loss.

The other horses in the field came over and investigated when we pulled the tarpaulin back the next morning, but Ben, a livery horse who came in at nights, was devastated when he found Joe lying in the field. He sniffed him all over and whinnied in distress, nudging him gently to try to get him up. He didn't leave his side, and when the transporter from the crematorium came to remove Joe, he was frantic, hovering around, getting in the way, trying to stop them taking his friend away. As the trailer containing Joe's body drove up the track, Ben's plaintive neighs were heartbreaking.

SEVENTEEN

Amber

(Adam)

'Yes, hello there,' said the voice on the telephone, 'I've bought a young horse, an Arab mare, for my daughter and she wants to, you know, break it in, I wondered if you had any advice.'

Breaking in a young horse. Advice.

For a moment I was so flummoxed I couldn't find a word to say. I couldn't think where to start. Finally I stammered, 'Yes. Don't let her do it, unless you don't like her very much.'

By now I had seen enough messed-up young horses to know that starting one is not something that most amateurs should be getting involved with. A young Arab mare, being a combination of notoriously difficult traits, was unlikely to be easy.

If I had known what was going to happen to her, I would have been as forceful as I could in my salesmanship, which would probably have scared my prospective client off in seconds. We seemed to hit it off, but there was a major stumbling block. The daughter was quite a good rider, she said, and she wanted to take part in the training as much as possible. In itself, that didn't seem a problem, but they lived in London. It would be very difficult for her daughter, a student called

Emily, to see and participate in much of the process, unless she stayed here, which was not ideal, especially as the horse, who was called Amber, had been moved recently. I offered to visit London, even for a few days at a time, training the two of them together, but this wasn't a great scenario either. It was a hard decision for my prospective client to make, so instead of trying to persuade her, I emphasised that I thought she should certainly get professional help, rather than letting her daughter do anything by herself, and sent her a letter outlining the various options we could offer, but heard no more.

I had all but forgotten about it when the phone rang a few months later, but I knew immediately from the tone of the lady's voice that things had not gone well with the training. The first time a saddle had been put on, it had not been done up tightly enough, and had slipped. Amber had got loose with it upside-down around her belly and had run around the school in a complete panic. The stirrups had banged around her feet, tripping her up, and she had become entangled in them. Eventually the saddle had ended up dropping down her body, and, after falling over, she managed to squirm, buck and kick until it came off. She was now extremely phobic about the saddle. I could hear a voice in the background, anxiously adding details to a disastrous picture. Amber had become unrideable, although the trainers had tried on many occasions. She had bucked everyone off, and they now thought she was incurable and should probably be shot. As I delved deeper, the story got worse. Although the yard was right on the edge of one of London's most scenic parks, Amber had been kept in a stable for twenty-three hours a day, as there was no pasture available, and her only time outside was half an hour in a patch of mud. Then she had been taken off to the school and trained – or tortured, as she must have seen it. We arranged for Amber to come and visit us. Emily, whose term was ending, would accompany her and stay for a few days while we assessed the situation and began work.

It was a warm day in early summer when they arrived. Nicole and Julia were off teaching on a course, which was perhaps why Jo and I were sitting outside in T-shirts, taking a break, delighted at no longer having to wear several layers and coats. A rented horsebox drew up, from which emerged a driver, and a slim girl in jeans and a huge polar coat with a fake fur hood. Her hair, long and barely controlled, was too blond and wispy for a horse to confuse it with hay, but this was about the only thing to indicate she might have anything to do with horses. Although I didn't think she could possibly be old enough to enter one, she looked more like she belonged in a nightclub than the Pony Club. It seemed she had just emerged from a state of hibernation, one not of sleep but late nights and urban energy, which had given her white skin an extra pallor, as if hardly ever exposed to the sun. We introduced ourselves to Emily, who looked otherwise as if she wouldn't have said a thing, then got the ramp down and let Amber out.

She had loaded and travelled reasonably well, but was obviously very tense, practically leaping down the ramp. A darker stain of sweat lay beneath her bright chestnut coat, and the tips of her ears, so inward-pointing as to look almost like crescents, darted in all directions as she took in her new surroundings, so different from those she had left. The constant hum of London's traffic and the endless stream of jets passing overhead had given way to the gentle shushing of the leaves in the trees and the acrobatic tumbling of swallows, recently returned from Africa. An appetising smell of wild garlic emanated from the woods, a welcome change from the polluted urban atmosphere. Getting away from the city had to be good for Amber, but it was obvious that she would need more than that to come right. Although she was well halter-broken, and never pulled on the rope, or did anything outrageous, I noticed immediately that she paid no attention to anyone, ignoring us, occasionally stepping through someone's space, quite subtly, more out of a lack of consideration than aggression, almost as if they weren't there. She tried to do it to me, and when she found I wouldn't let her, and pushed her back, she swished her tail in annoyance, and pulled the first of the many splendid ugly faces we were to get used to over the coming months.

As we took Amber up to the yard, Emily gave me a cheque for a thousand pounds – enough for almost two months' stay. This was more than most of our clients had ever paid, and I had hardly ever seen a cheque as big. In an attempt to break the ice, which backfired spectacularly, Jo and I quipped, 'Oh great, thanks, you can go home now.' Not the slightest hint of a smile showed in her face. The couple of days she was staying suddenly seemed a very long time.

Later that day, having unpacked enormous quantities of tack, rugs, ointments, remedies, feeds and supplements, and a crooked saddle, I showed Emily and Amber around, and took them up to the round pen. I had seen join-up make a difference so quickly to so many horses, I could not help hoping that she might be about to change her whole outlook, and allow me to wipe the slate clean. I led Amber around the pen for a while, letting her see the wood and valley dotted with grazing horses, while I explained to Emily about join-up. Amber's head was raised, and she snorted as she looked out, and began frantically to pop her lips open and shut in rapid spasms, in a grotesque impersonation of a goldfish. I had been explaining about how I would be looking for her to lick and chew, as she began to calm down and accept me. But this seemed uncontrollable, a nervous tick. She followed me well enough as I walked around, making sure not to put herself under any pressure from the rope, but steadfastly concentrating on anything else but me, and having trouble just staying in a walk. She began to empty her bowels, producing another little contribution for the muck heap about every minute for the rest of the session. I bustled about, giving her a rub, clearing up again, stroking her quietly, then leading her round, until eventually I let her loose and continued walking as if she should follow.

As soon as she realised she was loose, she ran off, as if I had made the most elementary mistake in the book, and rushed up and down the side of the pen, calling towards the field. Two horses were standing nearby, but they showed little sign of concern as Amber pranced along, desperate to find a way out. I let her keep running, and she charged around, heading vaguely towards where I was directing, yet somehow as if I wasn't in there with her at all.

This wasn't join-up, it was just a horse panicking. I soon started trying to invite her in, even though I had seen none of the signs I was looking for. Her lips never ceased to pop open and shut, but she held her jaws resolutely shut, eyes darting around, her head up as high as it could go. Only if I really blocked her strongly, or made a very sharp movement, could I get her to flick an ear at me for the briefest second before she made a last-minute change to her direction. She also kicked out a lot, mostly at the metal grill surrounding her, shooting off in a panic at the loud noise when she made contact. But she wasn't aggressive, and at first I couldn't put a finger on what she was doing. Only later did I realise that this was what she had learned as a way to cope with being trained. She was attempting to blank me out of her existence.

Eventually I managed to get her to look at me for a second, and I immediately turned away and retreated. She stopped, snorted loudly and the world seemed to stand still for a second, before she turned and ran off in the other direction. A few tries later and I got a lead rope on her, but she was so restless she couldn't keep her feet still. Her tail swished constantly – I felt sure she was using it on me deliberately, whipping me with it as I stroked her and picked up her feet. She pawed the ground, all the while making the popping motion with her mouth, holding her breath and then flying off, round me again and again, but without ever pulling against the rope.

After a while, she settled; at least, it wasn't getting any worse. I began walking her round the pen, trying to decide on a course of action. It seemed the saddle was a good place to start, but as soon as

Jo brought one in, I wasn't so sure. Amber swished her tail intensely, curled her nostrils and buried her ears into the back of her skull. She showed no sign of lashing out at us, but my favourite saddle wasn't so lucky. After her first swipe at it, Jo and I looked at each other, thinking the same thing. She went to get a cheap old one, which we never use for riding, but which nevertheless has its uses.

I had by now taught Amber to back up, faces or no faces. This was my main way of telling her I was unhappy with anything she did. But I tried not to take much action unless she did something really dangerous, for she had backed away from any direct assaults on me. I wanted to see how serious she was about her hatred for saddles.

It didn't take long to convince me she would happily rip every saddle in the world apart, given the chance. She bared her teeth and snatched a sharp bite at it, then ran around me again, trying to pretend it wasn't there. I hadn't failed to notice that, put in a stable, she would likewise try to tear that down, ferociously attacking the door, its frame, and even the old stone wall itself, until I eventually gave her an expendable bundle of sticks as an alternative. Strangely, she did not weave from side to side in frustration as so many over-stabled horses do; she simply wanted to destroy the thing that so tormented her, and was trying to do the same to the saddle. I didn't let her, but only because it would have set a very bad precedent, and one thing I was already sure of was that she needed a new saddle, which would not be cheap. Her viciousness didn't help me feel kindly towards her, but I couldn't blame her for wanting to take out her anger. When I went to move the saddle alongside her, she wheeled round me in some kind of a canter, desperate to escape.

It had been clear from the start that nobody was going to ride her that day, at the very least, so I decided not to press the matter. After all, we had several weeks to work with her. Next to the bridle and long-lines that we had rather optimistically brought up to the pen, Jo was sitting with Emily, putting a brave face on the prospects. I was glad for the encouragement even though I was beginning to realise that this was not going to be easy. Quite apart from her mental state, Amber's young body was tense from head to toe, her muscles tightly knotted in spasms. The top line of her neck felt like a steel rod. She was fixated with one hind leg, which bore a large, pink scar on the cannon bone. She frequently looked down at it, stamped it, or kicked out, paranoid that something would injure her leg again or get entangled round it. Nicole suspected foul play at some stage as Amber's behaviour was so similar to that of a horse which Kelly was training, who came to her after his leg had been tied up, in an unsuccessful attempt to subdue him and make him more compliant. There was no way of knowing what might have happened to Amber. But most of all, despite the major physical barriers that we would have to contend with, it was the scale of the mental barriers she had put in place, in an attempt to escape from the reality she had been subjected to, that really daunted me.

Eventually I managed to get some kind of follow-up, but it was still without any kind of acknowledgement that I existed. She went through the motions of following, as if she was just going there anyway and I happened to be in front of her, while she continued the mouth popping. I took her out of the pen, and we spent some time just letting her graze the thick, lush grass on the bank below Henry's cedar tree, and she gulped it down eagerly, but without a trace of gratitude.

I had arranged for Pennie Hooper to come down the next day, so at least we would have a good idea of what physical problems we were dealing with. Pennie arrived, full of smiles and the usual tales of ghastly London traffic, and after her customary strong coffee and hand-rolled ciggy, we proceeded to the yard and Jo brought Amber out for us.

In her own very special way, Pennie proceeded to give us her professional opinion about Amber's physical state. 'Shit!' she exclaimed, before remembering Emily was standing with us. 'Her brachiocephalus and trapezius, what kind of a saddle have they been using? And she seems to have spent the whole time holding her breath! God, I can't believe how tight these hamstrings are, they're like piano wire. She's in constant pain, all over ...' Pennie moved along Amber's body, her hands studying the muscles, hard as marble beneath the skin and hair. She started to work, amidst much tail-swishing and teeth-baring, but had to back off when she got to the loin area, as Amber started to lash out.

I had known as soon as I saw her that Amber was not in good physical condition, but I had not imagined that so much damage could be done to a horse in such a short time. Amber was young and had been perfectly healthy when I'd first heard of her three months before. But she was in a much worse condition than I had expected, and I felt I had been a bit dismissive of Emily's concerns the day before, in my efforts to keep her from becoming too despondent. I suddenly realised that a lot of her apparent coldness was down to a very sensible distrust of us, given that the last trainer had ruined her horse. It was perfectly natural for her to doubt that we would come up with a result, having made the same sorts of promises that he had spectacularly failed to make good. And it was plain that successfully training Amber to the point where she could be ridden by anyone, let alone enjoyed as a horse for Emily to hack around on, was now going to be a great deal less easy, if it would be possible at all.

'Adam, you mustn't do anything at all with her for at least a month, nothing the least bit strenuous. You can take her out for walks, and graze her in hand. Give her a gentle massage as often as you can, but be careful. She really is close to breaking point,' Pennie declared. Of all the horses she had looked at for us, she had never given such an extreme diagnosis.

Once she realised that we were not going to ignore her horse's needs and proceed without regard to her physical or psychological condition, Emily seemed to relax. So for the next two days of her stay, we took Amber out to see the estate and surrounding area. It was remarkable how good she was about some things, and how others sent her into an uncontrollable panic. She showed no sign of nervousness at being separated from the other horses, and was actually very relaxed for a young horse being led out around the village with its barking dogs, noisy children and light traffic. This confirmed my initial suspicions. Although she had huge problems, these had only been the result of the training she had been subjected to. In fact, she was a perfectly normal horse, or at least she had been. Her early education had been good – she was perfect about picking her feet up, for example, and to tie up to the wall.

About a week before Emily's visit, our new working pupil, Brian Mortensen, had arrived from Denmark. Partly due to his imperfect English, it had been difficult to break the ice with him, but I had been able to use the time-honoured tradition of asking him what his favourite band was. Expecting to have to grapple with the name of some Danish heavy rock outfit, I was surprised when he replied with the name of an English group, one of the top five biggest bands ever. Their songs are so well known that even my mother, whose rock credentials are nil, might be able to hum a few. Feeling buoyed by this success, when Brian and I gave Emily a lift that night to the pub where she was staying, I bought them a drink and tried the same thing on her. Unfortunately I had hardly heard of the pop stars she liked, so that line of conversation quickly dried up. But Emily was different in this environment, and much easier to talk to. Much like her horse, underneath a sceptical and spiky exterior lay a sensitive personality.

She was due to leave the next day, after lunch, and we were sitting outside in the sun, discussing the plan of action. We wanted to take Amber out for another walk, since it would be Emily's last chance to spend time with her for a while. She was due to go to Los Angeles for most of the rest of her summer holiday, with her family. I was somewhat anxious about this, as I was aware that if anything happened to

Amber while she was away, we would have to make all the decisions regarding veterinary treatment ourselves. In the event of a real emergency I did not want to have to make life-and-death decisions without consulting Emily and her mother. But, in spite of the fact that we seemed to be getting along much better, she was very reticent about giving me a contact number in the US. I couldn't imagine why, as every client I had previously worked for had given me a long list of phone numbers to enable me to contact them every step of the way when they went abroad. I thought it could only be that Emily didn't fully understand the desperate nature of the potential crises I might be calling her about, but I also didn't want her imagination to run wild over the possibilities. She had enough to worry about with Amber even if everything went as well as could be hoped for, without hearing details about all the potential nightmare scenarios of horse ownership. So the conversation went round in circles for a bit. I realised it was time to get going on our walk, as her father would be arriving to pick her up in only about an hour. So I explained to Jo that if we weren't back when he arrived, she should invite him in for a cup of tea and make him feel at home until we returned.

'He won't like that,' said Emily quickly, and an awkward silence fell.

'I could bring it out to the car for him,' Jo offered quickly, obviously remembering her gaffe about the man with no legs.

'No, it's not that,' Emily mumbled. 'He won't even get out of the car, he'll just want to pick me up and go.'

'Oh.' I looked at Jo and Brian, but they seemed to find this as unusual as I did. Again it seemed like there was nothing to say, but there aren't many situations in which I am genuinely lost for words (not that I can always be trusted to find the right ones). I mumbled that we wouldn't force him to drink tea, but it would be rude not to offer him one, having driven all the way from London. Again Emily said he wouldn't want to, leaving us all wondering what was wrong.

Just when I thought she was never going to fill us in on the reasons behind her father's mysterious aversion to hot drinks (and bearing in mind Nicole's conviction that a person who does not drink tea should never be trusted), she suddenly blurted out, 'You see, he's, like, a celebrity, and everyone always tries to get him to do things.'

It all began to make sense. But now, although my brain was telling me that I probably didn't want to know who he was, I was far too intrigued to let it go. 'What does he do?' I asked.

Emily hesitated, as if she was about to cross some sort of Rubicon. 'He's a musician,' She said. 'He plays bass for—' It was Brian's favourite group.

And so it was that I was able to give my working pupil a rare perk – his favourite bass player's autograph – and also, start to realise what made Emily tick. It was obvious at once that her father's fame, which he does not relish, had created a profound impact on her life. Her parents were exceptional by the standards of their peers in the upper echelons of rock's nobility, in terms of the stability provided by their long marriage. But it was also clear that, in spite of the fame and fortune, Emily had not necessarily had an enviable childhood.

There was, however, one real advantage to be had from all this. She did not have the financial constraints of most of our clients, who find themselves in the difficult position of having to make choices between spending money on treatments from people like Pennie, and other vitals such as a new saddle, after which there is usually very little left to pay for training. It was clear that helping Amber was going to take a long time, if it was feasible at all; but at least a lack of funds wasn't going to be the deciding factor.

It was one thing knowing that Emily's family had the money to pay for our services. But it was still going to be very difficult to find ways to work effectively. Her physical condition meant that we couldn't do the basic training that we normally would, teaching her to be saddled and then long-lined in the school and out on tracks and roads. That would have been the perfect way to gently strengthen her muscles, without the extra weight of a rider, while at the same time accustoming her to the sights and sounds of metropolitan Woodmancote. But it was absolutely out of the question to put a saddle on her, as she could go crazy and strain all her muscles again. I didn't realise at this stage that it would prove even more difficult to train her to be long-lined, than to be ridden.

So, for the first weeks, we did nothing but lead her out, taking her to find the best views and tastiest patches of clover, and groom and massage her. She was remarkably unspooky for a young horse, calming down very quickly if a pheasant came up nearby, flushed out by the dogs, and she was fine in moderate traffic. Pennie came back and Amber was noticeably less resistant to the excruciating treatment. Maybe our training methods were making her more manageable. Or maybe she was starting to realise we weren't trying to torture her.

Eventually Pennie gave us the go-ahead to begin working towards riding her. I took her up to the pen and tried another join-up. But, despite the considerable improvement in her physical condition, she was hardly any better mentally. As soon as she realised where we were headed, she began her goldfish impersonation, and you could almost see the adrenaline rise up in her. Immediately, she was back in survival mode, her attention everywhere but with me, her feet unable to cope with staying in a walk. It would have been unbearably frustrating for me, if I hadn't been aware that it was at least as frustrating for her. In spite of the fact that first join-up work had not made an impression, I was still hoping to see some good results. But she still seemed to panic altogether at being sent away, however gently, and then not to want to be with me, only going through the motions of following, without seeming to have any trust or confidence in me. For the first few sessions, it was a battle to keep her attention for more than a second or two. Even when I sent her away, she would just scoot around the pen or school, lips popping frantically, looking everywhere else but at me until I showed her the back of my shoulder. Then she would come directly in, still looking away, and stand next to me, but avoid being given a stroke on the head, pushing through my space as if I wasn't there. Every time she did it, I would go off in the other direction, and she would come round to me, like a barely-tamed barracuda.

In the next session, I tried long-lining her without tack, just using a headcollar, and found that having a line resting on her hocks was far too much for her. Her back end dropped nearly to the ground, like some great cat on springs, and then she bounded off before kicking out so ferociously that the line nearly left my hand, and flew forwards over her back as she pounded around me. No matter how carefully I did it, she could not tolerate the line going behind her. For a split-second she would catch her breath and freeze, and then she was in an unreachable state until well after I stopped. I could get her to stand still, stock still, but moving sent her into a frenzy as she fled the line on the back of her legs. She just couldn't cope with the idea, in spite of having a rug with straps that go around each back leg in much the same fashion as the long-line. And I knew that her body wasn't up to much more frantic running around. It just seemed so likely to end in disaster.

We were soon both in a sorry state, dripping with sweat and even more exhausted by the mental strain of it. Horses naturally react strongly to something they fear, but once they realise that no pain is involved, they'll usually overcome their anxiety, even if it takes a while. But the memory of the huge, ugly pink scar on her back leg seemed to live on in Amber's mind like a nightmare. She pounded that foot on the sand, her eyes rolling wildly above her mane as she glanced down at it in terror. This was not making it better, I told myself. Her mouth was almost in a spasm, and she stamped the ground and set off again, all by herself. Enough was enough. I reached out desperately, and grasped the end of her nose, as if I could somehow hold back her fear. She stood prone, holding her breath.

For a moment, it was like we were the only two beings on the face of the earth. I slowly relaxed my hand, and somehow got her back down. We walked for a long time, drying off the sweat.

Everything we asked her to do that she didn't like, she blamed us for with venom. After that day with the long-lines, she hated me for weeks. I could understand why she felt like that, but it made the prospect of making significant improvements seem remote. It even took some time to re-establish the small improvements we had started in the school. We went back to walking out around the farm, grooming and rubs.

At first it seemed as if, in her world, everything was in one of two categories: taken for granted, or utterly terrifying. Nothing much was in between. I was beginning to wonder whether there was any chance of anything in her 'terrifying' category ever being turned into 'accepted'. If there was any chance of her being ridden, by Emily instead of some rodeo cowboy, she would somehow have to get used to a saddle. Before that, she would have to accept the idea of working with a human.

So I had really high hopes that we might make progress if we worked with a tarpaulin. She was bound to find it quite worrying, but as she almost certainly would never have been asked to walk over one, she wouldn't have formed any negative associations. After I had just about accustomed her simply to being in the school, which was easier to do in body than in spirit, I set the blue tarpaulin out.

Without pausing for a moment she walked calmly over it. I could have screamed.

Unless I approached her with it aggressively, she found it only slightly disconcerting that I should want to shake it at her, more because it seemed such an odd thing for me to be doing than for any other reason. As long as I didn't do anything with the long rope, everything was fine. Back to square one.

It was around this time my ideas on driving horses with a single line began to change. I had never been a fan of lungeing, at least in the conventional sense. The idea seems to be that the person stands in the middle and asks the horse to go round in a circle. As anyone who has ever tried acting out the horse's role in this ritual will very soon realise, this is an extremely dull, repetitive task. Although it may exercise a horse's muscles, it certainly does not exercise his mind. It teaches him, in fact, that you want him to do 99 per cent of the work, while you twitter on and occasionally flick a whip. And even the muscular benefits of it are questionable, especially if devices like side reins are used inappropriately. I'd tried it with Sensi many years previously, in the fields in Milton Keynes when she was still fairly green. In spite of having lots of equipment, I was spectacularly unable to control her, at one point losing hold of the lunge line completely. It was easy enough to make her move, especially with the long whip, but making her move forwards was another matter. She had an expertly tuned ability to turn in towards me, and run back if I waved the stick. And when she finally did move forwards, it was all but impossible to get her to slow down, unless she decided to turn back in towards me again. All this meant I was quite ready to accept Monty's assertion that lungeing could be detrimental to horses, and much less useful than long-lining. But we were beginning to see how, in many situations, there could be great value in combining Monty's 'body language' techniques with a lunge line, when working in a bigger space than a round pen. There are clear similarities to how a horse behaves loose, and how he behaves on a single line if you do the right things.

So I considered trying something similar with Amber. She had already been at our place for several weeks. In the usual run of things, horses came and went, usually reformed almost out of recognition in less than a month. But with her, although we had put so much effort into getting her body to unwind a bit, and she was responding to Pennie's treatment, the improvement was painfully slow. It was not comforting to think that she had been here so long and we had hardly gained any ground.

So I got the rope out again. I decided to work mostly in the school, so she could move in a straight line more easily. When I gently asked her to move away on a 30-foot line the first time, it was just like the first join-up – she blasted off round me in a complete panic. I was expecting it, but it still shook me how manic she was, as she flew round, nearly falling over and kicking at the fence. It wasn't long before I started to remember the fact that lungeing has a particular weakness. It's a lot easier to get the horse to go forwards than it is to make it stop. In Amber's case this meant that whether or not I slowed down, she was on a schedule of her own, constantly evading the central issue, my existence. I tried another way – blocking her path so she was confronted by the fence. She panicked even more. Either she leaped forwards into the closing gap, almost falling over, or halted and turned, threatening to get herself tangled in the line. Putting her on a tighter circle just made me dizzy and put even more strain on her limbs. She could turn so tight that I could reach out and touch her shoulder, and she'd still be cantering, her legs at a 45-degree angle to the ground. I even tried making her speed up, then allowing her to slow down, but that nearly sent her out over the gate. Everything was either too subtle or far too much. There just didn't seem a way to reach her.

Finally, I tried something that I didn't really expect to work. I shook the line between us vigorously. She raised her head sharply, which slowed her down, and she looked down the line towards me, about to panic. I stopped in my tracks and she seemed to check herself. In a second she was off again. But it was a start, and I managed to build on it, until I could really get her attention when I needed it. This turned out to be probably the most useful trick I found to use with Amber. Big waves coming up the line right towards her eye were too much for her to ignore. Her natural inclination was to pull her head back away from the movement, which slowed her down. By stopping the movement of the rope instantly, eventually I got her really sensitive. Within about two weeks, a tiny jiggle on the rope was all I needed to get her to come down to a walk. It was the first and most important thing I taught her to do, for as she slowed down, she stopped panicking and began to come back to earth mentally, from where I could get through to her in other ways. Eventually I could get her to steer around the school quite accurately. It was an obvious improvement, and a viable substitute for long-lining.

Around this time Emily came up and attended a riding clinic. Although she had never done much groundwork with a horse before, she managed to get Amber to listen to her and go away calmly wherever she directed. Using a different horse, we soon got Emily a lot more stable in the saddle, and began to unpick a few major weaknesses, which previous instructors had taught her. Knees off, feet too far forward and too much weight in the stirrup through trying to push her heels down, Emily was already halfway to falling backwards and popping upwards before a horse even moved forward, and had no idea about how to 'bear down' (engage her abdominal muscles, while breathing steadily). Of course, she couldn't breathe deeply, or bear down, because she had been told to 'sit up', which had the effect of sticking her chest out and hollowing her back, as if she were doing ballet. Clearly, there was work to be done on Emily as well as Amber!

But Amber was a long way off being ridden. In the weeks we'd spent trying to loosen her muscles and connect with her mentally, we hadn't even looked at putting a saddle on her. Pennie came up again and we discussed her condition. After that first terrifying experience when the saddle had slipped, the trainer had girthed her up so tightly he had almost – perhaps actually – broken her ribs. But the damage was starting to heal. When Amber welcomed Pennie's massage and began to groom her back, showing where she wanted to be rubbed, we decided it was time to try to move on.

The first time I put a roller on her, she tried to climb out of her own skin. Her terror, her anger, was as bad as anything I have ever seen. I had taken advantage of the fact that she was blanking me out to just do it up as quickly as I could. When she realised what had happened, she threw herself around the pen, ten times worse than most horses with their first saddle. But she did not injure herself, and when she realised that the roller wasn't slipping around her belly like her first saddle had done, calmed down eventually.

But the next day it began almost the same. Now she knew what I was up to and squirmed about, trying to bite the roller, or me if I happened to be in the way. For about two weeks, she made improvements so slowly that I couldn't be sure they were real improvements. I was getting to the point where I dreaded training her, which was not something I had ever experienced before. Nicole took over for a while, and it was almost a relief to see that she had the same difficulties. Whether she got Amber to stand still, or put the roller on while she was cantering in that tight circle, it made no difference. Sometimes she would put the roller on and take it off twenty times in a session, other times she would put it on just once and reward Amber for her compliance by taking her out for a walk, but Amber's attitude hardly seemed to change. After a week, Nicole handed the job over to Brian. A week later, Jo took on the task.

By now, Amber would just about tolerate the roller, albeit with much tail swishing and grinding of teeth. It was time to introduce the saddle – my old one, of course – with a breast girth. By putting it on and off, again and again, I hoped that eventually she would be calm enough to think about what I was doing, and realise that it didn't actually hurt. We decided that it might help to limit her space.

One lovely afternoon, telling myself I really did have all the time in the world, I got her out of her field and took her up to her stable, where my tatty old synthetic saddle was waiting on the door. As I stroked her body all over, I told myself I was going to put on that saddle as many times as it took even if I set a new world record. Which I probably did. Every time she moved forward I made her move back, and if she started to trot on the spot, or paw the ground, kick, or bite, I made a sharp gesture with the rope. But the second she stopped, I instantly stopped my noisy movement, and after stroking her softly, I would go very gently back to work, lifting the girth up onto her belly and tightening and loosening it again and again.

After about one and a half hours, she was pretty good. The next day she got better. After the following session I began to work a bit in the school and found that if I was very tough, not letting her move her feet at all, she could cope with it. I wouldn't let her trot off without having to put up with the lunge line being shaken in her face, and finally, fighting every inch of the way, she reached the stage where it wasn't the end of the world.

At this time, we arranged for a saddle to be made for her. Kay Humphries, the only saddler we really trust, came out to take measurements. Her high standards have caused her to have numerous conflicts with manufacturers, and she's long been campaigning against the poorly designed, poorly made, poorly fitting saddles that cause so much pain for so many horses. Emily was in the fortunate position of being able to take her old saddle, which was badly twisted and very heavy, completely out of circulation instead of needing to sell it on, to damage another horse.

We still had to face the bit where the rider gets on. By now Jo and I were a pretty good team and we got better, going through each part of the procedure enough times to be sure that Amber would cope. To get her used to the sight of a person looming up above her, Jo jumped up and down next to Amber in what would have looked to an outsider like a variation on step aerobics. She immediately seemed to know what this was all about, but apart from trotting on the spot and pulling some spectacular faces, she accepted the process comparatively calmly. We walked around with Jo bellied over the saddle, many times, to get Amber used to the weight of a person on her back, letting her work out that the saddle no longer hurt her. In this position, Jo could easily bale out if anything went wrong. Amber tried to shoot off at first, and when I finally persuaded her to stand still, bunched herself up like a coiled spring, waiting to explode. It took several sessions before she would walk around calmly with Jo lying across her back, but when Jo finally went for it, and put her leg over, Amber was magnificent. Not only did it pass no more eventfully than it usually does with a starter, but the last thing I had most dreaded – having to tighten the girth once the rider was on – wasn't a problem at all, probably because it had never been done before. All my worst imaginings, of Jo being thrown backwards with her foot right up in the air while I fumbled with the straps, came to nothing.

Amber has turned out to be our longest-ever resident trainee, having lived with us since we met her in the summer of 2000. Despite a long series of niggling setbacks as she slowly regained her physical condition, she has come on so well, proving that with the right approach you can make progress with almost any horse. Turning her into a youngster who can be tacked up and ridden away with little more risk than any other horse is probably the most difficult, and certainly the longest work I have ever done. I say that not only because of the type of horse she is, the delicacy of her physical and psychological condition and the extreme depth of her phobias of the saddle, ropes, and being mounted and ridden. Most of all, it was because three of the most valuable training techniques I learned from Monty – release of pressure, join-up, and long-lining – had little impact. Amber already knew about pressure/release, and join-up did not have the usual effect on her – she responded, but only as if going through the motions. Long-lining her proved almost impossible. My research on spookbusting was pretty irrelevant, too. She really was never spooky. Her fears were grounded in her reality, not her imagination. The best thing I could take from

Monty's approach was his attitude – stay focused on the end result, and keep thinking of ideas until you get there.

Emily tells me she loves her pony more than anything else she owns, and although it isn't easy for her to get to Moor Wood, I'm sure Amber knows who her real owner is. I take them out for hacks around the countryside, and Emily spends hours just escorting her to the best grazing on the estate. Perhaps Amber understands something of what she's been through it all for. Or maybe Emily just gets to be the good parent and I'm the one who does all the disciplining. For sure, Amber likes her more than me. But I've never had a moment of greater satisfaction in my working life than the first time I gave Emily a leg-up, and she sat on her pony and just stood quietly in the closing gloom of a December afternoon, and did nothing else but breathe in a moment that seemed to last for ever.

EIGHTEEN

Flying high
(Nicole)

It's not unusual for us to fall in love with a horse we're training, often to the point that we get quite tearful when they leave. Sometimes one of us will fall more deeply for a horse than the other, and as a general rule, I prefer to work with nervous horses, whereas Adam seems to enjoy the challenge of big, bolshy horses who have no regard for one's personal space. Even horses like Amber, who at times was so frustrating and difficult to train that we had to take it in turns to avoid going mad, nevertheless very quickly found a place in our hearts. It's extremely rare, even when things are particularly difficult with a horse, that I find myself not liking them. In fact, I'm not sure I had ever really disliked a horse until High Flyer came on the scene.

Right from the start, I didn't like the sound of him. Adam had come across him, via another client, as a possible candidate for us to use for our first Open Day at Moor Wood. It was a typical scenario of an owner with a huge problem, but being the owner of a small stud, very limited finances. High Flyer was a bottle-reared yearling and had become almost impossible to handle. Adam went to see him to find out if he would make a good demo horse.

'So how was he?' I asked, when Adam got back.

'Oh, fine.'

'So what did you do with him?'

'I didn't touch him at all, didn't do any training. I wanted to see what his owner, Lynette, was doing. Apparently he is so pleased to see her, being alone in a field all the time, that he charges across and rears up in her face when she comes along. She seems really scared of him and practically offered to give him to me. He was near the gate when we came along, and didn't do much, but Lynette was practically shaking with nerves. At first, she just couldn't get him to take a single step in any direction. She put on his headcollar and held on to the rope just under his chin, stood by his shoulder and pushed his head as she told him to walk on, but he didn't budge. Didn't leap around or anything, just planted himself. Then she put a bridle on, and she could just about get him to move, but he was rearing up and striking out. It took ages to take him about fifty yards from the field, and even longer to get him back in. It was really hairy. At one point he practically tore her shirt off! I wanted to know if he could be sent away at all, so I went into the field and tried to move him away. He went off about fifty yards.'

'Oh, good.' Bottle-reared horses can be almost impossible to send away. Either they don't understand their own body language, or they resent being manoeuvred. Either way, it makes join-up an unsuitable process for many of them.

'Then I went passive. He stopped dead in his tracks, turned to face me, charged at me, reared, then wheeled away at the last minute, kicking out as he went. Only just missed me.'

'Ah.' I wasn't sure how Adam had reached the conclusion that High Flyer was 'fine' from this description, but quickly rearranged the allocation of horses on the Open Day so that Adam would be working with him. We decided to put this particular segment on at the end, so that if Adam were injured, I could take him to the hospital, if necessary.

It was our first summer in charge at Moor Wood and we were putting on our first Open Day, partly as a way of publicising ourselves, but also to raise money for the Brooke Hospital for Animals, a charity that does superb work in the developing world, providing veterinary care, water troughs and other facilities for working horses, mules and donkeys. Their owners often live in worse conditions than most horses do in this country, and not surprisingly, there is a great deal of ignorance as well as poverty to combat. As their publicity material was set up on display, it brought a few things into sharp focus. Although the potential is there – as Misty's tragic past shows – for an animal to be as badly treated in this country as any other, some of the cases the Brooke Hospital comes across are almost too horrific for words.

We worked with several horses to show join-up, spookbusting and other techniques, and Misty gave everyone who wanted one a hug. All the while I could hardly bear to watch when people approached High Flyer's stable, on which was posted a note advising that a distance should be kept, and that on no account should anyone go into the stable with him, no matter how friendly he seemed. The notice also mentioned that he was a Welsh cob, section D, for sale.

When it was High Flyer's turn last thing in the afternoon, I realised my precautions were not unreasonable. I don't think I've ever seen anything quite so dangerous as Lynette trying to take him from the stable to the pen, not even with all the bucking horses I've seen Monty and Kelly deal with. Those horses might be potential killers, but are generally quite safe so long as you don't try to ride them. But you literally couldn't do a thing with this High Flyer without being in mortal danger. Lynette had been trying to groom him in the yard, to smarten him up for his big day. He was getting increasingly het up, and whirling in circles. As a yearling, he was small, but strong enough to pull her around, and with his teeth, front legs and back legs all so close together, it was very hard for her to put herself in a safe place. He had clearly spent some time working on his repertoire. While snapping at Lynette, he would rear and strike out with his forelegs, and then a split-second later, curl his back end around and cow kick with his hind legs. He managed this while leaping and twisting almost continually, and rarely seemed to have more than one foot on the ground at a time. Lynette had a short lead rope on him, which she held tightly under his chin, and he kept pulling her off balance so that she was frequently in danger of getting right underneath his flying hooves. I'm not at all sure how helpful my 'they're ready for you in the pen, now' message was. As she tried to lead him towards the gate of the yard, he got even more frantic. It wasn't even clear that the circles they were spinning in were getting them any closer to the intended destination. At that moment, Adam appeared, armoured from top to toe with hat, body protector, long sleeves, gloves, chaps and steel toe-capped boots, in spite of the heat of the day.

The idea had been for Lynette to lead High Flyer to the pen so that people could see how difficult he was, and also that he had received no training at all from any of us. But it was clear that in doing so, Lynette would be risking serious injury. In the end, I took Finn, our Exmoor pony, to give him a lead, and Adam put High Flyer on a long rope, which he held at the end farthest from High Flyer's teeth and front legs. By now, the spectators were peering curiously around the corner, giving the odd gasp as High Flyer came a bit too close to one of the cars that lined the track to the pen. It was erratic progress, but thanks to the lead Finn gave, Adam got him there in one piece.

Once in the pen, High Flyer put on a display as impressive as the one in the yard. But he was frustrated when his usual bag of tricks didn't produce the normal results. Working with a longer rope, in the confined space of the round pen, Adam was able to stay out of the way of the thrashing hooves and snapping teeth, without having to worry about High Flyer actually getting away from him. Snaking the rope vigorously whenever his space was invaded, Adam could keep the yearling at bay, and only invite him closer on his own terms. By leading him from a distance, instead of by his shoulder, he was able to show that he wanted him to follow. And with careful application of pressure and release, soon he was getting the idea and began to lead and back up without all the tantrums. Once High Flyer had grasped the principle that Adam could control his movements with the rope attached, it was time to show him that the same principles held when he was loose.

Unlike many bottle-reared horses, High Flyer was actually relatively easy to send away. From time to time, he would swing his back end in and lash out at Adam, but it seemed more like a token protest than a well-aimed strike. When Adam invited him in, High Flyer was reticent, as if unsure about the new boundaries, and whether or not he was meant to approach. But by the end of the session, which in total had taken about forty minutes, the change in his attitude was quite extraordinary. He was no longer a piranha on legs, choosing instead to follow Adam around most courteously, as if that had always been his intention. The walk back down to the yard was spectacularly dull in contrast to the journey up. Following Adam politely, High Flyer walked calmly back down the path on a loose rope, without even trying to eat the grass.

High Flyer had certainly lived up to his name, and provided a fantastic finale to the end of a successful day. I was really pleased that Lynette had brought him along. But there was one niggling doubt at the back of my mind.

'When's he going home?' I asked Adam.

'Well …' he said shiftily, not looking me in the eye, 'she's hoping someone will want to buy him. Apparently a couple of people have expressed an interest. It would be good if he could stay here for a couple of weeks for a bit more training, and then he would be a lot safer in his new home.'

'Hmm. That's fine, but we're *not* keeping him. We don't need eight horses. Do we, Adam?' I said the last bit as emphatically as I could, more a statement than a question. It wasn't just that we already had seven horses, there was something about High Flyer that I just didn't like. It wasn't even particularly his behaviour, as I was confident he would soon be absolutely fine to handle. I couldn't put my finger on it. I just knew I'd rather he found somewhere else to live.

By this time, we had got quite used to people offering us horses. Probably the most unlikely candidate was a 17.2 hand high, eighteen-year-old thoroughbred, who needed remedial farriery every three weeks, couldn't live out, reared and bolted, was aggressive towards people and horses, and was prone to colic. Not exactly the ideal companion horse, which was how the lady on the phone was trying to promote him.

'I wouldn't want any money for him,' she hastened to add. 'It's just that I can't afford to keep a horse I can't ride, and this one is really dangerous.'

As a child, I would have been happy to take on anything, but as an adult I had learned to look a gift horse in the mouth. It didn't take long, working as professionals, to realise that however deserving each case might be, if we were to take them all on, we would be inundated with horses, without time to make much of a dent in their problems, only in our bank balance.

Apart from Karma, Free Be had been the latest addition to our herd, bought for just one pound with the intention of rehabilitating him and selling him on, or at the very least saving him from becoming dog food. I still can't imagine what made us think we'd be capable of selling a horse, let alone one with the traumatic history that Free Be had obviously experienced. So when I saw Adam falling for High Flyer, I knew I had to nip it in the bud.

Two years later, he's still here. Living out with our herd has brought out the best in him, and he seems to have discovered what being a horse is all about. The overhandling of his youth has been diluted by only receiving the most minimal handling since. Adam somehow managed to convince me that he would be a good prospect for selling on. The fact that we were paid £300 to take him helped sway the decision, although inevitably he has cost far more than that to keep. Now, of course, Adam's decided he might be a useful character to have around, and has visions of him being helpful on riding clinics. I have a strange suspicion he might be with us for a long time yet.

Just as we tend to become extremely fond of the horses we train, so too with the owners. Overwhelmingly, they have their horse's best interests at heart. Of course, it can be quite exasperating to receive a phone call at half past ten at night to check that 'little Jimmy' has settled in all right, but we understand the sentiment. It is dreadfully difficult to entrust the care of your horse to someone else, and I'm not at all sure how I'd feel about sending my horse away. The difficulty is compounded by the fact that everyone has such different views on how horses should be kept, and I'm sure this is a big part of the reason for the tense atmosphere of so many livery yards. One person will be tut-tutting at the poor horse stuck in his stable all the time, while the other will be tsking at the poor horse stuck out in the field in the rain. And each will feel that what they are doing is the best for the horse, and that the other practice is tantamount to cruelty or neglect. At the very first hint of disapproval, war is declared, and grudges are borne for ever. I've never heard anyone say, 'Oh yes, you're right, I am very slack with my horse care. I'll do it more like you in the future. Thanks for that.' It just doesn't happen.

Which is why we're often amazed at the open-mindedness of our clients when we (tactfully) inform them that certain aspects of their horse's care – the saddle, their riding, the feeding regime, the home environment, or their handling of the horse, for example – has actually been part of the problem, or even the entire cause of it. It's quite a leap for the owner to realise that to become part of the solution, something major has got to change.

We had become so used to dealing with people whose main

concern was for their horse's comfort and well-being, that when we came across someone who didn't think like that, it took us a long time to recognise the situation for what it was. One owner we dealt with gave us a horse to look after whose feet were in a terrible state, and whose mouth was black with ulcers and laceration. They seemed uninterested in the horse's well-being, merely wanting her to be trained. When we explained that we could do very little until we'd sorted her health out, the owner took her away. We didn't mind losing the business, but were just concerned for the horse's welfare.

I don't think we realised quite how different the life we had chosen to live was, until our friend Dan came up to visit. He'd been in the same college at university, and had played with Adam first in a duo called The Gypsy and Van Gogh (Dan was the Gypsy, Adam was Van Gogh), and then in another band called Industrial Accident.

When Dan came to visit us that autumn, he had been working in London for several years as a very successful computer programmer, variously self-employed as the owner of a limited company, and also doing contract work for larger clients. He loved driving on 'proper' roads, and had been meaning to come out and see us for ages, but it had been about three years before his executive lifestyle and our lack of available weekends had allowed a time to visit. As it was, we didn't think it was a particularly suitable time of year to come.

'Bring lots of warm clothes,' Adam suggested, 'and a waterproof jacket. Oh, and don't forget your wellies.'

But when Dan climbed out of his low-slung, turbo-charged, super sexy sports car, and pulled off his trendy sunglasses, he took a small hold-all out of the tiny space at the back of his car that masqueraded as a boot.

'I've brought all the warm clothes I own,' he said. This turned out to be one thick woollen grey jumper. 'I didn't bring my wellies, because I don't own a pair. This jacket is quite waterproof, though.'

We looked at it doubtfully. It was made of suede, with hippy tassles hanging off the arms like a horse's fly fringe. I could only imagine what short work High Flyer would make of it.

'What will you do about the mud?' we asked incredulously.

'Mud?' he replied. 'Why would I be near mud?' which prompted a sarcastic retort from us about earth, rain, and the general lack of concrete that more or less defines the countryside.

Nevertheless, he gave us each a big grin, and a hug, and we went into the house.

'Don't you have central heating, then?' he asked, almost managing to make the question sound merely conversational.

'Yes, it's on,' I assured him.

'Are you sure you've switched it to "heat" and not "air-conditioning"?' he asked.

'I know I only did one year of Engineering,' I replied, 'but I do remember a little about Thermodynamics. Heat would be the red bit on a thermostat, wouldn't it? Yes, the sensation you're experiencing is technically known as "a draught". It comes through the walls. This sitting room used to be a tack room. Still damp air encourages mould on leather, so they went for moving damp air instead.'

Dan looked around the walls, where the marks from the saddle and bridle racks were still visible. 'But isn't it rather chilly for a living room?'

'Not if you huddle against the radiator,' I demonstrated, 'with a duvet wrapped around your body. It's surprisingly toasty then. Anyway, don't worry, this is the only really cold room in the house.'

The next day we decided to go out for a walk, having asked permission from Henry to ramble through Moor Wood. In spite of Dan's irritated objections, we clucked around him like mother hens, making sure he would be adequately equipped for this unfamiliar situation, and not weighed down unnecessarily. In the clothing department he was woefully under-prepared, but on the technical gadgetry front he was well equipped, with his mobile phone. We laughed and asked if he was planning also to take a global positioning satellite receiver.

'I thought you were meant to be escaping to the country,' Adam said.

'Yes,' Dan replied, 'but you never know when you might need a phone. I can always ignore the call if I choose to. But the whole point of a phone being mobile, is that you bring it places with you.' He looked pointedly at our own mobile phone, where it was resting incongruously in the fruit bowl, switched off and covered in dust, patiently holding at least one message sent from Dan asking for more detailed directions on how to reach us.

'I suppose,' I said, not entirely contrite.

We had been sploshing merrily through the mud, Dan in a pair of borrowed boots, and were near the end of our walk, when we heard the bell. It was a familiar sound, but incongruous, and it took us a moment or two to realise what it was. It was the same sort of bell that Henry had on his hawk, clasped around its feet, but it was coming from a bird high up in a tree. It wasn't Henry's falcon though, and looked like a 'tame' buzzard that had escaped. We had no way of knowing whom it might belong to.

'Why don't you phone your landlord?' suggested Dan, grinning. 'He would know, wouldn't he?' And he held out his state-of-the-art mobile impishly.

'I doubt there'll be any reception just here,' Adam started to say, and then realised that the signal was clear and strong. Even there, in the middle of a wood that has stood since before the Domesday Book was written, out of sight of any dwelling and out of earshot from any road, we were still within the clutch of the modern world. Invisible and inaudible, the microwaves buzzed through the air around us as Adam sheepishly made the call.

Henry arrived a few minutes later, with a dead pheasant to use as bait, but the recently liberated bird wasn't hungry. That meant she was probably doing a good job supporting herself. 'She escaped from

Mrs Such-and-such last week,' Henry explained. 'But she doesn't look like she's lost much weight. That's it, now. If she's learned to hunt, she'll never come back. Which is a shame, because she's an American buzzard, and they're bigger than European ones. She'll probably contaminate the gene pool, but what can you do?'

Despite our failure to retrieve this retrograde raptor, Dan spent most of the rest of his stay revelling in the glory of his technological success in what he insisted must have been the most exciting incident to occur in Woodmancote since, well, the Domesday Book. This was, of course, a gross exaggeration, and it was to be eclipsed by an event that took place almost the next week.

This was the date set for us to negotiate a new lease with Henry. It was now a year since Sarah and Peter had left, so the remnants of their lease were now at an end, and we were dreading the expected increase, even though we felt sure Henry would be reasonable. But the rent had not, after all, gone up for five years.

The day we were due to see Henry, we found ourselves running late. We had several horses in for training, but had left the most difficult to last. This horse, Basil, had a mounting and bucking problem, caused by a brand new saddle that had a nail sticking out of it, which had damaged his back. By about 5.30 p.m. we were only just ready to work him in the round pen, leaving just half an hour before our appointment. By this stage, he had come on a long way. He had been ridden successfully several times by Jo, Adam and myself. Although he had shown definite signs of nerves, he seemed to have come through the worst of his fears.

Part of what had worked so well was the pace at which we had taken the work. It was clear that he had a severe phobia of being mounted from the ground, but after practising a lot with leg-ups and bellying over, we were able to introduce the idea to him gradually, and prevent him from blowing up. By the time I actually got on him properly for the first time, with Adam carefully leading him from the ground, he was able to cope with the idea, but it took all my effort, stabilising my body as much as possible, to keep him from setting off into the trot which I felt could so easily turn into a series of bucks. When I did trot him for the first time, it was as much as I could do to contain his anxiety, but gradually he calmed down and coped well with the process.

That evening, Adam mounted up, and Basil stood still, just as he had done for many times in a row, while I stroked his head. It was a still, balmy evening in late summer, and with not a breath of wind, there seemed no reason to suspect anything could possibly happen. After a couple of circuits being led around, Adam asked me to take off the lead rope, and he walked around again once or twice and then gently pushed Basil into a trot.

He had just come down from about his third rise when Basil simply erupted in about the worst fit of bucking I have ever seen. There was no chance that Adam, or almost any other rider, could have stayed on even if he had been expecting it and within a second he was flying through the air over Basil's shoulder, landing like a sack on his face.

Basil did not stop. His head so close to the ground that his nose was almost thrusting into the sand, he threw his entire body into the next buck and then let out the most anguished sound I have ever heard a horse make. Less shrill than a horse's neigh, it sounded more like a pig being stuck by a knife, a desperate, terrified scream of fear. He belted past me around the pen towards where Adam was lifting his body out of the sand, bucking wildly all the way.

I don't think there are many people around who are better at stopping a charging horse than Adam. I saw him turn towards Basil and prepare to block him. Shoulders square, eyes on eyes, raising his hands into the air, he took a confident step forwards, before leaping smartly out of the way as Basil galloped past like an express train ready to blast its way through anything.

After he had careered round the pen several more times, still in a blind panic, we managed to slow Basil down and eventually stop him. He was dark with sweat, which showed in lines of white froth around his tack and the folds of his skin, as he shuddered with the effort to breathe. Adam was shaking too, more from adrenaline than from exertion. He was all right, but it would have been very unpleasant indeed if he hadn't been so quick to throw himself out of the way. There was no question of getting back on Basil that evening, and it took quite some time just to cool him off sufficiently to put him back in his stable.

Not that we had planned it, but there was a bright side to all of this. Adam was still in a virtual state of shock by the time we got round to Henry's for our rent meeting. We had a pretty good excuse for being late, we felt, and it probably didn't do our cause any harm to attract sympathy from our landlord at this precise moment. As Henry fixed him a strong whisky, Adam described what had happened, before proceeding to slip into a dazed state, unable to participate very coherently in the discussion as the shock wore off and the whisky wore on.

Even with occasional little incidents like that, it seemed from the moment we first saw Moor Wood that we were meant to be here, belonged here. From the beginning, when I saw the ad in *Horse and Hound*, the first time we came down the driveway, or maybe even the day I went out for that bike ride and met Sensi, how could so many coincidences and chances have occurred without being scripted? Without Sensi, without Adam's chance comment, we would never have got involved with horses; instead we would almost certainly have been sucked into the rat race and moved to London to find work like most of our friends. Having a horse meant we couldn't stay in a city, and, all the time, Moor Wood was waiting, a destination where we could fulfil our lives in so many ways. Even Leslie, who drove us out of his yard, and Sarah and Peter, who left Moor Wood so suddenly, made it all possible.

But our landlord need not have seen it like that, and a great many would not have had the foresight and generosity to freeze the rent for yet another year, to enable us to establish ourselves more solidly, maybe even start to make a little money, hopefully without falling off too many horses in the meantime.

NINETEEN

Back to the sky
(Adam)

Clients come to Moor Wood in a variety of ways. We met Liz, a student who had started recently at university in London, because her cousin came to live in the village and walked down past the stables one day in January. There was an instant connection and it transpired that Liz was looking for a place to keep her two horses. Sky, an ex-race-horse, and her retired childhood pony, a venerable-looking arthritic Dartmoor pony called Koala Bear, moved in a few days later.

At first I thought Sky was going to be just another ex-racehorse. Indomitable, proud, majestic but vulnerable, with the kind of eye that tells you so much in an instant. By now, I was getting to see patterns in flesh, and even before I looked for it I was resigned to seeing the usual. The drawn muscles, tight all down the neck, that familiar dip behind the withers, and damaged legs all stood out as testimony to years of use. Not what most people would call abuse, I guess, just too much use, and from a very early age, which amounts to the same to me. Put it this way: if punters were given a sufficiently comprehensive history and veterinary analysis, and were sober enough, I don't think many would feel happy that a horse running for them had ended up like this. Sky looked incredibly like Joe, being a 16 hand high bay thoroughbred, but he was not in as bad a state. He hadn't met too closely with any buses, and his tendons hadn't been fired. And he had landed on his feet, so to speak, because he couldn't have asked for a more wonderful owner than Liz.

They settled so quickly, it soon felt like Sky and Koala had always belonged here. And not only them, but their entourage of admirers. There was Liz's cousin and her kids (often accompanied by friends), and three other friends of Liz who came to ride, working in shifts to keep Sky exercised. The problem was, riding wasn't exactly the kind of exercise we felt he needed at the time.

I am sure many people who keep horses will have stories like ours about nightmare livery yard managers. But most never make the transition to becoming yard managers themselves. It isn't easy. Your most natural instinct is to want to butt in. You have responsibilities for the animals that you look after, but it can be hard to find limits. Some things are massive welfare issues; for instance, where a horse is so sore from a piece of tack, or foot imbalance, that you have to recommend the saddle is fixed or a different farrier. But where to draw the line? Sometimes one's sense of responsibility gets totally out of control. I used to be able to see someone ride past on a horse, and just enjoy the sight in a perfectly normal way. Now I have to stop myself assessing the rider's shoulder-hip-heel line, and checking to see if the horse looks comfortable.

Unsolicited advice is not easy to give, but Nicole, Jo and I didn't really think it was wise for anyone to be riding Sky. He needed help from Pennie, to free up his neck muscles, a lot of quality groundwork to build up his hindquarters, and his saddle badly needed to see Kay. His teeth (and Koala's) were sorted out first. It wasn't as if there was any resistance from Liz, or her financiers, who were very supportive, but at first, we kept quiet about a few of the other things.

It wasn't long, though, before Pennie and Kay had seen Sky and he was on a completely different work programme. We weren't surprised that all his team just wanted the best for him, but the dedication they showed was fantastic, as they adjusted to not riding him. Within a couple of weeks, all four of his riders had taken lessons and learned to long-line him, and regularly did so around the school and out on tracks, and this work, combined with massage, began getting him to stretch long and loose, and to rebuild his outline. By the end of winter all the work was beginning to pay off. We were looking at a different horse, and everyone was looking forward to riding him in the summer, especially me, as I had never sat on him.

All the same, I remember the first few sessions I did with him, and they were some of the hardest I had ever done. For all the sweetness of his character and beauty of his appearance, he was one of the most cynical horses I've ever met. He would tempt me into letting him join-up with me, then just wander off or trot over to where he could see his buddies again. It took four sessions before I got to the point where I could just take him up to the school and he would follow me straight away without testing what I was all about. It was as if he could see through every bit of my motivation and took liberties whenever he could, especially if I was only going through the motions. The work he made me do to get his trust was good for my attitude, too.

But in the fourth session, something changed. He seemed to understand me, in a very conscious way, as if he was taking the time to reconsider whether we humans could actually be helpful to him, instead of simply getting something out of him. Most of the time, a superficial willingness would suffice as he went through the motions of being owned. In spite of the adulation he received from his devoted little group of carers, he had somehow not seen sufficient evidence that they would be all that much better than the rest of mankind.

This reappraisal of humanity seemed to happen on such a deep level for him. He became so willing to work, so grateful for massage, so easy to handle. The team and I moved on in his long-lining, taking off the saddle so that nothing would block his muscles. I taught them various different types of groundwork, trying to be inventive with single lines, using trotting poles and other tricks to best enhance his recovery. He never seemed to lack enthusiasm for anything, and we began to see just what he could have been.

Sky gave me a session that was the closest to perfection that I have ever achieved in groundwork. It happened one evening in early spring, and I must confess that working him was a bit of an after-thought at the end of a long day. He had come in for the night but there was still a bit of light. I was only working him once a week, as his fans were around so much, which suited me well enough. But I guess, in spite of having a variety of activities, we were lagging behind in our training. So that evening, when I led him up into the school, I guess he had a right to feel that this would just be more of the same. I got such a strong feeling that this was what he was thinking as I closed the gate behind me, that I stopped for a second and listened.

I stood for a moment and then hung my long-lines on the fence, feeling sheepish. He was only wearing a headcollar, and it wasn't as if it would have caused him any pain, he just seemed resigned to the fact that he would be working under the control of the lines, even though he was perfectly happy to work without them.

I stroked his head and ears and lifted his legs in turn, giving them a loosening stretch in each direction. Then I rubbed him to stimulate blood flow to his saddle-damaged area, the dips behind his withers where years of ill-fitting saddles had taken their toll. I walked off across the school and he came along by my shoulder. His steps beside me were alert and purposeful, and he seemed perfectly content a moment later when I turned and asked him, as politely as I could, to move away at a walk.

There he was, totally loose in the school, and yet as I danced around with him, he did absolutely every move I asked for, without hesitation, and flawlessly. Rein changes, figures of eight, tight serpentines, circles and straight lines, extending the trot as soon as I moved up a gear, slowing to a walk or approaching me and halting, he did exactly as I indicated. Of course, after a while, I started getting a bit breathless, but he was still up for more, so I let him finish his workout, directing him without moving so much. We finished by just walking around the school together. The whole time, we'd hardly put a foot wrong. It was like a form of dressage, and I felt I'd experienced a dance of perfect understanding and co-operation between man and horse. I was filled with a sense of wonder at what he had just shown me. Finally, Sky was almost free of pain, and showing me his love of movement. Movement for the sake of more than just freedom to move. Movement for the sake of expressing beauty. I'll never forget it.

Three days later I had an appointment, to see a woman called Emma who had a young horse she couldn't control. It was a lovely bright day in late April, and Nicole was off teaching with Kelly, and so was using the car. I had arranged with Jo for her to give me a lift to the appointment, and then Emma would bring me back afterwards.

Jo greeted me as I came out the door with so much less than her usual bubbly smile that I could see she was ill and wouldn't make it through the day, and probably shouldn't have even come in. But she had known I was relying on her for the lift. It was a bad coincidence that our working pupil at the time happened to be on that week's course, so she had gone in to Witney with Nicole. The horses were out for the day and Jo promised to clean the boxes ready for them to come in, but instead I told her that I would help her finish the yard before we left, so she could go home and rest. This would mean the fort would be unmanned for some time, which is something we hate to do, but on occasions it just can't be avoided. Anyway, I should be back well before coming-in time, so I could bring all the horses back in from the fields.

The horse I saw that day, a beautiful black mare called Poppy, was indeed a real handful. Young, barely halter-trained and completely lacking in confidence, she was practically impossible to lead, and Emma, who had several children, was in real danger of being seriously injured any time she handled her.

It was a tricky job, but by the end of the afternoon, Emma could safely lead and handle her horse, and it was clear the basis of their relationship had changed dramatically. But I had arrived late and we had gone on longer than expected, so we would have to pick up her kids from school and take them up to Cirencester with us when she took me home.

Strangely enough, given that I was in a car surrounded by kids, I rather enjoyed the journey. Not only because Emma's company was so pleasant, but her children were actually polite enough not to interrupt immediately if they had something to say. Which is why it was such a surprise when her little son Alfie suddenly announced loudly, with a ghastly edge of panic in his voice, 'I don't want to die! Why do we have to die!'

I looked at Emma across the car, utterly at a loss for words, and stole a glance back at Alfie. He was close to tears. His elder brother tried to say something reassuring, but all he could manage was, 'But we *all* have to die,' and he started to give examples, listing various famous people like the Queen and the Pope, and the trees and birds running past their window. This failed to lift Alfie's spirits.

I tried. 'Well, you know, Alfie, if nobody died then we'd have to make sure no one was ever born, because otherwise we would fill up all the world and destroy it even faster than we are anyway. So that would mean you wouldn't have any brothers and sisters and you wouldn't even be alive yourself, your mum and dad would just be getting older and older and never dying. Things could never change. Look out the window and see how all the life is just coming back to the world after the cold winter. All you see are the dead stems from last year's plants, but in the soil new seeds are just starting to come to life. And they'll grow and flower and be beautiful, but then they'll die too, and the whole cycle will start again. Everything passes, everything has to change. You just have to try to make the most of your time, because the moments that pass will never come back again.'

'But I don't want to die!'

In the end, I had to agree with him.

We drove quietly the last few miles past Cirencester and up into the heart of the Cotswolds, but as we came through the gates and down the driveway, the kids began to babble excitedly as they saw Moor Wood. The sun was going down and it was getting gloomy, as the huge silhouettes of the cedar and giant sequoias loomed impressively out of the valley, strewn with horses grazing quietly. When we got out of the car, of course the kids wanted to see the stream and the lines of rambler roses, and I took them to prove how you can punch the sequoia trees without hurting your hand, as the bark is so squishy. Finally they left, promising to come back at the next Open Day.

As I set off across the field, a half-drizzle was descending while the light slowly faded, and I lowered my face to the wind. At times like this, when it's getting dark and you're alone and dog tired from a hard day's whispering, and there are still several long journeys up and down to the field to fetch the horses in, even being the luckiest guy in the world doesn't feel like quite such a bed of roses.

The first thing that made me realise there was a problem was that the fence was down. The electric tape was broken in several places, and I could see there were no longer any effective boundaries between several fields, but everything looked somehow all right. There was a grey horse and a bay shape in the area above me and another grey shape as expected in Amber's field. She looked fine, as she stood grazing with her boyfriend Sky near the stream. But in the next bit of field it was clear there had been a stampede. The fields, naturally, had been rolled just a day or two previously, and they had resembled a golf course. Now there was a trail of ruts and destruction where a group of horses had galloped down the hill. I went and found all of them and checked them over, before going and seeing Misty, Sensi and the rest of my lot in the back field. Miraculously, everyone seemed intact, and I gathered up the first two to take back to the yard.

It was only when I reached the gate that I noticed Sky was standing oddly. He hadn't moved from where he had been several minutes before. He met my gaze and then looked deliberately down at his foreleg. I unclipped my two horses and went to look closer, an uneasy feeling creeping up my stomach as I noticed that the grey horse that was in with him and Amber wasn't the right grey.

It wasn't until I got round on the other side of him that I could see the hole in his leg. It was only about half an inch across, but it was clearly serious. A thick dark rope of blood oozed out. Somehow I managed not to recoil, but touched his neck softly and quietly asked him, 'What's happened, old boy?'

He looked down very carefully at his leg again, and as he moved a huge spurt of blood erupted from the wound, and he smarted from the pain. My heart plunged and I got back to the house as fast as I could, turning and talking to him as I went, in a desperate effort to reassure him that I wasn't just abandoning him.

I was on the phone to the vet when Nicole arrived back from work. Her bewilderment at the fact that the horses had obviously not been brought in yet, although it was by now almost dark, soon turned to horror when I told her Sky was injured. Gathering an armful of first aid stuff, I ran down to Sky while she found a torch and some headcollars.

I fumbled open a wound dressing and thought about whether I should try to put it on. Quite a lot of blood had come out but the flow seemed to be slower. Then he tried to put a bit of weight on it, and I knew with a shudder as I saw the leg bend limply that it was irretrievably broken.

The whole scene was a grim repeat of what had happened to Joe the year before. So alike in their lives, the details of their stories had echoed each other so much. Their physical resemblance was so strong that several times both Nicole and I had called Sky 'Joe' by mistake. And here was his exact reincarnation, a second chance, a horse just on the cusp of the really good life he deserved, waiting to die not 40 metres from the spot Joe had lain down for the last time only a year before. Every time I thought of what was happening my heart welled up. In the closing light I fed Sky fresh herbs from the other side of the fence, and a huge bowl of the most delicious mix of treats Nicole could rustle up, which he generously shared with Amber, who stood with us very quietly. He ate until he didn't want any more, although Amber seemed happy enough to keep going until she'd have colic. I talked quietly to him, supporting his body or head as best I could, while I gently massaged his beautiful face. We stood together for about half an hour and I held him until Greg, the vet we had met that night with Joe, appeared. He confirmed what Sky had been trying to tell me from the moment he managed to attract my attention.

By now we knew all too well what the procedure would be. Greg had arrived just in time. Having shown no great signs of distress until that point, Sky was growing weaker and had begun to slip into a state of shock. It just seemed like his time was up, that he had enjoyed himself as much as possible but that his sand had run out, and he had known it instantly, the moment he was injured, what had happened and what the vet would do. The last hour or more had been almost pleasant for him, as Nicole and I and Amber took care of his every whim, but now he had reached the end of the time he could enjoy. He made not the slightest effort to resist as Greg slowly pressed the needle into his neck and found a vein. For a moment he looked up past the woods, up towards the great sequoias, rising together like an obelisk into the sky. Then he sank back onto his quarters, and silently rolled onto his side.

Joe, like Sky had come to Moor Wood, his damaged body concealing a heart of gold. When Joe had returned to Moor Wood on loan to Julia, and Muggins found himself with an extra horse to bring in and out of stables, a horse too regal to be rushed, Muggins had at times overlooked what an amazing and dignified character he really was. It was not until he died, with such grace and dignity, that I really began to appreciate how privileged I was to be able to meet and learn from such a refined equine aristocrat. I was thankful I hadn't made the same mistake with Sky. I hadn't wasted any precious time in seeing what a noble horse he was. He made a real difference to my life; I hope I made a difference to his.

Epilogue
(Adam and Nicole)

It was a perfect English summer's day, and we had been keeping our fingers crossed for weeks in the hope that the weather would be just so. It was the last Saturday in June 2002, and the most important day in the year for us. We were holding another Open Day in aid of the Brooke Hospital for Animals, and we were expecting over a hundred visitors.

As usual, it was also the most important day in High Flyer's year. Having sorted out his extraordinarily wayward behaviour on the first Open Day, Adam had introduced him to his first roller and long-lines on the second. Now a three-year-old, we were planning to back him for his third star appearance.

Now that we were sufficiently well known to ensure that more people would turn up than we could fit around the round pen, we were going to have to use the school to back a youngster for the first time since we'd surfaced the pen. We both felt a twinge of apprehension at the potential difficulty of the job. For although he had shown very little of his previous behaviour since that first day Adam worked with him, we had recently seen Kelly dealing with another bottle-reared horse at a demonstration. It had been the most difficult horse she had ever worked with, and we'll never forget the sight of that big horse calmly rearing up and then leaping forward, neatly depositing the saddle on the floor every time Kelly managed to get it on her back. To finally secure the saddle, and then put up her brilliant rider, Grant, was a feat of consummate skill. We just hoped High Flyer hadn't heard about it and wasn't planning to put on his own impressive display.

It all went brilliantly. Although he had been in the school only a couple of times in the previous months, Fly showed neither concern nor surprise at seeing the bank of the school lined with people. He was a perfect gentleman when Nicole mounted him, and we felt so confident that nothing could go wrong that we even stopped for a photo! He was a little reticent to move forward on his own, so Finn saved the day, stepping out confidently to provide him with a steady lead.

High Flyer turned out to be the easiest starter we have ever backed. On the third occasion he was ridden, we took him out alone, with Nicole on board and Adam on the ground, and he didn't put a foot wrong. Instead of being shot, he has a bright future to look forward to. When Lynette, who hadn't been able to come to the Open Day, saw him a couple of months later, she could hardly believe it was the same horse. She watched three friends ride him around like he was an old schoolmaster, and it was immensely gratifying when, in spite of her old misgivings, she rode him too. It was the first time she'd been on a horse in over two years.

Finn has now started helping Adam to give lessons, and seems highly amused by the whole concept of working 'on the bit'. He clearly can't understand why the other horses should bother to use their bodies in such an energetic way. 'Don't bend your knees, and make sure you stretch your nose out horizontally,' seems to be his motto. When he has to come in from the field to look after horses that are in for training, he wanders loose around the estate and does a fantastic job mowing the lawns, although his rose pruning may be a little over-zealous.

Misty maintains her role as chief hug-giver, and is getting confident to the point of naughtiness. She gets whiter, and wiser, every year.

Karma has developed into a lovely three-year-old, ready to be backed at four, perhaps at the next Open Day. We're tremendously proud of her, especially as she is our first homebred youngster and is so well adjusted. We attribute this mostly to Sensi's brilliant parenting, and the education given to her by the rest of the herd. Having her integrated into the group meant she didn't have to be forcibly weaned, saving her and Sensi from what can be a very traumatic experience.

Sensi has recovered brilliantly from all her misadventures, and at fifteen seems to be in the prime of her life. This year, Nicole achieved a long-standing ambition to take her on a Mary Wanless course, where Sensi proceeded to show us up by being the naughtiest horse there.

Amber goes from strength to strength. She's changed shape so radically that her saddle has had to go back to Kay Humphries four times to be made wider, and instead of being tense and hard and wiry, she's round and soft and relaxed. She was visited recently by a healer, named Margrit Coates, who seemed to help her come to terms with the events of her past, enabling us to revisit areas of her training that we had abandoned, for fear we might set her back. Adam has now successfully longlined her, something neither of us ever really expected to see. This confirms our impression that no horse is untrainable if you have the right attitude and resources.

Jo and Julia have, however, moved on. Jo left us recently when her boyfriend went back to live in New Zealand. Having passed her Preliminary Certificate in 2001, and retrained a very difficult remedial starter, we have every confidence she will go on to be a successful trainer.

Julia became pregnant, and she and Danny moved back to Hertfordshire to live near their families, having decided that the annexe simply wasn't big enough to raise a baby. Seeing her apply the same high standards to nappy fit that she had to saddles was an eye-opening experience for Nicole. Emma Rose was born in 2001 and has already backed a young horse! Although we miss Julia and Danny terribly, it has meant the annexe is now unoccupied, and can be used by clients wishing to come and learn at Moor Wood, which is probably our favourite and most satisfying way of working.

The most unusual and challenging venture of 2002 has to be the coaching day we put on for the Oxford Boat Club. Stifling our natural sense of loyalty to Cambridge, this day was designed to be a motivational, inspirational workshop. Using sports psychology techniques, we tried to demonstrate to the rowers the importance of being willing to change in order to achieve greater success. We showed them join-up, and Karma duly obliged by being a recalcitrant teenager, kicking out at Nicole and charging around the school like a wild horse. We'll have to wait for the result of the race to see how successful the day was, but the rowers reported having enjoyed themselves, the coaches were pleased, and it was a rare treat for Nicole to be surrounded by so many young men, making up for our predominantly female clientele the rest of the time. We hope to do similar events in the future.

2003 is the centenary of Moor Wood Stables, and we often wonder what happened to the people and horses who lived here before us. They must have had many stories to tell, with triumphs and disasters, just like us. It's funny to think how different the world was a hundred years ago, but they would have looked out across the same valley and seen the same trees, and lost boots in the same mud. Every May we commemorate our arrival here, and every September we celebrate with Henry our holding the lease at Moor Wood. Each time, we're just a little bit astonished that we've been lucky enough to spend another year here. And as our finances have become that little bit more secure, the quality of the bubbly has steadily improved from that first bottle we shared in the annexe with Henry.

There have been so many stories we've had to miss out, so many horses that have moved us and changed us, and we've learnt from them all. The riding clinics and Kelly's courses continue to go from strength to strength, and we're looking forward to meeting new people, new horses, new challenges, and doing what we can to help.

Useful Addresses

If you wish to contact us, you can do so through our website, www.whisperingback.co.uk or by post at Moor Wood Stables, Woodmancote, Cirencester, Glos GL7 7EB.

For details of the other practitioners in this book, or to find out more about the Intelligent Horsemanship Association, contact Kelly Marks's office. The office can be contacted on 01488 71300, or through the website, www.intelligenthorsemanship.co.uk, which also has details of all the demonstrations and courses available.

For some quality feedback, visit SCSI on-line at www.scsi-official.co.uk

Also available in Ebury Press Paperback